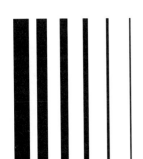

CRIME AND
JUSTICE
IN TWO SOCIETIES
JAPAN AND
THE UNITED STATES

Ted D. Westermann
Valparaiso University

James W. Burfeind
University of Montana

Brooks/Cole Publishing Company
Pacific Grove, California

For Florence
—TDW

For Linda
—JWB

Brooks/Cole Publishing Company
A Division of Wadsworth, Inc.

Printed in the United States of America

10   9   8   7   6   5   4   3   2   1

Library of Congress Cataloging-in-Publication Data
Westermann, Ted D.
    Crime and justice in two societies : Japan and the United States /
Ted D. Westermann, James W. Burfeind.
        p.   cm.
    Includes bibliographical references and index.
    ISBN 0-534-15516-2
    1. Crime—Japan.   2. Criminal justice, Administration of—Japan.
3. Crime—United States.   4. Criminal justice, Administration of-
-United States.   I. Burfeind, James W.   .   II. Title.
HV7113.5.W47   1991
364.952—dc20   90-21527
                                                            CIP

Sponsoring Editor: *Cynthia C. Stormer*
Editorial Assistant: *Cathleen S. Collins*
Production Editor: *Penelope Sky*
Production Assistant: *Micky Lawler*
Manuscript Editor: *Joan Atwood*
Permissions Editor: *Carline Haga*
Interior and Cover Design: *Roy R. Neuhaus*
Art Coordinator: *Lisa Torri*
Interior Illustration: *Lisa Torri*
Typesetting: *Kachina Typesetting, Inc.*
Printing and Binding: *Arcata Graphics, Fairfield*

ABOUT
THE AUTHORS

Ted D. Westermann grew up in Seattle, Washington. He received his B.A. degree and a theological diploma from Concordia Seminary in St. Louis, Missouri; he earned his Ph.D. in sociology at Emory University in Atlanta, Georgia. He was an independent scholar at the University of Sydney, Australia, and did post-doctoral work at the University of Louisville. Currently professor of sociology at Valparaiso University, Dr. Westermann also taught at Concordia Senior College in Fort Wayne, Indiana.

The Raiapu Enga of New Guinea resulted from anthropological research in the Western Highland of Papua–New Guinea. Dr. Westermann's research and teaching interests continue to range from cultural anthropology to the sociology of law, but focus on cross-cultural issues in criminal justice.

James W. Burfeind was raised in Rochester, Minnesota, and received his B.A. in criminal justice and sociology from Moorhead State University. He earned his Ph.D. in criminology and urban sociology from Portland State University. An assistant professor of sociology at the University of Montana, Dr. Burfeind teaches courses in criminology and criminal justice studies. His research focuses on cross-cultural and comparative criminology, and on causal analysis of the family's role in delinquent behavior.

Dr. Burfeind has been a probation officer in Scott County, Minnesota, and an administrator for a nonprofit agency that provided services for delinquent youth in Hood River, Oregon.

PREFACE

The idea that led to our writing this book emerged about a decade ago, when Ted Westermann saw a television documentary about policing in Japan. The narrator attributed Japan's exceptionally low crime rate to the effectiveness of the Japanese police, implying that if police in the United States would adopt the strategies and tactics of their Japanese counterparts the war on crime would quickly be won. No mention was made of the fact that the Japanese police were operating in a very different cultural system, nor of the likelihood that the intrusive police presence portrayed in the film would be in sharp conflict with basic American ideas about privacy and civil rights. No mention was made of the very different characters of the Japanese and American peoples. It was frustrating for someone trained in sociology and anthropology to be unable to respond to an obvious oversimplification.

Westermann later researched the influence of cultural values on policing in Japan and the United States; when James Burfeind joined him the scope of the work was expanded to include the entire justice systems of both societies. What we present here is the result of this collaboration.

We have taken what Terrill (1984, p. x) calls the "anthropological–historical approach," making a comparative analysis of crime and justice that crosses disciplinary lines. Shelley (1981, p. xxii), observes that "comparative criminologists, motivated by the desire to explore the multidimensional question of the relationship of crime to society, have been forced to pursue an interdisciplinary perspective." The text reflects our extensive review of the relevant scholarly literature, including historical materials on the development of institutions of justice and analyses of Japanese and U.S. criminological data. We integrate the work of historians, theologians, sociologists, legal scholars, anthropologists, statisticians, psychologists, and experts in criminal justice studies. These areas are all essential to understanding both how culture influences crime and how society responds.

ORGANIZATION

The anthropological–historical approach is *functional* in character, focusing on the effects of structural elements (such as values) on human social behavior. In Chapter 1 we discuss the value and use of the comparative method and show why Japan and the United States are prime candidates for cross-cultural comparison. In Chapter 2 we analyze the core cultural values in each society, showing how the very different combination of land, people, and historical sequence have produced quite dissimilar core values. In Chapter 3 we demonstrate how these differing values have influenced formal and informal social controls, and how each society's control mechanisms have influenced crime rates. In Chapter 4 we trace the history of legal development in the two countries, examining criminal law as a social control mechanism. In Chapter 5 we describe policing, especially law enforcement at the local or municipal level. In Chapter 6 we outline adjudicatory processes, showing how the core values have affected both the court structures and the legal climates in which they operate. In Chapter 7 we focus on correctional philosophy and practice in each society, again seeing how core values shape both the goals and the practices of corrections. In Chapter 8 we summarize what can be learned from a cross-cultural study of crime and justice.

Over the past few years this project has taken on a life of its own. It has led us in directions we had not intended to travel. Many of the areas we entered were *terra incognita*. But the result has been a great learning experience that has led to new horizons and, at times, to surprising insights into American and Japanese societies. Much of the work is reflected in our teaching. We come to our courses with a new awareness of how important cross-cultural approaches are to understanding crime and justice in our own society as well as in the rest of the world.

ACKNOWLEDGMENTS

No project of this sort is ever completed without the help of many people. We are especially grateful to colleagues and friends who read portions of the manuscript and whose comments and suggestions were of great value; they include Gary Sykes and Don Gibbons, and our colleagues at Valparaiso University, James Albers, Bruce Berner, Ted Ludwig, and Keith Schoppa. We appreciate the valuable help given by a number of our students who served as research assistants: Dawn Jeglum–Bartsch, Debra Hill, Beverly Rivera, Diane Prather, and Eric Beatty. We wish to thank the interlibrary loan staffs at both the Moellering Library at Valparaiso University and the Mansfield Library at the University of Montana for their invaluable services. Shari Linjala cheerfully and competently provided word processing assistance; she was a great help. We are indebted to Valparaiso University for a summer research grant in 1988. We acknowledge our reviewers: Steve Brodt, Ball State University; Dae H. Chang, Witchita State University; W. Byron Groves, University of Wisconsin–Green Bay; Rom Haghighi, University of Dayton; John Haley, University of Washington; Hillard Trubitt, Indiana University; and Charles Wellford, University of Wellington. Finally, we express our appreciation to the editorial staff at Brooks/Cole including Cindy Stormer, Cat Collins, Joan Atwood, and Penelope Sky. Their work has contributed greatly to the quality of this book.

We thank our families, especially our wives, Florence and Linda, for their support and understanding, which made this book possible. We promise that next year we *will* rake the leaves or maybe even plant some trees!

Ted D. Westermann
James W. Burfeind

CONTENTS

1 INTRODUCTION: A CULTURAL ANALYSIS OF JUSTICE SYSTEMS

The use of comparative and cross-cultural approaches has a long history in the social sciences. From the time of Auguste Comte and Herbert Spencer, scholars have used the comparative method extensively. This is reflected in the works of Max Weber, Emile Durkheim, Karl Marx, William Graham Sumner, Vilfredo Pareto, Charles H. Cooley, and others (Chang 1976).

Despite this legacy, the use of comparative and cross-cultural approaches in the study of crime and criminal justice has increased substantially only within the past few decades. As crime rates rose in all of the industrialized nations, scholars belatedly began to turn to these approaches in an attempt to understand both the causes of crime and societies' attempts to control it.

Why has there been this hesitancy to use comparative methods? To begin with, Shelley (1981, xx) has pointed out that "[b]efore World War II world criminology was dominated by the European school, which employed medical–biological, psychological, and legalistic approaches to crime." Because this approach focused on crime as the product of individual characteristics, there was not much interest in examining what social and cultural factors might be related to crime. As a result, cross-cultural studies of crime and criminality were largely precluded.

Following World War II, the rapid growth of sociological criminology in the U.S. produced a switch in focus from an "emphasis upon the criminal to a new emphasis upon the contribution of the social and political order of society to criminality" (Shelley 1981, xx). However, Leavitt (1990) points out that criminological thought has been largely relativistic, arguing that criminal behavior can be understood only in the context of the social setting within which it occurs. This perception, together with the serious lack of adequate data sources, has limited comparative approaches until relatively recently.

Today there is a rapidly growing literature focused on comparative and cross-cultural crime and justice.* The attention this cross-cultural approach has received

---

*Although we cannot begin to list all the works that have been produced during the last few decades, the following appear to be important contributions to this growing literature. Early works by Mannheim (1965) and Cavan and Cavan (1968) were followed by the works of a host of scholars. The 1970s saw

(continued)

1

at meetings of professional groups such as the American Society of Criminology and the Academy of Criminal Justice Sciences also attests to the growing appreciation for and use of comparative methods.

This growth has occurred because a larger number of criminological scholars have come to recognize that if "crime is inherent in the structures of society and that changes in criminality can be ascribed largely to social, political, and economic conditions of society," then the comparative study of different social systems provides us with better insights to the dynamics of this process (Shelley 1981, xxi). In this way, cross-cultural comparisons should help us better understand the nature of crime and to answer questions such as: Under what conditions does crime occur? Are these conditions the same in all societies? What are the social, political, and economic influences on criminal behavior? Are some of the answers we accept today universally applicable? Or do we find that some theories of criminality apply only in specific social and cultural settings?

Researchers have also begun to see that studies that examine the relationships between culture and behavior foster the development of theory that "transcends the one-dimensional explanation of criminality rooted in the unique characteristics of an individual society" (Shelley 1981, xxi; see also Leavitt 1990). Archer and Gartner (1981, 78) put it this way: "While . . . investigations of an individual society are of great descriptive value, they do not by themselves result in general explanation or theories."

Certainly one of the great values of comparative, cross-cultural study is that it helps us overcome our ethnocentric perspectives. By examining cultures other than our own, we can move to more objective understandings of how our own culture shapes criminal behavior and our society's response to it (Chang and Blazicek 1986).

Finally, some researchers now recognize that scholarly cross-cultural comparison can yield very pragmatic results. We can learn a great deal not only about crime but also about methods that societies can use to combat crime. As we will see in the final chapter of this book, one of the most recent and important innovative concepts in policing in the U.S. has been influenced strongly by comparative studies in law enforcement. By looking at both crime and social responses to it in a number of nations other than our own, we may develop new and innovative ways of dealing with one of our society's most vexing problems.

works published by Clinard and Abbott (1973), Chang (1976), and Gurr, Grabowski, and Hula (1977). In the 1980s, substantive studies were produced by Shelley (1981), Cole, Frankowski, and Gertz (1981), Johnson (1983a), Adler (1983), and Chang and Blazicek (1986). While these more general works were being published, many works with more focused interests, such as Bayley (1976a), Ames (1981), and Parker (1984), were being produced.

Other scholars have been more concerned with questions of methodology. These include Wolfgang (1963), Meyers (1972), Skogan (1974), Gurr (1977), Krohn and Wellford (1977), Vigderhous (1978), Wilkins (1980), Archer and Gartner (1981, 1984), Kalish (1988), Huang and Wellford (1989), and Bennett and Lynch (1990).

Mention should also be made of the growing list of journals that focus on cross-cultural comparison. These include the *Journal of Comparative and Applied Criminal Justice, Criminal Justice International, International Journal of Criminology and Penology,* and the *International Annals of Criminology.*

COMPARING JAPAN AND THE UNITED STATES

Japan appears to have become a focal point within this growing literature on comparative criminology. Perhaps the major reason for scholarly interest in Japan is that, in contrast to most industrialized nations, the rates for major crimes in Japan have been fairly stable or declined since 1950 (Ministry of Justice 1989; Nakayama 1981). Property crime dropped from a rate of 16 per 100,000 in 1948 to a rate of 9.98 in 1980. In this same period, despite a 46 percent increase in population, the actual number of bodily injury crimes declined by 37 percent (Suzuki 1985).

These trends become even more impressive when the rates of violent crime in Japan are compared with those in the United States. Data reported in a recent study of international crime rates (Kalish 1988) reveal that:

- There were over five times as many homicides per person in the United States in 1984 as there were in Japan—a rate of 1.5 per 100,000 in Japan compared to a rate of 7.9 in the United States.
- Rape was committed twenty-two times more frequently in the United States in 1984 than it was in Japan—35.7 per 100,000 in the United States, 1.6 per 100,000 in Japan.
- In 1984 the rate for armed robbery in the United States was 114 times the rate for that crime in Japan—205.4 per 100,000 in the United States, 1.8 per 100,000 in Japan.

These amazing statistics come from a nation that has become a major industrial society only within the past few decades. Scholars have long contended that crime is a consequence of the social disorganization that accompanies rapid industrialization and urbanization. After World War II, assisted by the United States, Japan quickly began to rebuild its war-shattered industry. This resulted in a massive influx of people into the cities. Today, Japan is one of the most urbanized societies in the world. Its population is about one-half that of the United States, yet it is crowded into a land mass no bigger than California. When forested and uninhabitable lands are excluded, "there are 2,326 people per square mile in Japan and 83 per square mile in the United States. . . . Almost one-fourth of all Japanese live within thirty-seven miles of downtown Tokyo—25 million people" (Bayley 1976a, 9–10). Yet, despite this rapid industrial and urban growth, which started just after Japan lost a major war and was under the control of a foreign power, Japan's crime rates have declined (Smith 1983).

This situation has attracted a number of scholars seeking to understand Japan's success in preventing crime. Several have included Japan in surveys of the criminal justice systems of a number of societies (Terrill 1984; Cole, Frankowski, and Gertz 1981). Other studies focus on a single justice institution in Japan. Ames (1981), for example, offers a detailed description of the Japanese police and the unique cultural setting within which they carry out their task. Bayley (1976a) and Parker (1984) add a cross-cultural component, comparing police organization and operations in Japan and the United States. Skolnick and Bayley (1988a) include Japan in a survey of policing in a number of societies.

We intend to present a cross-cultural study that will differ from previous comparative studies in both scope and perspective. Rather than focusing on a single criminal justice institution, this study examines the complete criminal justice systems of Japan and the United States. Furthermore, instead of surveying criminal justice systems in a number of countries, we will focus our attention on only these two societies. We believe that by limiting the scope of the study to Japan and the United States, we can move beyond simple description to the analysis of how cultural values influence the formation, structures, and operational processes of criminal justice systems.

CULTURAL VALUES AND SOCIAL CONTROL

Every society develops ways to guarantee conformity to social norms. Through the processes of socialization, individuals learn the norms and customs of their society which then serve as internal and informal means of controlling social behavior. However, as societies grow more heterogeneous and complex, informal means of control become inadequate and need to be augmented with formal institutions and processes of control. Criminal justice systems have become the standard structures of formal social control in modern society. In the terms of Talcott Parsons, the institutions of the criminal justice systems help to meet the functional prerequisite of "pattern maintenance" or "latency"—the need for society to maintain social continuity and order. As such, the component parts of the criminal justice system—the law, police, courts, corrections—are institutional structures that form around the central values of a society to protect and perpetuate these same values.

This study will focus on the organizations and processes of social control in Japan and the United States. While these nations share the commonalities of urban and industrial development, major differences in geography, population, and history have produced different clusters of cultural values. These core values, developing out of how land and people interact over time, have resulted in quite different patterns of social control, criminal behavior, and societal response to that behavior.

Using such a comparative analysis provides an understanding of how cultural values affect patterns and rates of crime and shape the unique institutional structures of social control which have developed in each society. Thus the cultural context of these justice systems is the analytic theme which informs this comparative analysis of the criminal justice systems in Japan and the United States.

The approach that we use might at first seem to be circular: If central values for each society were deduced from the observation of social behavior, and it was then argued that behavior sprang from those values, this approach would indeed be tautological. However, we argue that the core values of a society are the product of history—that they develop as people interact in time and place. We will provide historical evidence which shows that the cultures of Japan and the United States are distinctly different because each has developed out of a different mixture of environment, population, and history.

The functional perspective with which we work is one which presupposes that there is a general consensus about values within a society. This is, indeed, the general picture that the so-called *Nihon-jiron* literature presents. It portrays the

Japanese as a placid conformist people, so dominated by the groups to which they belong that there is little room for individualism.

We would disagree most strongly with this portrayal. No one—not even the most convinced functionalist—would suggest that Japan is a society without conflict. Any complex society with more than a single socioeconomic group is bound to have a measure of conflict and competition. We would certainly agree with Masatsugu (1982), Krauss, Rohlen, and Steinhoff (1984), Mouer and Sugimoto (1986), and Upham (1987) who argue that the Japanese are a very competitive people whose history has been replete with conflict, often violent and destructive.

Yet at the same time, there is little evidence to suggest that the Japanese people are sharply divided over major social issues or enter into open conflict over central values. The instances of organized conflict that we found involve such things as strikes over salary and working conditions, litigation over environmental issues and damages suffered from industrial pollution, demonstrations about the U.S.–Japan security treaty (probably the closest instance of conflict over a central issue), disagreement over the construction of an airport that threatened farm land, or student conflict over issues related to their university or college. It is interesting that conflict in Japan does not appear to be closely related to issues involving social class, although there is the continued struggle by the *Burakumin* (the traditional outcast group, also known as the *Eta*) to confront the age-old discrimination they have faced (Upham, 1988). Increased litigation by women who seek equal employment opportunities appears to be a relatively new development. The absence of any large racial or ethnic minorities other than the Korean minority also influences the character of conflict in Japan, and there is little evidence of any relationship between racial conflict and criminal behavior. Instead, there is strong evidence to suggest that the Japanese are a racially and ethnically homogeneous people, united by a strong sense of tradition and common values.

Our argument asserts that a criminal justice system is shaped by the cultural environment of the society and that the study of the criminal justice system in any society must begin with an examination of the central values of that society. Comparisons between countries like Japan and the United States must begin with a comparison of the cultural values that have developed in each nation. The central argument that informs this work, then, is that U.S. and Japanese systems of justice differ because the primary values which shape the arenas of justice differ.

2 CULTURAL VALUES IN JAPAN AND THE UNITED STATES

SIMILARITIES AND DIFFERENCES: CONTRASTS IN LAND, PEOPLE, AND HISTORY

An American entering Japan for the first time would not immediately be aware of all of the differences that exist between the United States and Japan. The physical environment of Tokyo is not really all that different from Chicago or New York. Masses of people, traffic moving at a hectic pace, overcrowded streets, skyscrapers, professionals carrying attaché cases, department store windows displaying the latest fashions—except for the language and the oriental features of the people, Tokyo is like any other world-class city.

However, one would not have to be in Japan very long for the differences in behavior to become more and more apparent. For Japan, a society built on an ancient culture, has survived through its amazing capacity to absorb the new, to adapt itself to new situations and conditions, but at the same time to cling to values that have developed over nearly two thousand years of history (Smith 1983). The result is that although there are similarities between Japan and the United States, there are also major differences—differences that relate to the land, differences in the character of the people, and differences in the history of how land and people have produced the values that characterize each culture.

Geographic Differences

The United States is the fourth-largest country in the world. Its land mass covers more than three-and-one-half million square miles of territory that is richly varied in climate and terrain (Shane 1980). Seacoast, mountain, prairie, desert, farm lands, semitropical areas, and lake-studded glacial terrain—all can be found within its borders. The United States is a land that is rich in resources of minerals, timber, and fertile land. It has always been a self-sustaining nation and today produces more foodstuffs than any country in the world.

Japan is an isolated nation that lies some distance off the Asian land mass. Its 142,305 square miles of territory stretch over a distance equal to the distance

6

between the Canadian border and the Gulf of Mexico. In total area it is the size of Montana or California. It is an intensely mountainous country with less than one-fifth of its territory suitable for agriculture or other commercial use. Only about 15 percent of Japanese land is used for food production. Its major resources are limited, but they include the seas that surround this nation of many islands and a climate that allows for an unusually productive system of agriculture. The climate is similar to that of the eastern United States with about the same variation from the temperate north to the semitropical south.

Despite its productive agriculture, the shortage of arable land causes Japan to suffer about a 30 percent deficit in food production. This plus the lack of other natural resources has had a strong impact on the Japanese economy (Reischauer 1988).

Demographic Differences

Major differences also exist between the populations of these two societies. The population of the United States numbers about 246 million, while the population of Japan is about half that number, approximately 123 million. But size of population is relevant only in relation to the size of geographic territory. Japan is one of the most densely populated nations in the world, about thirty times more densely populated than the United States.

Even more important is the difference in the makeup of the people. The U.S. people are a polyglot mixture, born of almost continual migration from every corner of the world. There is probably no other nation as diverse in its mixture of race and ethnic characteristics. The city of Chicago boasts of having more people of Polish descent than live in Gdansk or Kraków, Poland. More Jewish people live in New York City than live in Haifa and Tel Aviv, Israel, combined. Flourishing communities of Chinese are found in most of America's major cities. The people of the United States are a mixture of very different racial, geographic, and linguistic backgrounds.

The Japanese, on the other hand, are a singularly homogeneous people. According to Reischauer (1988), the modern Japanese are a mixture of Asian peoples who flowed into Japan from northeastern Asia, through Korea, especially during the first seven centuries of the Christian era. However, since the eighth century, there has been no infusion of new people. For over a thousand years, immigration into Japan has been infinitesimal. During those years, the original inhabitants, ancestors to the ethnic group known as the Ainu—which today number less than 20,000—were slowly pushed to the north.

As a result, the Japanese today are a people who perceive themselves as a racially and ethnically pure and homogeneous people. With the exception of the Ainu, a Korean community of about 600,000, and small numbers of other non-Japanese residents, there are no ethnic divisions in Japanese society. Reischauer (1988) estimates that the total number of non-Japanese comprise less than 1 percent of the total population.

One factor that has contributed to this homogeneity is Japan's isolation. Until World War II, Japan had never been successfully invaded by a foreign power. Its location was an effective barrier to contact from without. Further, from the twelfth to the nineteenth centuries, Japanese rulers effectively maintained their isolation by preventing any major influx of other peoples. With the exception of some European contact in the sixteenth century, Japan remained an isolated country whose homogeneous people developed a culture that was uniquely Japanese (Reischauer 1988).

History

The history of these two societies is also a study in contrasts. Four elements of history are important for the purposes of this comparative study: time span, political development, economic development, and the evolution of religious belief.

Time span   The United States is a relatively young nation, if its history is reckoned on the basis of its inhabitation by Europeans. Although European settlers came to this country in the sixteenth century, its establishment as a political entity did not take place until near the end of the eighteenth century. This late date, plus the fact that its population continued to develop through an immigration–aggregation process, means that the United States has not developed a strong historical tradition. The average person in the United States is not very conscious of history. For most, concern focuses upon the present and future rather than the past. For many Americans, family history is tied to other countries. The result is that few people attempt to understand the present through the analysis of what has happened in the nation's history.

Japanese written history extends back more than 1400 years. Japanese are conscious of that history. They see themselves in historical perspective and celebrate that perspective through ritual and drama. They are intensely proud of a distinctive cultural heritage that has become a living tradition (Hall and Beardsley 1965).

One of the implications of that shared historical tradition is that the Japanese see themselves as a united people. When people in the U.S. are asked about their heritage, many respond in terms of the nation from which their forefathers migrated. In Japan, this could not happen. Because they share one historical tradition and one common language, they feel bound to one another as an entity distinct from any other people (Ishida 1974).

Political development   The second important historical element is the nations' political developments. American political history begins with the struggles of a colonial people who started a revolution in order to develop a democratic system of government. Despite the institution of slavery and the racial inequality it spawned, the ideals of democracy and individual freedom play a significant role in the nation's unfolding history. The perception that the United States was the "land of the free" helped draw to this nation the millions of immigrants who provided the labor for its development. The goals of freedom and economic independence fueled the westward expansion. The ideals of freedom and democracy were contributing factors in the nation's only civil war.

Because the United States was dominated by that democratic tradition, it never fully developed the sort of political and economic aristocracy characteristic of Europe. Major differences in wealth and power? A social class system that sharply differentiates between rich and poor? Yes. But in its development, U.S. society has clung to a belief in the ideals of equality and independence. Its economic system has provided sufficient opportunity to maintain that belief.

Japanese history presents sharp contrasts. For the purposes of the present analysis, we trace the political history of Japan from the sixth century, when a group of military aristocrats, proclaiming superiority over a number of semiautonomous tribal units, established a court in the Yamato area. While most of the lands remained under the control of individual tribes, they were joined to the Yamato court by ties of kinship, real or fictive. In A.D. 645, a group of innovators seized power in the Taika Reform. Borrowing extensively from China and Korea, the reformers attempted to transform Japan from what had been a tribal-centered society into a centrally organized society, complete with an emperor and a bureaucratic state mechanism. A system of court ranks attached to the emperor's family developed still further the idea of aristocracy that had come into being during the Yamato period (Reischauer 1988; Varley 1984).

This centralized system was never truly successful. By the twelfth century, the bureaucratic imperial system had atrophied, and Japan moved into a feudal system that was destined to control Japanese history for the next seven centuries. This period was one of continued intergroup struggle and conflict as rivalries between feudal leaders led to intermittent warfare. While the emperor remained as a symbolic figure, political control was in the hands of local warlords who struggled to develop more tightly organized feudal domains. During this period the samurai tradition came into being (Reischauer 1988; Ishida 1974).

In the sixteenth and seventeenth centuries, a centralized form of feudalism slowly developed, giving rise to what is called the Tokugawa Period. Once again, the emperor remained as titular head of state, but real power was held by the Tokugawa family who divided the country between their own estates and those of vassals, the *daimyo*. During this period, to eliminate all possibility of change, all foreigners were expelled. The Christian religion, which had established missions in Japan, was ruthlessly suppressed. All foreign contact was cut off, and Japan entered into a period of self-imposed seclusion that lasted more than two centuries (Reischauer 1988).

During the Tokugawa Period, the distinction between commoners and the aristocracy became even more sharply defined. To preserve the status quo, rigid distinctions among social classes were reinforced by sumptuary laws that stipulated dress and other consumption patterns (Tsunoda, de Bary, and Keene 1958). A time of relative peace, the Tokugawa Period witnessed both the development of Confucian philosophy and historical scholarship and the flowering of Japanese art and architecture. The samurai tradition emphasized the soldier–scholar and encouraged the samurai to master such arts as calligraphy and poetry. Schools of painting developed at the courts of various daimyo. But this cultural outburst was not limited to the upper classes. The rise of an urban merchant class in trade centers such as

Edo, Osaka, and Kyoto spawned an urban culture that produced the ukiyo-e style of art and fostered the popular Kabuki theater (Reischauer 1988).

It was not until the second half of the nineteenth century that the Tokugawa system began to collapse. Western industrialism and the concomitant hunger for new markets eventually brought great pressure upon the Japanese. In 1853, the United States sent a fleet commanded by Matthew Perry to force Japan to open its ports to foreign vessels. By 1868—a mere fifteen years after Perry's arrival—the Tokugawa system had collapsed, and the period known as the Meiji Restoration was ushered in (Reischauer 1988).

Of primary importance in the Meiji period was the development of a strong centralized government and the dissolution of the feudal estates. The emperor took on new significance as the symbolic head of state, but power was actually held by a number of powerful men from the middle samurai rank. Thus the stage became set for a transformation in which status would be determined largely by education and personal achievement rather than by ascription (Reischauer 1988).

By the 1880s Japan had developed to the point where it was ready for the adoption of a new constitution, modeled after those of Britain and Germany. This period also marked the beginning of the industrialization of Japan and its initiation into the modern world.

Two things appear to be important consequences of this historical development. First, for more than twelve hundred years Japan has had a system of hierarchy and ranking. In contrast to the American ideal of equality, Japanese tradition has recognized ranking and hierarchy as the natural order of human relationships.

Second, Japanese history has emphasized authority and subservience to authority. Japan did not begin its national experience with democracy until the last decade of the nineteenth century. As a consequence, egalitarianism and individual freedom are not deeply ingrained in the Japanese tradition (Masatsugu 1982). Where people in the United States stress their individual freedoms and rights, the Japanese stress duty and obligation (Clifford 1976).

Economic development   The third important historical element is economic development. The economic history of the United States is one of rapid growth in technology and industry. The United States began as an agrarian society, its people living in a land well suited to large-scale farming. But within six decades of its founding, it was caught up in the beginnings of the industrial revolution. That revolution, in large part made possible by agricultural productivity, in turn influenced the practice of agriculture through development of mechanized farming. A relatively small number of people, working independently and using machinery, were able to produce vast amounts of foodstuffs. Today, as a result of continued scientific and technological innovation, 2½ percent of the U.S. population produces enough food and fiber to meet the needs not only of the United States but of a significant portion of the world's population as well.

That agricultural productivity is what enabled the United States to become one of the world's industrial giants so rapidly. People, freed from the land, could move to the cities to work in the factories and offices spawned by the industrial revolution. Agriculture in Japan has developed as a consequence of an entirely different set of conditions. Because of the scarcity of arable land, the Japanese very early adopted the system of wet-rice cultivation that had originated in Southeast Asia. That system requires small-scale farming that is labor-intensive. Further, it is a system that entails cooperative effort. Large-scale efforts are necessary in the building of the canals and dikes that allow water to be distributed. Cooperation becomes essential in the allocation and control of this necessary resource (Ishida 1974; Burks 1981; Smith 1983).

Eiichiro Ishida suggests that rice cultivation may be the major factor in the differences between Eastern and Western civilizations. It is not the grain itself that is a factor, of course, but the basic skills and the systems of daily living that developed around its cultivation (Ishida 1974).

What is important is that rice culture engendered a cooperative rather than a competitive spirit. If a village was to survive, then individual desires and wishes had to be repressed for the common good. As technology advanced, smaller communities became linked together. An isolated village could not carry out the labor needed to provide irrigation for the paddy fields. In time, demand for the cooperative administration of waterways allowed for the rise of centralized leadership (Ishida 1974). Further, as feudalism developed, control became increasingly centered in the local daimyo who was titular owner of the village lands. The daimyo's demands for taxes and labor reinforced the development of hierarchy and central control.

Japan's agricultural practices have improved greatly over the centuries, and today the relatively small areas that are left to agriculture produce prodigious quantities of food. Yet, despite the use of advanced techniques, about 15 percent of the Japanese population is needed for agriculture production. However, for Japanese society, the historic impact of its agricultural system has been to help individuals recognize that their best interests are served when they work in cooperation with others.

Religious belief   The development of religious beliefs in Japan and the United States has had important influence on the value structures that have developed in each nation. Martin Marty (1987, 33) notes that:

> One would not think of interpreting cultures that derive from Buddhist, Islamic, Hindu, or similar influences without some awareness of their religious grounding. Every visitor to American shores who wishes to make sense of life in this nation also finds it important to reexplore the religious roots of this culture.

Early U.S. history is bound up with the colonists' religious beliefs and convictions. Although the colonies were sponsored by trading companies as commercial ventures and many of the colonists came to America seeking economic gain, the thread of religious faith and piety runs deep in the story of this nation's beginnings. It is true that some of the colonies were anything but models of religious toleration. Many of the colonists were dissenters who came to America seeking to find a place where they could worship according to the dictates of their own conscience, but, at the same time, they were intolerant of the beliefs of others (Johnstone 1988). The result was that religion in colonial America was a patchwork of differing beliefs—Dissenters from the Church of England, Quakers, Roman Catholics, Anglicans, Dutch Reformed, Moravians, Dutch Calvinists, Baptists, Lutherans, as well as Jews and free thinkers who had no religious affiliation (Chalafant, Beckley, and Palmer 1987).

One major influence on religion in America was the individualism and independence that became such a strong theme in the nation's life. The idea of freedom, of people being able to choose for themselves where they would live and what work they would do, became a core value of the new land early on. It bred a spirit of independence, a people who could and would make their own decisions and who would tolerate no interference with that right. That spirit of independence carried over into religion in what Marty (1987) has referred to as "Voluntaryism," the belief that religion should rest on voluntary principles.

Wilson (1978) and others (Marty 1987, 1970; Chalafant, Beckley, and Palmer 1987) have suggested that, because of this religious diversity and the spirit of independence that had emerged, any attempt to establish a single national church would have been politically and socially disruptive. As a consequence, developing sentiment supported the separation of church and state and the freedom of individual religious choice.

Although overwhelmingly Protestant during the colonial period, the guarantee of religious freedom and the doctrine of the separation of church and state established a set of conditions which encouraged the development of religious pluralism. Today there are more than twelve hundred different religious denominations in the United States (Melton 1978). They include a wide variety of religious groups, ranging from the traditional—such as Protestant, Roman Catholic, and Jewish organizations—to avant-garde sects and cults.

Religious pluralism and the ideal of religious freedom have influenced the character of religious belief and practice in the contemporary United States. First, American religion is highly individualistic. It stresses the individual's right to believe what he or she wants to believe or to believe in nothing at all. It is also a private matter, in the sense that what the individual believes is rooted in the individual's consciousness and is not a public matter (Berger 1967). As a result, American religious character is tolerant of the differences that exist among denominations and groups. While people may not accept or approve of some religions' teachings, the vast majority is willing to live and let live where beliefs are concerned, so long as religious practices do not interfere or conflict with constitutionally guaranteed rights.

At the same time, paradoxically, religion in the U.S. must be seen as both fragmented and competitive. Many of the twelve hundred religious groups practice an intense kind of proselytism. This can be seen in the highly competitive form of television evangelism in which various religious leaders seek to develop large followings to their particular version of the faith or in the growth of the fundamentalist sects (Hoge and Roozen 1979). This kind of proselytism stems from a perception of religion as exclusive. For example, a person in the United States cannot be Protestant, Catholic, and Jewish simultaneously. While individuals have the right to believe what they wish to believe, religious groups have the right to try to persuade people to their version of religious truth.

Religious beliefs in the United States vary widely, but they generally share a common emphasis on individualism. People may practice their religion as members of a group, but the focus of that religious practice is the salvation of the individual. Piety is enjoined in the hope of individual reward in the hereafter rather than for the benefit of the community in the here and now.

As a consequence of that emphasis upon individual piety, most mainstream religions in the U.S. accentuate guilt rather than shame. Failure to live up to a religious ideal is perceived as a sin for which the individual should feel a sense of failure. But it is a personal failure rather than failure to meet the expectations of a group. Because of this, the predominant emotion one feels is guilt, not shame (Wilson 1982; Pruyser 1968; Weatherhead 1951).

While there are some common denominators in American religious life, such as the shared commitment to the Mosaic law among Catholics, Protestants, and Jews, there is also great diversity in beliefs and practices. Each religious group provides a somewhat different set of beliefs and religious norms. As a result, there is no commonly accepted religious ethical code in U.S. society, and the sanctioning power of religious norms is thus weakened (Berger and Luckman 1967; Winter 1977). Further, the doctrine of the separation of church and state has prevented the public schools from serving as an agency which teaches American children a common code of morals or ethics.

The result is that religion in U.S. society does not speak with a common voice and does not appear to serve as a strong central source of social control. To be sure, religious beliefs strongly influence the behavior of those individuals for whom religion plays a significant role. However, the diversity and privacy of religion in America prevent it from becoming a major unified force for sanctioning behavior. Even Robert Bellah (1975), a strong proponent of what he called "Civil Religion," now speaks of this as a "broken covenant" that fails to provide a consensus of belief and values.

Religious belief in Japan differs significantly from its counterpart in the United States. While the central core of ideas in U.S. religions stems from the Judeo-Christian tradition, Japanese religious beliefs develop out of a more diverse framework. Yet, as we shall see, there is probably a greater unity of religious ideas in Japan today than there is in the United States.

Japanese religious history involves three ancient belief systems: Shintoism, Buddhism, and Confucianism. It is impossible in the space available to do more than sketch an outline of fourteen centuries of the development of religion in Japan. Our purpose here is to try to distill the influence of these religions' history on contemporary Japanese culture.

The early religious practices of Japan, which later came to be called Shintoism, were based on the worship of natural phenomena (Reischauer 1988; Forbis 1975). Developing early in the history of Japan, Shinto was not really concerned with immortality or transcendental concepts. Instead, it sought to bring people into a right relationship with the world as they perceived it—a world filled with gods and spirits (Anesaki 1963). By A.D. 500 Shinto had coalesced around the idea that Japan was the land of the gods and stressed loyalty to that land and to the emperor who sprang from the Sun-Goddess to rule over the land (Tsunoda, de Bary, and

Keene 1958). Shinto thus became a religion in which patriotism became religious sentiment.

By A.D. 700 Buddhism, introduced from Korea, had begun to supplant Shintoism as the most important religious movement in Japan. Although these two religions were very different, Shintoism and Buddhism were both transformed and turned out to be very complementary systems of belief. Buddhism provided a sense of the transcendental absent from the pragmatic and "this-worldly" Shinto. In time, the two became so syncretized that Shinto shrines became administratively linked with Buddhist groups (Reischauer 1988).

When Buddhism was introduced to Japan, Japan received far more than a second major religion. Reischauer (1988) argues that Buddhism played a role in Japanese history similar to that played by Christianity in northern Europe. It became the means by which an entire higher culture—that of China—came to Japan. Buddhism flourished in Japan from the ninth to the sixteenth centuries and influenced virtually every area of Japanese life: social, intellectual, political, aesthetic, as well as religious (Tsunoda, de Bary, and Keene 1958).

One of the prime reasons that Buddhism was so successful was that at the time it was introduced to the Yamato court, the prince regent, Shotaku, was trying to enhance his power by importing many new ideas from China. Perhaps equally important was the fact that Buddhism, instead of conflicting with the native Shinto beliefs, supplied some basic concepts Shinto lacked, especially that of an afterlife (Tsunoda, de Bary, and Keene 1958; Kitagawa 1987).

By the beginning of the twelfth century, groups struggling for political power had begun to challenge the established order. For the next four centuries Japan became embroiled in a period of great political and religious unrest that finally culminated in the founding of the Tokugawa Shogunate in 1603 (Kitagawa 1987).

During the Tokugawa Period the need to unify a badly divided society, to find an ideology that would consolidate Tokugawa power, led Ieyasu Tokugawa to shift from a Buddhist to a neo-Confucian emphasis (Smith 1983), combining elements of Confucianism with Buddhism and Shintoism. To associate his reign with the unbroken succession of power that stemmed from the Sun-Goddess, the Tokugawas built the great Shinto Shrine at Nikko to house Ieyasu's soul. At the same time, to eradicate the influence of the Roman Catholic missions, the Tokugawa rulers outlawed Christianity, and, in time, ruled that each Japanese household had to be registered at a Buddhist temple (Kitagawa 1987). The combination of Confucian philosophy with Buddhist and Shinto religious ideas was to become the dominant pattern of Japanese religious and moral life.

Although Ieyasu remained a devoted follower of Amida Buddhism, he recognized that Confucianism provided a philosophy which would help him establish peace and order and, equally as important, maintain the hierarchical order (Noda 1976b). Neo-Confucianism, introduced to Japan by Zen Buddhist monks, stressed the substantiability, order, and intelligibility of the world. It expressed the belief that consistent laws of human behavior and political morality could be discovered in the study of human history. Further, it stressed that morality consisted of obedience to those laws and of faithful service to one's position. Confucianism was essentially a humanistic philosophy which focused upon human relationships rather than the supernatural order. Because it provided a code of ethics based on the ideals of loyalty and obedience, it became the basis for the social order imposed by the Tokugawa (Tsunoda, de Bary, and Keene 1958; Smith 1983).

Neo-Confucian ethics remained the most important moral force for the entire Tokugawa Era. As Smith (1983) observed, the Tokugawa leaders believed that the golden age of Japan lay in the distant past and were convinced that the way to maintain peace and order was to prevent innovation. Thus, they strongly supported a conservative polity based on Confucian ideals. More than 200 schools for the children of samurai of the middle ranks promoted a system of morality based upon obedience to the leaders of the state. It was a system which reinforced the status hierarchy and the idea of the individual's responsibility to the corporate group. The rules of *giri,* which spell out the duties and responsibilities inherent in the various kinds of *kobun–oyabun* (subordinate–superior) relationships, became a central part of the moral way of life.

By the end of the nineteenth century, under pressure from the Western world which sought to open Japan to trade, the Tokugawa Shogunate had collapsed and Japan had entered the Meiji period. The leaders who had forced the collapse of the Tokugawa system, seeking to return Japan to what they saw as its rightful place of prominence in Asia, were eager to restore the emperor to a position of power. To do so, a system of "State Shinto" was given strong political and economic support, and Buddhism was relegated to a subservient position (Kitagawa 1987). The Shinto emphasis upon respect and veneration for the emperor was reinforced by the neo-Confucian stress upon filial piety and obedience.

When foreign protests over the establishment of a state religion forced the government to grant a qualified freedom of religion, "a way to instill the virtues of imperial loyalty and filial piety in the people was already in place. It was the system of compulsory education, established in 1872" (Smith 1983, 31). The Meiji government simply turned over the responsibility for the moral education of Japanese youth to the schools. The purpose of education became increasingly that of producing citizens who would be loyal to the emperor and obedient to his edicts (Smith 1983).

The textbook for this neo-Confucian approach was the *Imperial Rescript on Education* of 1890 (Tsunoda, de Bary, and Keene 1958). This document, outlining the responsibilities of subjects loyal to the emperor, was, by imperial edict, read every year in each classroom in Japan. Framed copies hung on the wall in each school room, and students and teachers were required to make obeisance before it. As Smith (1983, 16) tells us:

> The drafters of the rescript defined the virtues of the subject in terms provided by Confucianism's central truth as Nishimura saw it: "It taught that the meaning of social life lay not in seeking salvation in another world . . . but in cultivating the relationships among members of society built on trust, a fundamental sense of one's humanness, and, above all, a commitment to loyal action on behalf of others."

This combination of State Shinto and Confucian ethics was an important force that legitimated the increasingly militaristic stance taken by Japan in the 1920s and 1930s that culminated in World War II. Japan's defeat and the occupation by U.S. forces were to produce profound change in the religious foundation of Japan.

Joseph Kitagawa (1987) points to three major consequences of American postwar occupation policy. First, the principle of religious freedom, insisted upon by the U.S. authorities, upset the accepted belief that the first duty of every Japanese was loyalty to the emperor and the nation. Freedom of religion allowed the individual to obey principles higher than state law. Second, the disestablishment of religion—especially the removal of all government support for State Shinto—effectively undercut the idea of the emperor as a divine being. Third, the principle of the separation of church and state canceled the time-honored unity of religion and government. This was enhanced by the publication of the imperial rescript of 1946 in which the divinity of the emperor was officially denied. As Kitagawa (1987, 281) argues:

> This rescript made it clear that the Japanese people's traditional world of meaning and their understanding of history, which counted the ancient Shinto myths as historical facts, could no longer be preserved in postwar Japan. This meant that the Japanese people were cut off suddenly and abruptly from their own past and their own historical experience.

Small wonder then that religion plays only a peripheral role in Japan today. Reischauer (1988, 204) describes Japan as a society whose secularism is rooted in its essentially Confucian philosophical background:

> Contemporary Japanese obviously are not Confucianists in the sense that their Tokugawa ancestors were, but Confucian ethical values continue to permeate their thinking. Confucianism probably has more influence on them than does any of the traditional religions or philosophies. Behind the wholehearted Japanese acceptance of modern science, modern concepts of progress and growth, universalistic principles of ethics, and democratic ideals and values, strong Confucian traits still lurk beneath the surface, such as the belief in the moral basis of government, the emphasis on interpersonal relations and loyalties, and the faith in education and hard work.

Although Christianity has made some small inroads in Japanese society, its adherents number only about 1 percent of the population. Many new religions, such as Soka Gakkai, have developed since World War II. However, observers like Kitagawa (1987) seem to question their potential for making a strong and lasting impact on Japanese religious life.

All in all, the development of religion in Japan, especially the role of Confucian ethics, has influenced Japanese culture in ways significantly different from the way religion has influenced U.S. culture. First, religion in the United States is fragmented, competitive, and exclusive. In Japan, the three great religions are syncretistic. In Japan one can celebrate at a Shinto shrine festival, pray at a Buddhist temple, maintain the Confucian values of filial piety and loyalty, and never sense any conflict whatever. As Noda (1976a, 170) explains:

> Ideas are for the Japanese nothing more than tools that can be used for different purposes. If a saw does not do the job, you can use the axe. In the same way, if Confucianism does not give the desired result, resort may be had to Buddhism.

The result of this is that there is little of the competitive element in the religious world of Japan with perhaps the exception of some of the new cults. In the absence of any wide variation in beliefs, there appears to be greater unanimity of religious opinion in Japan than in the United States. One of the consequences of this is that religious or moral and ethical beliefs may have a stronger influence in controlling behavior.

The emphasis upon freedom of individual choice was a potent force in making religion in the U.S. both pluralistic and privatistic. Japan's long history of Confucian influence, combined with its history of hierarchical structure, has had an opposite effect. Japanese morality has always focused upon the group and the individual's responsibility to the group. To go contrary to the moral code in Japan is not so much a private matter as it is an offense against society. The consequence is that although the individual may feel some sense of guilt for his actions, the primary emotion is shame.

The fragmentation of American religion has also resulted in the fact that there is no common ethical code that is accepted by the entire society. The Confucian philosophy has provided the Japanese with a moral and ethical code that has been in existence for centuries. While the doctrine of the separation of church and state prevents morality from being part of the curriculum in U.S. schools, this is not the case in Japan.

Confucianism—with its emphasis on tradition and loyalty to that tradition, its acceptance of hierarchy and position, and its teaching that morality is to be found in the fulfilling of the duties and obligations of status—has profoundly affected Japanese values. The Japanese sense of belonging, which gives identity to the person, certainly develops out of the ideas of corporate responsibility found in Confucian ideology. The Confucian desire for peace and order has also strongly influenced the Japanese concept of *wa,* or harmony. These ideas have remained very much a part of the secular religion of modern Japanese culture.

CULTURAL VALUES

In the preceding chapter we contended that Japan and the United States are characterized by different clusters of core values. Given the geographic, demographic, and historic differences between Japan and the United States that we have just described, it is only to be expected that there would be major differences in the cultural values that influence the behavior of their peoples. However, before we can analyze these differences in core values, it is necessary that we more specifically define what we mean by *values.*

Our basic understanding of values and *cultural values* stems from the work of Talcott Parsons (1951) who postulated that values are structural components of social systems and help to shape human relationships and behavior. We perceive cultural values to be social conceptions of what is right or good, statements of belief, or shared perceptions which

> indicate what is a good society, what is good social action, what are good social relations, what is a good person as a member of society; these values regulate individual attitudes as well as the way social relationships are phrased in any society. These values limit choices; they make some choices more likely; they make some choices almost

impossible in the realm of social action. That is, the social value system creates a set of possibilities and impossibilities for social action (Bellah 1970, 115).

These values develop out of a society's historical experience as land and people interact over time. While they are subject to change, core values tend to persist over time. This does not mean, however, that everyone within a society perceives or accepts the basic value structure in exactly the same way. The existence of core values does not automatically preclude either disagreement or conflict over central issues. Social groups who have different historical experiences may have very different perceptions about a common value and its interpretation. For example, people in the United States who value freedom and the civil rights of the individual may have quite divergent views about the issues of abortion or the Equal Rights Amendment. Further, people within a society may hold strongly opposing views about some values yet find common agreement on others. Every society develops its own unique set of values with some societies having greater consensus than others.

While it is always risky to attempt to develop a thumbnail sketch of a complex values system, we have argued that values shape a people's response to crime and criminal behavior. Keeping in mind the critical differences in each country's historical and cultural development, we will try to outline what appear to be the central values in Japanese and American society that are most relevant to a discussion of crime and criminal justice.

Central Values in American Society

One of the major problems in dealing with values is how to define and describe the important values in a society. From de Croevcoeur in 1782 to Robert Bellah and his associates in 1985, many people have attempted the difficult task of outlining the values central to American life. We know of no accepted methodology for accomplishing that task.

Bellah and his associates (1985) conducted several research projects examining a number of aspects of middle-class life. They sought to determine major themes in both the private and public life of people in the United States. Robin Williams (1960), in an earlier attempt to outline American values, argued that core values could be determined by using the four criteria of (1) the extensiveness of an idea's acceptance, (2) the length of time it has been accepted, (3) the intensity of the emotion it arouses, and (4) the prestige of those who are its carriers. He then proceeded to use these criteria to examine what he and others had perceived as major themes in American culture.

Lee Coleman's (1941) earlier work was an attempt to get at what was essentially "American" by reviewing a large number of scholarly essays and reviews that dealt with "the American way" in order to see what these authors felt were distinctly U.S. traits. Although Coleman did not find complete consensus among his sources, he was able to develop a list of traits or values that have been consistently mentioned or agreed upon by various scholar/authors over a period of more than one hundred years.

Other attempts to get at American values have grown out of the attempt to describe the American character. Works such as David Riesman's *The Lonely*

Crowd (1950) and William H. Whyte Jr.'s *The Organization Man* (1957) have attempted to determine major value themes in U.S. society. Seymour M. Lipset's (1961) essay, though critical of Riesman and Whyte, argues that U.S. values derive from the nation's historical experience. He points out that:

> It is obvious that American society has changed, not only in its technological and ecological aspects such as industrialization, urbanization, and population growth, but in family structure, education, religion and "culture" also. But these changes have not altered the social character or the principal values radically (1961, 321).

Sidney Verba and his associates (1987) reinforce the idea of the stability of cultural values in their work, which seeks to compare the values of equality in Japan, Sweden, and the United States. Although this work focuses upon the elite members of these societies, it provides a model for the cross-cultural comparison of values. Importantly, Verba and his collaborators stress that "the beliefs and values we deal with have historical roots" and that "[s]uch data run the risk of being inadequately understood when isolated from their contextual background" (1987, 20).

Finally, we refer to the work of Gordon Heald (1988). Heald, using materials from an international study of social values, compares American, European, and Japanese core values. What makes Heald's work of particular value is the extensive data base developed in the international survey. Conducted under the auspices of Gallup International, the study asked a carefully selected random sample of at least twelve hundred persons in each of sixteen nations to respond to nearly 150 questions dealing with central values. This empirically based study appears to present strong evidence that there are major definable differences in central values in Japan and the United States.

What we have attempted is to become acquainted with what these and other scholars have said and to explore how their ideas appear to be reflected in the developmental history of American culture. We are certain that we have not outlined all of the values that inform U.S. society. That was not our intent. Rather, we were concerned to outline those values that we feel most strongly influence people's attitudes toward the law and lawful behavior, factors which shape crime and society's response to crime. While other values may have been outlined, we gain a sense of confidence from the fact that many of the previously mentioned observers of U.S. life seem to agree with our basic outline.

Other values can be attributed to American culture, but four major values, or value clusters, appear to be important influences on American social behavior: freedom, individualism, and equality; diversity; decentralization of authority; and a pragmatic, utilitarian approach to life.

If there is one primary value in American society—other than the value of success—it must be the value of freedom. The United States boasts that it is the "land of the free," and though it is in no way perfect, no other society in the world has done so much to structure individual freedom and liberty. Constitutional guarantees of the freedom of the individual have continued to expand, limiting the authority of government and its agents.

As a consequence of that freedom, Americans are conscious and protective of their individual rights. That notion of *rights*—that the individual is endowed with certain basic privileges under the law—is central to any understanding of the value of freedom.

Further, that concept of freedom is associated with individualism. Rights are endowed to individuals apart from any relationship they may have to any group, religion, race, or social status. Individuals are free to travel where they wish, speak as they please, assemble with others where they will—these and the other rights they hold through citizenship are individual rights.

This, in turn, leads to a deeply ingrained belief in equality. United States citizens are equal before the law. That understanding of equality expands to the sentiment that every person, whatever class differences may exist, is as good as any other person.

The second important value in the American cultural milieu is diversity and the values that cluster around diversity. As has been pointed out, the United States was framed from the timbers of a polyglot immigration that has continued to bring a mixture of peoples and cultures from virtually every land.

At one time, people in the United States believed in a melting pot theory of cultural assimilation, predicting that the sharp differences of ethos and culture would ultimately be blended into a new synthesis. Today, they are more likely to speak about cultural pluralism and to value the diversity it brings.

From one perspective, the United States is a crazy quilt of diversity, patched together out of a multitude of racial and ethnic groups, each with its own perspectives and values. Compounding this is the complex division of labor and specialization of our industrialized economy and the diversity of life styles brought about by the socioeconomic distinctions this division brings. People in the United States are all different, and they value those differences.

A third major value in American culture is the belief in the autonomy of the local community and the decentralization of authority. In many ways, this is a product of the first two values as they shaped the nation's historic development. Because people in the United States value their freedom, they have produced a form of government in which local control—the right of diverse communities to determine their own future within the limits of the constitution—is emphasized. The framers of the constitution, remembering vividly the autocratic rule of monarchy, gave only limited power to the central government, retaining all other powers for the individual states and communities.

Further, that desire for decentralized authority derives from an inherent distrust of centralized power. Not only did the colonial founders abhor autocracy, but later many families in the United States were founded by immigrants who fled to this country to escape tyranny. This society's inherent distrust of central power has not only shaped the U.S. political institution, it has influenced every other institution as well.

Finally, culture in the U.S. reflects a pragmatic and utilitarian emphasis that results in an entrepreneurial spirit. Americans value "what works" and reward those willing to take risks because they believe they can make something work. Long before the age of high technology, America rewarded the risk-takers who dared to cross the prairies and conquer the mountains. That frontier spirit became a part of a U.S. mentality that still believes there are no problems that technology cannot solve. Technology reflects the American belief in the pragmatic and the utilitarian, and it is both producer and rewarder of the entrepreneurial spirit.

Central Values in Japanese Society

If it is risky to attempt a shorthand description of American cultural values, it may be foolhardy to attempt to do this for the Japanese. Japanese culture is very different from American culture, and because we are aware of that contrast, there is a temptation to look for clear-cut, black-and-white differences between them. Japanese values should not be seen as the obverse of U.S. values. Instead, Japanese culture should be understood in its own terms as a distinct and different blending of ideas and values.

Perhaps the most obvious difference is the emphasis people in the U.S. place on individualism and the strong value Japanese place on the group. This is not to suggest that Japanese are without a sense of their own individuality. It is, rather, to suggest that the Japanese sense of individuality, of self and self-worth, derives from the person's sense of belonging to the group—the family, the work group, the nation-family (Burks 1981; Masatsugu 1982). As Nakane (1970, 4) points out, one of the basic characteristics of Japanese society is a firmly rooted group consciousness, expressed in the notions of family and household "which penetrates every nook and cranny of Japanese society."

That sense of group-relatedness may stem from at least two things. First, the subsistence system of Japan—wet-rice cultivation—demanded cooperation and the interaction of small groups of people who were willing to place corporate welfare above personal interests (Masatsugu 1982). As Reischauer (1988, 15) suggests, "Probably such cooperative efforts over the centuries have contributed to the notable Japanese penchant for group identification and group action."

Second, socialization patterns in Japan tend to produce strong affiliative needs (DeVos 1973; Doi 1973). Child-rearing practices produce an attitude that "begins with physical and psychic dependence for gratification on the mother and grows into psychic dependence for gratification from the warmth and approval of the group" (Reischauer 1988, 144). As Smith (1983, 71) notes:

> This process of socialization produces a self that is not independent of the attitudes and expectations of others. . . . Japanese achievement motivation, which is very high, is based not on training for independence and self-reliance as in the west, but rather in instilling of affiliative and dependency needs.

Whatever its source, virtually every commentator on Japanese life and culture emphasizes the importance of the group in determining individual behavior. If the group provides the individual with self-identity, then the group also provides the individual with the basic guides for behavior. Feelings of self-worth are dependent upon the approval of the group (Masatsugu 1982).

This is especially seen in the work group. Nakane (1970, 7–8) notes that:

> Kinship, which is normally regarded as the primary and basic human attachment, seems to be compensated in Japan by a personalized relationship to a corporate group based on

work, in which the major aspects of social and economic life are involved. . . . The equivalent in modern society of *ie* (the household) . . . is a group such as "One Railroad Family," which signifies the Japanese National Railways. . . . A company is conceived of as an *ie,* all of its employees qualifying as members of a household, with the employer at its head.

The result is a society in which individualism is expressed through corporate membership and action, in which individuals develop self-identity through interaction with the predominant group to which they belong. It is a society in which to "do one's thing" is to be guided by need for the approval of the group. If the United States stresses individualism, independence, and rights, Japan places emphasis upon dependence on the group and the duty that this entails.

The second major value cluster is homogeneity and *harmony,* or *wa.* The Japanese today are "the most thoroughly unified and culturally homogeneous large bloc of people in the world" (Reischauer 1988, 33). It is a society singularly free of racial and ethnic divisions. Further, major social distinctions of caste and class based upon wealth are extremely weak. The feudally based differences of samurai and peasant have long disappeared. Japan's custom of recruiting people to occupational position on the basis of education and its system of educational testing, which allows anyone who qualifies into its universities, have further eroded a system of ranking based on ascription. While there are both wealthy and poor people in Japan, the economic system provides for a more equitable distribution of income than is found in the United States (Reischauer 1988).

In the absence of sharp racial and ethnic distinctions, Japan has developed an unusual degree of cultural homogeneity. Although there are differences of opinion and approach, there is central agreement on the core values. This cultural homogeneity, influenced heavily by the Japanese identity with the group—and the community and nation-family should be included here—has produced the value of *wa,* or harmony.

Robert Smith (1983, 44–45) describes the value of harmony in this way:

> In the conduct of their daily lives, the Japanese are at pains to avoid contention and confrontation. Reciprocity is a virtue taught to children from an early age, and much of the definition of a "good person" involves restraint in the expression of personal desires and opinions, empathy for the feelings of others, and the practice of civility.

Harmony involves a basic reciprocity among people that can exist only when there is a solid agreement on central values. It involves a basic respect not simply for the rights of others but for their opinions and approval. This does not mean that competition, aggression, and self-assertion are absent from Japanese life. They are present and are powerful forces in the achievement orientation that has led to Japan's economic revitalization. However, the value of harmony helps to channel those energies, to direct them to forms of cooperation and interaction which recognize that the interests of the individual are best served in seeking the welfare of the group.

Perhaps the most subtle, and difficult to define, core value in Japanese society is that which is known as *hierarchy*. Chie Nakane (1970) has provided a thorough and illuminating explication of the role of hierarchy in Japanese life. Growing out of

. the value of group-relatedness, Japanese society can be best understood as being structured vertically rather than horizontally. In the United States, social class distinctions structure the society in horizontal layers or tiers. Japan's stratification is not based on class, however. Instead, it is based on institutions which become the focal point of status distinctions. Thus, for example, the universities in Japan become ranked on the basis of reputation. Within the universities, departments are also ranked as more or less prestigious. University teachers' positions in Japan are dependent upon the schools in which they teach, the departments in which they hold membership, and finally, their academic rank. While there is some similarity to this in the United States, the difference is that, in Japan, position in the institution establishes the person's position in all other social relationships. Where you fit into the total scheme of things is in large measure dependent upon the institution from which you derive basic status. Thus a person in a government position has more prestige than a person in industry who, in turn, is rated somewhat higher than a person in the professions (Varley 1984).

Horizontal ranking occurs within the institution. Here age and tenure, as well as education, specialization, and office, become important in the ranking process. But this ranking is not perceived to be a barrier-creating form of stratification; rather it provides people with a clear understanding of social relationships and allows them to interact with a minimum of discomfort. Each knows what to expect from the other (Nakane 1970).

This hierarchy then extends outward to guide even casual social relationships. As Reischauer (1988, 154) notes:

> Hierarchy . . . remains fundamental and all-pervasive throughout Japanese society, giving it its shape and character. . . . it is as natural for a Japanese to shape his interpersonal relations in accordance with various levels of hierarchy as for an American to attempt to equalize his interpersonal relations despite differences of age and status.

The final core value that appears to be important is that of respect for tradition and authority. It is a common assertion that in the course of creating its economic miracle—its rapid rise to become one of the world's great industrial and economic powers—Japan has become westernized. Nothing could be further from the truth. In that modernizing process, Japan has taken a great deal from the West and adapted much of its economy and social structure. However, modernization has taken place on the basis of Japan's own traditional culture (Reischauer 1977).

Respect for tradition does not mean a slavish conformity to the past. Instead, Japanese respect for tradition has been demonstrated by employing the ancient values of Japanese society in the adoption of modern ideas and technology. Nowhere can this be seen more clearly than in the structure of administration used in Japanese industry. Here modern technology is managed by techniques which are rooted in the traditional forms of group-relatedness, consensus, and hierarchy (Burks 1981; Nakane 1970).

Ardath Burks (1981) reports that between 1953 and 1978, Japan's Institute of Statistical Mathematics conducted six polls to determine Japanese "national character." The results showed a strong consensus on attitudes that indicated modern Japanese (1) are nationalistic, valuing the nation as family, (2) have attachment to groups as a continuing value, (3) have strong feelings supporting conformism, hierarchy, and filial piety, and (4) recognize the primary value of the family. Burks notes that while this respect for traditional values declined in the immediate postwar years, the survey shows a strong resurgence of respect for traditional values.

This respect for tradition, the value of hierarchy, and the strong group affiliative tendency combine to produce within the Japanese a deep respect for authority. While it is true that Japan has been the scene of a good deal of civil disobedience—primarily student unrest attributed to leftist political groups—the vast majority of the Japanese respect authority. Even the politically restive students, once they have graduated and entered the world of work, come to accept the more conservative norms of Japanese political culture. This is so consistent that the Japanese have developed a term for it: *tenko,* "a 180-degree reversal in which the rebel after graduation ardently embraces the whole establishment he has been valiantly fighting" (Forbis 1975, 17). It is not an unthinking obedience to whatever authority demands, but rather the acceptance of the need for coordination and cooperation. The Japanese value of harmony evokes a need for order. Their value of hierarchy leads to the acceptance of authority in order to reinforce control.

3

CULTURE, CRIME, AND SOCIAL CONTROL

SOCIAL DISORGANIZATION AND CRIME RATES

Despite their superficial similarities, Japan and the United States are very different. As we have seen, differences in land, people, and historical development are reflected in the core cultural values of each of these nations. It is our basic premise that these central values establish a climate of social control that strongly affects the way in which the people of each society respond to law and order.

To be sure, the crime rates differ greatly between Japan and the United States. As indicated earlier, Japan's crime rates are a fraction of the U.S. crime rates. What makes this even more startling is the fact that Japan's extremely low crime rates defy conventional thinking about crime in contemporary society. From Durkheim on, many sociologists have taken the position that crime in modern society is a function of the social disorganization and disorder which is believed to accompany the displacements caused by industrialization and urbanization (Durkheim [1893] 1984, [1897] 1951; Thomas and Znaniecki [1920] 1985; Shaw and McKay 1929; Park, Burgess, and McKenzie 1967; Webb 1972; Clinard and Abbott 1973; Wellford 1974; Krohn and Wellford 1977; Clinard 1978; Krohn 1978; Messner 1982; Scott and Katz 1982; Kick and LaFree 1985; LaFree and Kick 1986; Fiala and LaFree 1988). As Archer and Gartner (1984, 99) summarize:

> At least six theoretical explanations for higher rates of deviance have appeared in the literature on urban crime. These six hypotheses can be stated in abbreviated form as follows: (1) cities foster the development of criminal subcultures; (2) cities produce class, cultural, and racial conflict as a function of greater population heterogeneity; (3) cities increase criminal opportunities because of population size and the concentration of commercial establishments and consumer goods; (4) cities have relatively impersonal police-civilian relations, which leads to rigid law enforcement and arrest practices; (5) the age and sex composition of cities has been altered by the arrival of immigrants (from rural areas, other nations, etc.) who are predominantly young males, the population most likely to commit crimes; and (6) the greater population density and crowded living conditions in cities increase the likelihood of pathological behavior.

25

Conventional wisdom argues that as people move into the urban areas, the social bonds forged in the family and small community weaken. The division of labor and the specialization that accompanies technological development further diminish the ties of family and community. Then too, as new ways of thinking and doing develop, the older social norms weaken and lose their power to constrain behavior. As Durkheim (1951 [1897]) expressed it, *anomie* develops, in which older norms lose both their clarity and bonding power. These traditional norms are not vigorously enforced, and competing norms are often introduced. The net result is a sort of moral laissez-faire—social control is greatly diminished and crime and delinquency flourish (Gibbons 1987; Pfohl 1985; Clinard and Abbott 1973; Cavan 1968).

But this has not occurred in Japan. Although crime rates increased immediately after World War II, they later declined (Ministry of Justice 1989; Ames 1976); despite the fact that all the conditions of social disorganization, which theory says are conducive to the growth of crime, were abundantly present. Japan had lost a war in the most devastating way. Its cities lay in ruins, its factories and industries in total shambles. Economically and spiritually, the Japanese people were destitute. Their political way of life had been tested and had been found wanting. For the first time in over twelve centuries, a victorious, invading power was present in Japan and was in complete political and economic control of the country. The perception of Japan as a superior power, an image carefully cultivated by the military faction in control of the prewar Japanese government, was totally shattered. The Japanese people were forced to confront hunger, unemployment, poverty, and the psychological consequences of total defeat and unconditional surrender.

In this situation of economic and political chaos, crime rates in Japan rose. The war-imposed poverty and hunger and the disorganization caused by the bombings and destruction of home and industry led to rising levels of theft and burglary. Unemployment, shortages of food and housing, the collapse of many of the patterns of everyday life, the return of servicemen who had experienced the shame of defeat—all of these elements helped to fuel the increase in crime. This was a period in which the traditional moral values of Japanese society were in disarray. Not only was Japanese industry devastated, but the moral and social climate in which traditional values influenced behavior was deeply affected also. It would require some time before the central values would once again assert a measure of control.

The task of rebuilding the nation also added to the social disorganization. Although Japan had been an urban nation for centuries, the rate of urbanization in Japan increased sharply during the immediate postwar years. The postwar increase in birth rate plus the growth of new industries provided added impetus to the growth of the great metropolitan centers of Japan. By 1980, 80 percent of the population was living in cities, with more than 57 percent of the total population occupying only 2.2 percent of the total land mass (Befu 1971). As increasing numbers of people flooded into cities like Tokyo and Osaka, both the ties with native villages and families and the power of tradition weakened. Table 3.1 reveals the tremendous increase in Japan's population and density between 1945 and 1985.

The developing industry itself contributed to the conditions of social disorganization. Japan was a nation that in many ways benefited from what White (1959) has referred to as the "advantage of backwardness." As Japan began to rebuild its

TABLE 3.1 Japanese Population and Density, 1945–1985

Year	Total Population	Density Per Square Km.
1945	72,147,000	195
1950	83,200,000	225
1955	89,276,000	241
1960	93,419,000	252
1965	98,275,000	265
1970	103,720,000	280
1975	111,940,000	300
1980	117,060,000	314
1985	121,047,000	324

SOURCE: *White Papers of Japan, 1984–85*, Institute of International Affairs, Tokyo.

war-shattered industries, it could take advantage of the latest technologies. As a result, the Japanese labor force became more and more specialized, more and more technologically sophisticated. In the period from 1950 to 1975, the proportion of those employed in tertiary industries grew from 29 percent to 51.7 percent of the labor force (Befu 1982).

According to social disorganization theories of criminal behavior, these conditions should have produced a continuous upward spiraling of crime rates. Although crime rates in Japan did rise during the immediate postwar years, they peaked within about ten years and then declined. Table 3.2 shows that crimes of violence increased from 1945 until about 1959. Rates of assault, for example, increased from 7.11 per 100,000 in 1945 to a rate of 78.25 in 1954. Similarly, rates of robbery grew from 1.80 per 100,000 to 6.65 in that same period. But beginning in the early 1960s, violent crime rates began to decline—a trend that continued until the mid-1980s, when violent crime rates became quite stable (Ministry of Justice

TABLE 3.2 Number and Rate of Violent Crimes* Reported in Japan, 1945–1965

Year	Violent Crimes*	Rate per 100,000
1945	7,363	10.2
1947	29,530	37.8
1949	51,530	63.1
1951	61,413	72.9
1953	69,190	79.8
1955	89,336	100.5
1957	94,530	104.2
1959	97,485	105.5
1961	92,951	98.8
1963	80,264	83.7
1965	80,287	82.0

*Violent crimes include homicide, robbery, and assault.

SOURCE: "Comparative Crime Data File: Nations" in Dane Archer and Rosemary Gartner, *Violence and Crime in Cross-National Perspective*, New Haven, Conn: Yale University Press, 1984.

1989; Archer and Gartner 1984). Conventional criminological theory simply does not provide an adequate explanation for what occurred in Japan.

The issue becomes even more intriguing when we begin to compare the record of criminal behavior in Japan to that of the United States. That comparison yields at least two puzzling facts. First, there is the startling difference in the crime rates of the two countries. Second, Japan's consistently lower crime rates have declined overall, while the United States has seen significant increases in crime.

Before we can begin to examine that comparison, it is necessary to consider some of the problems inherent in making cross-national comparisons of crime data. Despite the fact that there has been a growing interest in the cross-cultural study of crime, few data bases have been developed that allow for adequate comparison of crime rates. Scholars who have assessed the comparability of cross-national crime data have been quick to point out significant differences in legal codes which define crime, in crime reporting, and in methods and procedures of gathering crime data (Bennett and Lynch 1990; Huang and Wellford 1989; Messner 1989; Kalish 1988; Kick and LaFree 1985; Archer and Gartner 1984; Wilkins 1980; Vigderhous 1978; Krohn and Wellford 1977; Friday 1973; Meyers 1972; Wolfgang 1963). Nevertheless, several international data sets have been developed, and there is a growing literature on the methodological problems of comparative crime data. One of the most ambitious pieces of scholarship on comparative crime data is Archer and Gartner's (1984) work that produced the Comparative Crime Data File. They address many of the problems of generating and using comparative crime data. While urging caution in the use and analysis of such data, Archer and Gartner provide what appear to be valid guidelines for making comparisons.

Archer and Gartner point out that there are two basic problems in cross-national crime data. The first is underreporting, or the failure to report all incidence of crime. Much of the research on underreporting has focused on data generated in the United States, comparing the differences between the Uniform Crime Reports (UCR) and the National Crime Survey (NCS). However, the kinds of problems reported for the U.S. materials may be presumed to be found in data reported for any other society. Given some of the problems inherent in the way crime data are gathered, Archer and Gartner (1984, 39) suggest that "simple cross-national comparisons of the levels of crime are at present imprudent or even unwarranted."

However, Archer and Gartner also argue that underreporting is not equally serious for all levels of crime. Following Skogan (1974) and Ferdinand (1967), they suggest that reporting errors are minimal for the most serious crimes and that "homicide is the most valid of offense indicators in that official statistics on this offense are immune to underreporting" (1984, 35). Citing evidence from Verkko (1953, 1956) and Phillipson (1974), they also assert that underreporting is simply not an issue in the cross-national records on homicide and that "offense seriousness and underreporting are inversely related—that is, most serious offenses *are* reported" (Archer and Gartner 1984, 56, emphasis added; see also Kick and LaFree 1985; Hansmann and Quigley 1982). Archer and Gartner applied this line of reasoning to the Comparative Crime Data File, the international data set they developed. This data set reports data on serious offenses—including murder, rape, robbery, assault, and theft—in 110 nations and 44 international cities. They also developed a composite index of "violent crimes," which includes the crimes of homicide, robbery, and assault.

The second major problem in using cross-national crime statistics, according to Archer and Gartner, is variation in measures of crime. This problem begins with differences in the legal definition and subsequent categorization of criminal acts. For example, most criminal codes in the United States identify interpersonal violence not resulting in death as "assault," and different degrees of seriousness are usually specified. In order to gather data on crime rates, the Federal Bureau of Investigation (FBI) requests local police departments to classify assaults into one of several categories, ranging from assaults with a firearm to simple, nonaggravated assault (Federal Bureau of Investigation, 1980). However, these data classification categories do not always correspond to the legal definitions of the various states. Japan's Penal Code, on the other hand, distinguishes similar acts of violence as "bodily injury," "violence," and "intimidation," based upon the amount of physical harm committed. These legal categories are the ones used to record assault offenses in Japanese crime data. Thus, similar types of offense behavior are defined and classified differently in the two countries.

Another dimension of this problem is the variety of indicators for crime rates used in different countries. Some of the indicators which have been used include "offenses known to the police," "arrests" or "cases cleared," "number of persons brought to trial," and "convictions." Obviously, what is used as the indicator of crime will significantly affect the reported level of crime. Data using "convictions" will yield a much smaller figure than data using "offenses known to police." While each of these indicators may be relevant for different types of studies, direct comparisons between societies is certainly not meaningful if different indicators are used.

Because of these data comparability problems, some researchers have concluded that descriptive analysis, comparing crime rates of particular countries, cannot be done legitimately using existing international data bases (Bennett and Lynch 1990). However, in focusing on crime rates in Japan and the United States, we can carefully consider differences in definitions of crime, differences in reporting practices, and differences in data-gathering methods and procedures in order to assess the comparability of crime data from these two countries. Huang and Wellford's (1989) recent research on the comparability of international crime data supports this approach. Because we are dealing with only two nations and because we have information on the crime reporting definitions and practices used, we can assess the comparability of crime data from these two nations with a good deal of accuracy.

Furthermore, even crime indicators that have comparability problems can still prove useful in analyzing crime trends in different countries. If it can be assumed that both the levels of reporting and the selected indicators have been used consistently for the time period in which the data have been gathered, the data may present valid portrayals of trends in criminal behavior even when used in cross-national comparisons (Archer and Gartner 1984).

The data presented in this chapter were collected by the Federal Bureau of Investigation in the United States and the National Police Agency in Japan. Both data sets are based upon reports submitted by local police agencies. We have several reasons to be relatively confident in making comparisons using these crime data. First, when we develop a *violent crime index,* which includes homicide, rape, robbery, and assault, the range of criminal behaviors encompassed appears quite similar. Such a composite index is much less subject to definitional issues associated with single categories of crime. While Archer and Gartner (1984) suggest that homicide is the most accurately reported criminal event, comparison of murder rates is possible only if the same definitions of murder are used in the countries being studied. Unfortunately, that is not the case for Japan and the United States. Homicide data in the United States include only instances where death has occurred—attempted homicides are classified as assault. Japan, on the other hand, classifies death that occurs as a result of assault or robbery as an assault or robbery, not homicide (Kalish 1988). Subsequently, if the single category of homicide were used as the basis for comparison, significant differences would exist in what was counted in each country, making comparison invalid. A violent crime index, however, allows a very similar range of offenses to be measured and compared. This usage reflects the pattern followed by Archer and Gartner (1984) and should provide data that allow for valid comparisons.

A second reason to be reasonably confident in the comparability of these data is that the indicators used to describe levels of crime are consistent between the two countries. One indicator used in both Japan and the United States is "offenses known to the police." This is the crime indicator that we use.

Third, although there are differences in the levels of underreporting crime in Japan and the United States (Ministry of Justice 1989), the patterns of underreporting that exist in each country add credence to comparisons of these data. It is generally agreed that U.S. crime data are more consistently and heavily underreported than the data reported for other nations (Archer and Gartner 1984). Some of the reasons for this include: the U.S. public's tendency to neither cooperate with police nor report minor property crimes, the decentralized pattern of American law enforcement, and the lack of a nationwide criminal code. The Japanese police, however, are a nationally organized force that enjoys unusual rapport with and cooperation from the public. They enforce a national criminal code and use a centralized crime reporting system. This should produce a much more accurate estimate of crime. As Fishman and Dinitz (1989, 114) put it, "Insofar as any criminal justice data, from any country, can be used with confidence . . . Japanese figures are undoubtedly more reliable than crime trend data from elsewhere." If this is the case, then the comparison of the low crime rates in Japan to the crime rates in the United States becomes a very conservative measure of the differences between them.

Despite these reassurances on the comparability of these data, direct comparisons of crime rates in Japan and the United States must be done cautiously. The study of cross-national crime rates is relatively recent, and confidence in comparative data, especially comparisons of crime rates between specific countries, is tentative (Bennett and Lynch 1990; Kalish 1988).

As was suggested earlier, two generalizations stand out when the crime data of Japan and the United States are compared. First, rates of violent crime are tremendously greater in the United States as compared to Japan—the sheer degree

TABLE 3.3 Violent Crime in Japan and the United States, 1988

	Japan[1]		United States[2]	
	Number	**Rate per 100,000**	**Number**	**Rate per 100,000**
Homicide	1,441	1.2	20,675	8.4
Rape	1,741	1.4	92,480	37.6
Robbery	1,771	1.4	542,968	220.9
Assault	21,516	17.5	910,092	370.2
Total Violent Crime	26,469	21.6	1,566,215	637.2

[1]*Summary of the White Paper on Crime—1989*, Research and Training Institute, Ministry of Justice—Japan (1989), pp. 66–68, tables I-4, I-5, I-6.
[2]*Sourcebook on Criminal Justice Statistics—1988*, U.S. Department of Justice, Bureau of Justice Statistics (1989), p. 427, table 3.115.

of difference is startling. Table 3.3 reveals that in 1988, when the rate of violent crime per 100,000 population was 637.2 in the United States, it was only 21.6 in Japan. The United States' rate was almost thirty times greater than Japan's. Homicide rates, which must be used cautiously given the differences in definitions, show a rate of 8.4 per 100,000 in the United States compared with a rate of 1.2 in Japan.

The second generalization that stands out when these crime rates are compared is the difference in crime trends. Figure 3.1 depicts the patterns of violent crime in Japan and the United States between 1960 and 1988. Far different trends of violent crime emerge from these data. Official data from the United States indicate that violent crime increased fairly dramatically throughout the 1960s and 1970s and then decreased in the first half of the 1980s, only to begin another upward trend in 1985. In contrast, Japan's official crime rates indicate that violent crime began to decline in the early 1960s after reaching a postwar high in the late 1950s. Japan's violent crime rate declined steadily throughout the 1960s and 1970s. In the latter part of the 1980s, the rate of violent crime appears to have leveled off.

What makes these differences even more dramatic is that much of the violent crime in Japan is directly attributable to the *Boryokudan*—the organized criminal gangs which are often referred to as the *Yakuza*. We should note that a considerable amount of violent crime in the United States is also attributable to organized gangs, especially street gangs. Within the past few years, violence committed by groups such as the "Bloods" or "Crips" of Los Angeles or groups like the El Rukns of Chicago has certainly been a significant factor in violence in the United States (Huff 1989). Unfortunately, law enforcement agencies in the United States do not seem to have the same level of information about gang membership as do similar agencies in Japan, and the U.S. system of crime reporting does not focus on crime resulting from gang activity.

Japan, however, has been able to detect what portion of crime is related to Boryokudan members. Because Japan's law enforcement methods and the gangs'

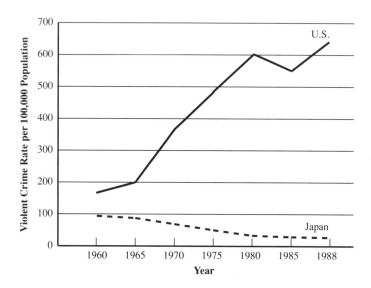

FIGURE 3.1 Trends in Violent Crime Rates in Japan and the United States, 1960–1988
SOURCES: *Japan Statistical Yearbook, 1986,* Japan Statistics Bureau, p. 712, table 22-1; *Summary of the White Paper on Crime—1988 & 1989,* Research and Training Institute, Ministry of Justice—Japan, 1988, pp. 61–62, tables I-4, I-5, I-6; 1989, pp. 66–68, tables I-4, I-5, I-6; *Sourcebook of Criminal Justice Statistics—1988,* U.S. Department of Justice, Bureau of Justice Statistics (1989), p. 427, table 3.115.

way of operating enable police to know who Boryokudan members are (Ministry of Justice 1989; Ames 1981; Bayley 1976c), the police are able to specify which crimes were committed by gang members.

The Japanese Ministry of Justice (1989, 7) estimated that 3,197 Boryokudan groups existed in 1988 with membership totaling 86,552, or about .07 percent of the total population. Examining the data in Table 3.4, we see that in 1988 this small group was involved in 25.3 percent of all arrests for homicide, 22.8 percent of all arrests for bodily injury, 19.5 percent of all arrests for assault, and 64.3 percent of all arrests for intimidation. In addition, Boryokudan offenders were involved in 45.2 percent of all arrests for violation of stimulant drug laws, 31.1 percent of all arrests for firearms and swords violations, and 38.2 percent of all arrests for gambling.

If the relatively few members of organized crime are involved in such a large portion of violent crime, we can only conclude that Japanese society is even less prone to violent criminal behavior than the composite data indicate. This in turn leads us to ask, "Why?" Why do we see such differences in the rates of crime for these two modern industrialized and urban nations? Why is the rate of violent crime almost thirty times greater in the United States than it is in Japan? Why has Japan's violent crime rate declined since the early 1960s while the United States' rate continues to rise? Conventional criminological theory simply does not provide a satisfactory answer.

TABLE 3.4 Number of Arrested Boryokudan Members by Selected Offense,[1] and Their Percentage of All People Arrested,[2] 1984–1988, Japan

Type of Offense	1984	1985	1986	1987	1988
Total	29,859	28,604	26,764	24,396	24,577
	(6.7)	(6.6)	(6.7)	(6.0)	(6.2)
Homicide	516	598	564	493	356
	(28.9)	(32.6)	(33.3)	(29.9)	(25.3)
Robbery	392	367	388	271	310
	(19.3)	(20.7)	(21.1)	(15.9)	(18.8)
Bodily Injury	8,339	7,814	7,392	6,144	6,321
	(25.8)	(26.2)	(26.0)	(22.4)	(22.8)
Assault	3,447	3,227	2,899	2,260	2,287
	(19.5)	(20.5)	(21.1)	(18.6)	(19.5)
Intimidation	655	728	556	720	683
	(63.9)	(59.8)	(59.2)	(65.0)	(64.3)
Extortion	4,519	4,753	4,412	4,544	4,532
	(38.0)	(39.4)	(35.9)	(40.6)	(41.4)
Destruction of Property	699	659	600	531	520
	(23.6)	(21.8)	(21.4)	(19.3)	(18.0)
Gambling	4,285	3,470	2,965	3,182	3,671
	(43.5)	(54.7)	(38.6)	(35.4)	(38.2)
Firearms & Swords	1,554	1,774	1,599	1,439	1,255
	(28.6)	(33.6)	(32.8)	(31.5)	(31.1)
Stimulant Drugs	11,352	11,183	10,711	9,307	9,221
	(47.3)	(48.7)	(50.9)	(45.1)	(45.2)

[1]Offenses in which arrest of gangsters accounts for an average of about 20 percent of total arrests for this offense.
[2]Figures in parentheses indicate the percentage of Boryokudan members among total offenders cleared by the police.

SOURCE: *Summary of the White Paper on Crime—1989*, Research and Training Institute, Ministry of Justice—Japan (1989), p. 78.

SOCIAL CONTROL THEORY

We believe that the answer to these questions may be found in an examination of the ways in which the culture of Japan has influenced the processes and mechanisms of social control. The concept of social control has a long history in sociological thought. Coser (1982) and Janowitz (1975) note that the concept of social control was introduced by Edward A. Ross in 1901 with the publication of *Social Control*. Although a great many sociologists have used the term, there does not appear to be any coherent theory or even commonly accepted definition of the term. Janowitz (1975, 82) pointed out that the classical use of the concept of social control referred to "the capacity of a society to regulate itself according to desired principles and values." Most scholars who used the term in this way paid explicit attention to institutions and institutional analysis. Their concern was to see how the structures of society influenced the development of conformity.

By the early 1940s, however, other scholars, using a social-psychological approach, began to perceive crime as a consequence of social interaction (Janowitz 1975). This group of scholars, influenced by theoreticians as diverse as Cooley, Mead, Freud, and Durkheim, argued that the essence of social control was found in the individual's internalization of the norms and values of the society—that social control was a kind of self-control developed within the individual through a socialization process in which the structured patterns of social values and norms shape the alternative choices of action for the individual (Coser 1982, 16).

These two basic approaches to the concept of social control, the structural and the interactional, are clearly reflected in mainstream theories of crime causation. Thus, theories that emphasize social disorganization, cultural conflict, and anomie focus on the structural factors in crime causation, while theories that deal with differential association, control, and labeling reflect the interactional approach. Crime causation theories and social control theories appear to present two sides of a single idea. While reflecting a common approach, they address criminal behavior from somewhat different perspectives. One examines how social systems prevent— or attempt to prevent—crime, while the other explains why crime occurs.

Social control theorists, however, have been reluctant to combine structural and interpersonal or interactional elements into an integrated theory of control. To be sure, it is not our intent to develop such an integrated theory at this point. At the same time, however, we feel that in the context of this comparative study of crime in Japan and the United States, both structural and interpersonal approaches to theories of both social control and crime causation are needed to provide adequate understanding of the very obvious differences that exist. What we propose to do is to define social control and to suggest how the processes and mechanisms of control are related to the historical and cultural contexts of the two societies, resulting in very different rates of criminal behavior.

By *social control*, we refer to a set of processes that develop within a social system and among its participants to guarantee or maintain conformity to societal norms and values. The processes of social control and the forms they take are dependent upon the social and cultural character of the social system. In simpler societies, characterized by homogeneity of population and simplicity of technological development, the processes of social control tend to be primarily informal. These societies, which Töennies (1975 [1887]) described as having a "gemeinschaft" mentality, are relatively small in size and tend to utilize custom and traditional norms of interaction. As society becomes more technologically sophisticated and structurally heterogeneous, what Töennies would refer to as "gesellschaft" types of relationships tend to predominate. In this situation, where populations become larger and more structurally differentiated, societies tend to rely more upon formal processes and structures of social control.

Informal Social Control

Informal processes of social control are those which develop apart from any formal, institutionalized structures created for the specific purpose of guaranteeing conformity to social and moral norms. These are control mechanisms that originate from interpersonal relationships.

There appear to be at least two types of *informal controls*. The first are the controls the individual has internalized, operating independently of the physical presence of others. These are the mechanisms within the actor that are commonly referred to as *self-control,* or what Gibbons (1987) has called "personal controls." Similarly, psychologists speak of the *conscience,* or superego, of the individual that leads him or her to conform to basic norms whether or not others are aware of the individual's behavior. These controls are acquired during the socialization process when the individual, in interaction with others, internalizes the norms and expectations associated with the approval and acceptance of significant others. Developing within the individual through a learning process, these norms, once internalized, help structure the self and the self-image. They become so central to the individual's self-perception that to violate these norms and expectations is to threaten the very image of self.

Obviously, the character of what has been learned, as well as how deeply it influences the person, will shape the individual's behavior. Further, patterns of what is internalized will vary both between cultures and between the subcultures within a larger society.

The second type of informal control is based on *responsive interaction—* behavior influenced by others, either in direct contact or in terms of what Hirschi (1969, 88) calls a "psychological presence." We are speaking about the influences of family, peer group, reference group—especially in their ability to provide approval for right behavior or to sanction inappropriate behavior. Without question, Hirschi's (1969) idea of *attachment* is central to this type of informal social control. The degree to which an individual becomes bonded to others—to groups—provides a strong source of control over individual behavior. If the group has power to sanction the individual's acts through mechanisms such as acceptance or rejection, inclusion or exclusion, praise or condemnation, then the group has power to influence how the individual will behave.

It follows, then, that the strength of the individual's attachment to the group is an important factor in informal control. If an individual's bond to a group is weak or if a group has little meaning in his or her life, then the group will have little influence over behavior. Further, as Hirschi (1969) suggests, the degree to which an individual has invested time and energy in the group will also influence the level of control the group can exercise, as well as the level of personal commitment to that group.

Formal Social Control

Although informal control is important, as societies increase in size and complexity, the need for more formal types of control also increases. By *formal control,* we mean those institutionalized structures that have developed or been created for the specific purpose of guaranteeing conformity to social norms (Clinard and Meier 1989). Formal mechanisms of social control include law and legal systems, law enforcement, the courts and systems of adjudication, penal or correctional systems, as well as all other regulatory agencies that have developed to impose constraints on behavior.

It should be recognized that, in addition to these institutions that are deliberately structured to control behavior, many other structures in society have control functions as well. Thus, institutions such as the family, the schools, and religion—important agencies of childhood socialization—also play an important role in developing social control. However, equally important is the role they play in developing consensus within a society. As Crane (1982) suggests, these institutions help to shape and maintain a widely shared set of values—a strong consensus—that exercises social control.

Formal agencies of control can be effective mechanisms for guaranteeing conformity to the extent they can successfully bring negative sanctions to bear upon miscreants. The classical theory of Beccaria suggested that the objective of what we have called formal social control was to deter criminality, and that would occur only when negative sanctions were "certain, swift, and slightly more severe than the fruits of deviation would be pleasurable" (Pfohl 1985, 57).

As Gibbs (1982a) has noted, most of the recent theories in criminology have paid scant attention to the importance of these formal control mechanisms. It is our assertion, however, that differences in criminal behavior in Japan and the United States cannot be understood without reference to both the formal and informal structures of social control present in each society. In fact, we will argue that the formal structures of control are effective only to the degree that informal structures of control are operative within the society. We propose to outline the control mechanisms found in both societies and to discuss how these relate to the core values of each country as well as their relationship to criminal behavior.

CULTURAL VALUES AND SOCIAL CONTROL

We have argued that every society develops central or core values as its people interact over time with each other and with the land and its resources. These values play a formative role in shaping social relationships and in establishing accepted social behavior patterns. Because they are important to the members of a society, various mechanisms evolve to maintain and perpetuate these patterns of conduct, belief, and relationship. Talcott Parsons (1957) argued that the components of society that function to maintain social order fulfill "pattern maintenance" functions. This is what we have referred to as social control.

What is important to the argument at this point is that social control is directly related to the culture of a society, for culture not only establishes the basic patterns that are to be maintained, but also influences the structures of social control. The character of social control in any society will be shaped by the nature and character of that society's culture (Cavan and Cavan 1968). This becomes clear as we examine both informal and formal types of social control in Japan and the United States.

Informal Social Control in Japan

As Gibbons and Jones (1975, 123) point out, social control theorists argue "that conformity is produced through the ties of the person to the conventional moral order which bind him to other persons and exact pressures on him to refrain from deviance." In other words, the more closely knit the society and the more tightly bonded the structure of the group, the greater the power of social control to restrain deviant behavior. Japanese cultural values have created a social climate in which informal means of social control exert unusually strong pressures for conformity.

One of the values in Japanese culture that has helped to produce conformity is homogeneity. There are two aspects to this value. First, Japan is an unusually homogeneous society in that its population is racially quite unmixed. Earlier we pointed to the fact that under the Tokugawa, Japan was isolated from foreign contact for over two hundred years. By carefully controlling immigration from then until modern times, Japan has maintained a population that has less than 1 percent non-Japanese people. Forbis (1975, 17) notes that the Japanese have the conviction

> that Japan is a unique nation-family, a concept that in turn comes from the country's racial homogeneity and isolated geography. Japan has no shared borders, no common frontiers with any neighbors. Other nations may be melting pots, but from Hokkaido to Kyushu the Japanese derive from more or less the same set of genes.

This racial and ethnic isolation has allowed the Japanese to develop a strong shared tradition. To be sure, it was a tradition that changed over the centuries as the ideas of Buddhism and Confucianism were introduced. But the new traditions, especially Confucianism's strong emphasis upon loyalty and fidelity, helped maintain a homogeneous world view. When Japan's isolation from the world was finally ended in the nineteenth century, the older Confucian values remained intact, and through the medium of Japan's educational system, they were passed on to succeeding generations.

Japan's emergence as a world economic power—her exposure to the broader world of ideas—has no doubt had an effect on her people. As new concepts and values are introduced, we might well expect that Japan will become more and more heterogeneous, at least in the realm of ideas.

However, homogeneity in Japan is not simply the fact of racial or ethnic purity, nor is it simply a matter of a people being like-minded. The second aspect of homogeneity is that the Japanese consider it a value to be sought. They are a people who actively seek to blend themselves into the group. Forbis (1975, 19) suggests that "the characteristic of the Japanese that lies under all the other national traits is the submission of the individual to the society. Nobody wants to stand out." A common saying in Japan is "the nail that stands out is hammered down!"

Homogeneity—both in fact and in desire—plays a role in social control for the Japanese. The consensus that develops out of this desire for homogeneity is something the Japanese seek to preserve. This can be seen in the Japanese value of *wa,* or harmony.

The Japanese notion of harmony may have developed from and been reinforced by the basic living conditions of Japanese society. As we have seen, the Japanese, for all of their history, have been forced by economic circumstance or population density to develop forms of cooperation and interaction in which the interest of the individual becomes best served when he or she seeks the welfare of the group. *Wa* involves both a basic respect for the rights of others and a willingness to subordinate one's personal wishes when they conflict with the common interests. Harmony is a central value in Japanese society where homogeneity of population and tradition provide a strong consensus that defines right and wrong. To violate that consensus is to act against harmony.

The desire for harmony is reinforced by Japan's reverence for and loyalty to its tradition. Adler (1983, 95–96) notes that despite Japan's modernization, the historic traditions which guide social behavior have been maintained:

> While undergoing political upheavals, wars, social revolutions, urbanization and mod- ernization, the Japanese have clung to their time honored and traditional code of social behavior. Intricate, rigid, and ancient norms exist side by side with open-minded and cosmopolitan life style.

That tradition, passed down through twelve centuries of Japanese history, has developed within the people a keen sense of what it means to be a Japanese. Their homogeneity—the very absence of cultural diversity—has strengthened that aware- ness.

Two prominent features of that tradition seem especially important in develop- ing the processes of informal social control. These features are group-relatedness and the acceptance of hierarchy. While these two concepts are interrelated, we will deal with each separately.

Virtually every commentator who has tried to describe or analyze Japanese culture has focused on the importance of groups in Japanese life. We noted earlier that the emphasis on groups in Japanese culture may stem from the earliest times when survival strategies demanded that group interests supersede individual desires. Historically, that pattern became reinforced at various times, such as when, in the Tokugawa era, the shogunal government created the *gonin-gumi,* or five-family association. This group was composed of five neighboring families who bore collective responsibility for the behavior of its members (Ames 1981).

That emphasis upon the family and the group has been reinforced over the centuries through the use of child-rearing practices that develop strong feelings of dependency and a need for affiliation (DeVos 1973). Reischauer (1988, 144) discusses how *amae,* the attitude of dependence upon the group, develops through child-rearing practices and helps to explain the modern Japanese attachment to the family and work group. As was pointed out earlier, emphasis on the group and the individual's need for the group is further inculcated in the Japanese schools.

This group orientation means far more than the fact that Japanese are aware of and structure their lives in terms of group memberships. Masatsugu (1982, 62) and others (Wagatsuma and Rosett 1986) argue that the group is so important in Japanese life that the concept of self, or self-identity, derives from group mem- berships:

> The most important feature of the self in Japan is its dissolution into the group, as scholars from various disciplines have pointed out. We are clearly reminded here of the ancient Buddhist and Confucian concepts of losing one's identity by merging with the larger unit through enlightenment. But the most significant point is that dissolution of the self is essentially an act of will—of self-control and self-discipline.

This sense of self is one that involves dependency upon the group. It is the group that provides self-image and with that self-image a sense of acceptance, recognition, and belonging that gives life meaning and purpose. Clifford (1976, 18) points to the reciprocal character of the relationship between the individual and the group:

> It is not possible to translate adequately the word *Amaeru* by which Japanese describe their great dependency on those they feel are responsible for them. . . . The word relates to the bonds within a tightly knit group that impose conformity but that also, as a group, especially as leaders of the group, carry responsibility for the happiness and well-being of its members. . . . The conformity is imposed and policed by group standards and scrutiny, but its individual acceptance is made a great deal easier . . . because it provides for the great sense of dependency and imparts not only a sense of belonging but an assurance of understanding and solutions in time of stress.

Given that sense of dependency, behavior becomes controlled by the expectations of the group—whether it is the family, the school, or the work group. This then becomes a powerful form of social control. Individuals live under the constant scrutiny of the groups to which they belong. How one is regarded by these groups, one's need to be accepted and approved, motivates behavior. Ruth Benedict (1946), in her classical study of Japanese national character, *The Chrysanthemum and the Sword,* argues that the basic motivation for conformity in Japanese society is shame. In a society where the opinions of others become the criteria for behavior, failure to live up to the expectations of the group produces shame. She notes:

> The Japanese ask a great deal of themselves. To avoid the great threats of ostracism and detraction, they must give up personal gratifications they have learned to savor. They must put these impulses under lock and key in the important affairs of life. The few who violate this pattern run the risk of losing even respect for themselves. Those who do respect themselves *(jicho)* chart their course, not between "good" and "evil," but between "expected man" and "unexpected man," and sink their own personal demands in the collective "expectation." These are the good men who "know shame" *(haji)* and are endlessly circumspect (1946, 293).

Benedict and others thus suggest that conformity in Japan is produced because individuals wish to avoid the shame they would experience if they failed to measure up to group standards. But the notion of shame is extensive. Clifford (1976) argues that to understand crime in Japan we need to see how individuals, caught up in the web of group affiliations, are also under great pressure not to allow their actions to bring shame upon the members of their group. The individual in Japan has a part to play, and is expected by associates to play it. Failure to do so brings a sense of failure—and shame— on everyone.

This may be one of the reasons for the relatively high rate of suicide in Japan. Japanese suicides are seldom anomic. Many commit suicide because they have failed to live up to the expectations of family and friends, others because they perceive that their actions have brought shame upon the group. Clifford (1976, 8) reports that the fathers of radical students who had been arrested for murder killed themselves out of a sense of shame:

> It was not just the shame brought on them by their children, but the shame brought on the rest of the family and perhaps on companions in the same factory or place of work,

and it was done to bring home to the offender the real enormity of his outrageous behavior.

While some scholars such as Doi (1962) and DeVos (1960) suggest that the dichotomy between shame and guilt may be oversimplified, Forbis (1975) reports that most Japanese scholars agree with Benedict's basic appraisal. Perhaps one unfortunate result of this perception of Japan as a tightly controlled society is that some have written as though there are no disagreements, that individuals in Japan are not free to deviate from the expectations of the group.

Obviously, this is not the case. Given the right motivation, the Japanese can and do rebel. However, because of the nature of Japanese society, an individual who breaks free to live a different lifestyle can expect to find censure, ridicule, and the withdrawal of supporting groups. To dare to be different is to risk ostracism and rejection. This is why rebellion is so often a group phenomenon in Japan. If a local group of neighbors and friends unite to defy authority, then individuals linked with them will "conform to the nonconformity" (Clifford 1976, 31).

This phenomenon of group deviance is clearly seen in the case of the Yakuza, or Boryokudan. Earlier we reported on the extent of crime committed by these organized deviant groups. Iwai (1986) has reported that the history of the Yakuza can be traced to the earliest period of Japanese history. Made up primarily of professional criminals, the Yakuza from that day until this have operated in a highly organized fashion. Using the imagery of a family, a Yakuza group is composed of unrelated individuals who enter into a tightly knit community through rituals of initiation in which they pledge strict obedience to the gang leader and to the rules of the group. Iwai argues that today's Yakuza share the social relationships and customs that were part of the cultural life of the medieval period. They are structured to provide a place in society, an opportunity to participate, for persons who would otherwise be excluded from group membership.

Kelly (1986b), Ames (1981), and Clifford (1976) all note that members of the Yakuza are drawn from the lowest strata of Japanese society. Kelly (1986b) asserts that the gangs are made up of the deviants in Japanese life—the failures and dropouts who refuse to accommodate themselves to the very competitive and rigidly structured patterns of Japanese life. Ames (1981) reports that many of the gang recruits come from the ranks of delinquents who have been rejected by the broader society and who find it difficult to find jobs. Thus, the Yakuza groups become surrogates for the groups that members have left and have their own codes of behavior and expectations.

Within the gangs, the same reciprocal expectations are found as in the groups of the larger society—the commitment of the individual to the group in return for the group's acceptance and support of the individual. In this context, the behavior of the Yakuza gangsters, seen as delinquent or deviant from the perspectives of the larger society, is behavior in conformity with the expectations of the deviant group.

The controlling influence of the group is reinforced by the cultural trait of hierarchy that is so dominant in Japanese life. Adler (1983, 96) notes that:

Since ancient times Japanese society has been hierarchical, with each individual occupy-ing a given position which carries with it specific obligations. . . . There is an intricate network of behavioral norms which subjects individuals to the needs of the group.

Hierarchy in the Japanese context does not refer to caste or social class. Edwin Reischauer (1988) has taken great care to point out that, despite its social rankings, Japan has an amazingly egalitarian quality. Hierarchy in Japan developed out of the Confucian concern for harmony and order, and, as Clifford (1976, 8–10) notes, it has created a social world in which each person

> has a proper place; everyone fits into the hierarchy of a vertical society; everyone . . . has a recognized position to fill in the scheme of things, and he is expected to live up to it. The Japanese society is so constructed that if he does live up to it, then he will benefit; if he does not live up to it, then he will be despised and bring shame on all those connected with him.

That sense of place is taught to children virtually from birth. Ruth Benedict (1946) describes how a Japanese mother whose infant is still being carried on her back pushes the child's head down with her hand, teaching the "respect rules" that express the differences in the social hierarchy. The impact of that training, the knowledge of where you fit in the society, of what is expected of you and what you can expect from others, still provides a sense of security and encourages conformity to the norms that govern social relationships in present-day Japan.

Social control theories have argued that conformity is produced when the individual is bound to the conventional moral order through close ties to other persons. These ties encourage individuals to refrain from deviance because they want and need the good opinion of the group (Gibbons and Jones 1975). These conditions are a part of the social structure in Japan and are reinforced by core values of the society. The homogeneity of the Japanese people and their cultural heritage have produced a strong cultural tradition that contains clear and consistent prescriptions for moral conduct. Further, the emphasis upon hierarchy and group relatedness ties into networks of security and support that strongly encourage the individual to conform to group and societal expectations (Vago 1988; Pfohl 1985).

As a consequence, both forms of social control that were discussed earlier are reinforced by Japanese culture. Because there is a single moral tradition, internalized in the home and reinforced by the educational system, the Japanese appear to be people with strong self-control. However, that self-control operates within the context of a social order in which the desire and need for the approval of others have created what Clifford (1976) has called "The Internal Policeman." Because individuals are embedded in the group, they are under constant surveillance; failure to live up to the expectations of the group may result in gossip, criticism, ridicule, reprimand, or rejection. As a result, much of that control is self-imposed. Because self-image is dependent on the group's response, individuals must constantly monitor their own behavior. The desire and need to maintain a sense of self-worth become an internal censor.

Informal Social Control in the United States

Social control mechanisms in the United States differ from those in Japan not so much in type as in degrees and levels of effectiveness. This is a result of the sharp differences in the cultural values of the two societies.

While Japanese prize their homogeneity and common tradition, people in the

United States celebrate their diversity. As we have pointed out, our polyglot population presents us with a richly diverse texture of heterogeneity.* We are not a people who have developed historically out of a common racial stock, knit together with a single historic tradition. The belief that the United States would become the great melting pot society in which a hundred cultures would be blended never came to fruition. Japan is the blend society; the United States is not. Instead, ours has become the first truly international society.

Although its citizens share such common elements as language, the desire for success, and the love of freedom, the United States remains a society of great diversity. We are divided by race and ethnic heritage, religious belief, occupation and social class, political ideology, and the hundred and one divergent opinions that stem from all of these differences—differences easily seen in the current struggles over issues such as abortion and gay rights. This is not to suggest that the Japanese have complete consensus on all issues. However, people in the United States are not linked by a common tradition and a common racial heritage. Almost every commentator suggests that U.S. citizens are far more diverse—in opinion as well as in social structure—than the Japanese. Put simply, a clear-cut consensus on many issues is not apparent in the United States.

We would argue that this diversity and lack of a strong moral tradition or consensus lead to a situation in which there is uncertainty about social norms and confusion over how deviant behavior is to be treated. Social disorganization and anomie theories of social control suggest that when there is a lack of strong consensus about values and norms, traditional rules no longer apply, and the amount of "deviance" is likely to increase (Sellin 1938; Traub and Little 1985).

Three factors of American life and culture seem to be important here. First, because of the social class and ethnic diversity in the United States, there is wide variation in the interpretation and application of norms. Norms that seem important in one community may be seen as inappropriate or meaningless in another neighborhood. For example, an upwardly mobile, middle class family might be horrified to discover one of its children dealing drugs; a disorganized family, living in poverty, may see it as a relatively normal part of ghetto life. Also, a subcultural norm of "manliness" may lead to behaviors viewed as deviant by members of the dominant group.

Second, these differences of class status and ethnic heritage are not modified by any effective system of socializing children into a common set of moral and ethical values. The strong feelings we have about the freedom of religious expression and our desire to keep church and state separate have prevented public education from becoming an agency for moral and ethical training. The consequence is that children learn, or fail to learn, basic moral values in the home, and the diversity of opinion,

---

*There is abundant literature on the relationship of social heterogeneity to crime, much of it attempting to explain variation in crime rates—often homicide—across cultures (Gartner 1990; Hansmann and Quigley 1982; Messner 1982; Krohn 1978; McDonald 1976; Clinard and Abbott 1973; Webb 1972). The work of Emile Durkheim (1893, 1897), who sought to explain the social consequences of societal development, provides the theoretical basis for much of this research, which supports the notion that greater levels of cultural heterogeneity are associated with higher rates of crime, especially violent crime.

belief, and value is perpetuated. Stephen Pfohl (1985, 161–162) summarizes the effects of social disorganization on the socialization process in this way:

> Socialization, the process through which one generation of people passes on its beliefs, values, and normative constraints to another, is disrupted by social disorganization. The power of traditional beliefs, values, and norms is dissipated by a disorganized moral climate in which "anything goes." At the individual level this means that many people will fail to develop the self-censoring consciences which are said to regulate behavior in the well ordered society. Simply stated, disorganizational theorists assume that (1) the presence of normative chaos results in disrupted socialization, and (2) disrupted socialization results in weakened normative constraint.

A third factor of life in the U.S. that influences the ability of norms to control behavior is the uncertainty with which our society has dealt with the problem of criminal sanctions. Policy has shifted from an emphasis upon due process rights to a "get tough" crackdown on street crime. However, that shift in policy represents only one aspect of a decentralized system of justice in which there appears to be little consistency of approach across either time or state borders. Failure to provide consistent definitions of crime coupled with unequal treatment of criminal offenders have helped weaken the respect for law as a control mechanism (Walker 1989).

The values of diversity and heterogeneity are closely related to the core values of freedom and independence. In stressing the American value of independence we do not intend to suggest that the Japanese are a people devoid of an appreciation of freedom and individualism. Reischauer (1988) is at pains to point out that the Japanese, despite their attachment to groups, retain a deep sense of self-identity. However, they express that individualism with self-discipline and inner control.

On the other hand, although residents of the United States prize their individualism and freedom, they, too, are a people who must live out their lives in the context of group relationships. But there are distinct differences in the two societies. The images that U.S. culture projects are those of the rugged individual who operates in self-directed independence—the entrepreneur and the pioneer who strike out alone to achieve a dream or vision.

These may be fitting images for a nation composed of people who came seeking freedom from the control of others—whether that be religious, economic, or political control. Central to these images are the concepts of freedom, liberty, independence, and individualism. These values were translated into an emphasis upon civil rights that contrasts sharply with the Japanese emphasis on the group, hierarchy, and duty (Conklin 1986). As Ruth Benedict (1946) noted, the Japanese reliance on order and hierarchy is poles apart from the U.S. faith in freedom and equality.

However, the emphasis upon "rights" in our society at times becomes interpreted to read, "My rights!" or "What pleases me." We would argue that our emphasis upon freedom, independence, and individualism, in the absence of any strong moral tradition or social consensus, leads to a situation in which freedom centers on the satisfaction of the self. In Japan the individual's actions are subject to the group's relentless scrutiny and control. In the United States that control becomes weakened by our insistence on the priority of the individual.

This difference became central in Benedict's guilt versus shame treatment of social control. Because people in the United States were less tightly bonded to groups, informal control operated on the basis of guilt rather than shame. However, if the individual had been improperly socialized or if the traditional moral values had little meaning for the individual, control by guilt was not effective. As U.S. society became more diversified, religion, family, and other social forces of community and neighborhood lost their capacity to exercise strong control upon individual behavior (Shaw and McKay 1929). As a result, people relied increasingly upon formal or external control mechanisms.

However, the emphasis upon freedom and diversity in the U.S. leads to a distrust of political power and less respect for centralized forms of social control. The United States was formed by people who sought freedom from control, and that distrust of centralized power has translated into an ambivalence about any agency that has the power to restrict freedom. As a result, we seem to have a love–hate relationship with law and order. We recognize the need for order—indeed, whenever crime rates have soared in this country, we have insisted on stricter controls (Kramer 1982)—yet few people welcome the restrictions law imposes. Fishman and Dinitz (1989, 113) point out that:

> Nourished in the principles of the French Revolution, which, on the American soil, neatly complemented the Protestant ethic laissez-faire motif, a nation of outcastes and strangers feared statism more than unbridled freedom, the fraternity of law enforcers as much and at times more than the fraternity of violaters.

As a nation, the United States—from the very beginning—has known the constant tension that arises when people desire complete freedom but know they also need some form of corporate social control. This weakens social controls because law and law enforcement are not given adequate respect.

An example of possibly weakened social controls is the struggle to control drug trafficking. Japan's record in suppressing drug trafficking may in part be explained by the fact that Japan is a nation of many islands lying hundreds of miles off the Asian mainland. Arguably, that situation may make drug smuggling easier to contain than the open borders between the United States and its neighbors. But the problem of drugs in the United States does not continue simply because drug smugglers have easier access. Despite massive effort and huge expenditures of money, labor, and resources, the United States has been unable to control the drug traffic.

In 1987, 13,423 defendants were convicted of drug offenses in U.S. District Courts. This represents a 161 percent increase over the 5,135 persons convicted for drug offenses in 1980. In 1987 drug offenses constituted 33.1 percent of all the cases prosecuted by the federal district courts, a 10.1 percent increase over 1980. Drug offenses accounted for over 50 percent of the total increase in federal convictions during the period from 1980 to 1987. By contrast, public order offenses increased only 21.9 percent in that period (Hester and Kaplan 1989).

The market for drugs in the United States is so great—the profits so large—that efforts to control it have failed. Could it be that the inability to control drugs is rooted in the nation's lack of strong informal controls? Because so many "average"

Americans, including people in the middle and upper middle classes, tolerate drug use—because the United States has no clear consensus on this issue—social control has broken down.

Thus, informal social control appears to be much weaker in the United States than in Japan. Lack of homogeneity has prevented the development of a strong moral consensus based upon a common tradition. Further, even if such a tradition were available, U.S. society has no public agency to educate children in a commonly accepted moral order. The result is a population that varies widely in its understanding of and respect for social norms, and, consequently, in those norms' ability to control individual behavior.

Equally important is the effect of the emphasis upon freedom, independence, and equality in the United States. The group-centered character of Japanese society provides strong controls over individual behavior, but although life in the United States is certainly group-related, the group seldom has the same power to control. Some groups, such as the family, are very important to most Americans, but they do not appear to provide the same sort of ego-defining relationship, and as a result, they become much weaker sources of informal control.

Formal Mechanisms of Social Control in Japan and the United States

Formal social control refers to efforts to maintain order through the use of institutions or organizations specifically developed for that purpose. This includes the law and the legal system, law enforcement, the courts, and corrections. Because the materials in the chapters that follow will deal extensively with each of these sectors of formal control, the discussion here will be limited to the relationship between formal and informal controls.

Informal social control influences formal mechanisms of control in at least two ways. First, the stronger and more effective the processes of informal social control, the less the need for formal control processes. Steven Vago (1988, 145) argues that

> if there is intense social interaction on an intimate face-to-face basis, normative consensus and surveillance of the behavior of members of the community, informal control will be strong to the extent that legal or formal controls may be unnecessary.

While Vago's argument is logical, no modern industrial society has been able to operate without formal control mechanisms. That is certainly also true of Japan. However, far fewer police are employed in Japan than in the United States. In Japan there are approximately 2.17 policemen for every 1,000 persons, while in the United States there are 2.85 (Bayley 1985, 81). Further, given Japan's extremely low crime rate, Japanese police are employed in a much broader range of activities than are police in the U.S. Japanese police, for example, play an important dispute resolution role and are more extensively involved in crime prevention.

The second influence of informal social control on formal control is indirect but important. Adler (1983) points out that the almost adversarial relationship between citizens and police found in many Western cities is not found in Japan. Instead, Japanese police enjoy the respect and admiration of the civilian population. This respect may stem in part from the Japanese tradition in which government employment is seen as prestigious, but it is also influenced by the Japanese notion of hierarchy which encourages respect toward persons who exercise legitimate authority.

The Japanese tradition of citizen participation that was seen in the five-family, or *gonin-gumi,* of Tokugawa times (Clifford 1976), the respect for police, and the value Japanese place on harmony have combined to encourage an amazing degree of citizen participation in law enforcement activities. Bayley (1976c), Ames (1981), and Parker (1984) all make note of the important role citizen groups play in crime control. Adler (1983, 103–104) remarks, "The most extraordinary aspect of the Japanese Criminal Justice system is the amount and intensity of popular participation, at virtually every level of the process." Bayley (1976a, 91) reports that "every neighborhood in Japan has a Crime Prevention Association composed of resident volunteers who work closely with the local police station." There are 1,200 associations in Japan which coordinate the activities of 560,000 contact points— residences or businesses, marked with a distinctive sign—where police information or assistance can be sought. In addition, there are 8,000 associations based on occupation or work place which are concerned with crime prevention and are linked into a National Federation of Crime Prevention Associations (Bayley 1976c).

These are functional groups which become involved in a variety of prevention activities—distributing leaflets, erecting signs, selling locks for windows and doors, alerting people to dangers such as unguarded canals, maintaining surveillance, and accompanying officers on street patrol.

Perhaps the presence of these groups, motivated by the same values that produce the strong internal forms of social control, makes it possible for the Japanese police to be an effective control agency. If effectiveness can be measured in terms of crime clearance rates, then the Japanese police are among the most efficient in the world, as indicated by Figure 3.2.

We would argue that formal systems of control are strongly influenced by the level and kinds of informal control mechanisms present in a society. Law enforcement agencies in the United States are often met with a great deal of suspicion and even hostility by a public that is ambivalent about the police role. For most people in the United States, the police are an intrusive force whose presence is needed to keep the peace but resented because it represents an unwanted control. Because U.S. society lacks a tradition of respect for public authority, police–citizen relationships are very different from those found in Japan.

While informal controls influence formal controls, the opposite is also true. For example, the respect many U.S. citizens have for the law may be diminished because of the criminal law's emphasis on what might be termed laws of morality— laws governing activities such as gambling, prostitution, and use of alcohol. These activities are viewed by many as a private concern, a matter of individual right, and the interference of the state in the pursuit of these activities is resented. When government agencies seek to punish these so-called "victimless crimes," some people withdraw their support. Disrespect for law in one area tends to weaken respect for law in other areas as well. As a result, weakened formal control may lead to weakened informal control mechanisms. This is clearly seen in the experiment with prohibition. An unpopular law that was broken by millions who saw no harm

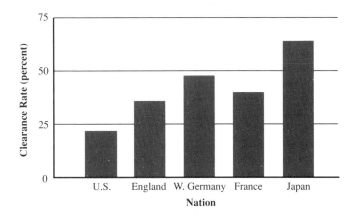

FIGURE 3.2 Clearance Rates of Major Crimes in Five Nations, 1985
SOURCE: "Annual Report on Crime, 1987," Ministry of Justice, Foreign Press Center, Japan, p. 1.

in the use of alcohol, prohibition may well have played a central role in the decay of the people's respect for the law in the United States (Walker 1989).

Finally, a pervasive response to increasing U.S. crime rates in the 1960s and 1970s was "get-tough" legislation that led to the incarceration of more offenders for longer periods of time. This was an effort to use the mechanisms of formal social control to maintain law and order. However, what has happened is that U.S. prisons quickly filled to overflowing, and the federal judiciary was compelled to act to maintain humane standards in the prisons. The result has been that corrections officials have been forced to use early release of felons to reduce prison overcrowding. Another consequence has been that some judges, aware of the burgeoning prison population, have made more generous use of probation and suspended sentences.

This has impacted informal social control. Classical theorists argued that punishment would have a deterrent effect—that is, would control deviance—if it was swift, sure, and sufficiently harsh to make the deviant action unrewarding. We would suggest that current penal policies in the United States have resulted in the loss of deterrent power and have weakened the informal mechanisms of social control.

CONCLUSION

Japan and the United States may be seen as societies which contrast sharply in terms of both social control and criminal behavior. Despite their similarity as modern, urban, and industrial nations, great differences in history and culture, in land and people, have produced major differences in the values and norms governing behavior. Japan's homogeneous society, deeply loyal to a historic tradition that provides a sense of moral order, is knitted into a network of group relations that provides its people with both a sense of place and a sense of self and that creates a strong commitment to social norms. The result is a people whose respect for law and order is reflected in one of the lowest crime rates in the world.

On the other hand, the heterogeneity of American society has not allowed the same sort of moral order or tradition to develop. If the United States has a tradition, it is that of the individual, the pioneer, the entrepreneur who goes it alone. Individualism and independence, based upon the value of freedom, have placed a heavy emphasis upon individual rights rather than corporate responsibility. Distrust of strong central government and power has fragmented our justice system and weakened its ability to exercise control. The consequence is a rate of violent crime that is almost thirty times higher than in Japan. Is that crime rate the price that people in the United States are willing to pay to maintain a sense of freedom and individualism? We would argue that basic values in the United States structure both criminal behavior and the society's response to crime.

4

DEFINING CRIME: CRIMINAL LAW

Differences in the core values of American and Japanese societies have important implications for criminal law as it has developed in each country. As Gibbons (1987, 49) suggests, "Laws are social phenomena which have roots in the social and economic conditions of the nations from which they emerge." While some law develops from the need to reinforce the social mores and some law stems from the power structure of the society, law develops overall as a reflection of the central values of the society. As the system of values within a society changes, law changes; and as values vary from society to society, so also does the law.

Lawrence Friedman (1984) provides a useful framework for studying the differences in American and Japanese law. Friedman suggests that legal systems can be examined in terms of three basic elements: the structures of law, the substance of law, and the *legal culture* of a society within which the law operates.

LEGAL CULTURE

In our discussion of law in these two societies, we use a somewhat expanded form of the concept of legal culture, which Friedman (1984, 6) defines as "people's attitudes toward the law and the legal system—their beliefs, values, ideas, and expectations." We use the term to refer to popular assumptions about law and its use, and also about the central values that help structure the law. Legal culture is a part of society at large, shaped and influenced by the same factors that affect other cultural components.

Legal Culture in the United States

Legal culture in the United States grows out of the same interaction of environment, population, and history that was discussed earlier. Four elements appear to be important in its shaping.

Constitutionalism: Diversity and the Colonial Heritage   As Allan Farnsworth (1963, 2) notes, "No adequate comprehension of the American legal system is possible without an understanding of the way . . . [the] individual colonies were welded together under a constitution."

Although the original colonists were predominantly English-speaking peoples who shared a common culture, peoples from many different nations came to the colonies during the first half-century of settlement. Germany, Holland, Spain, France, and the Scandinavian nations, as well as Africa, all contributed to the ethnic, racial, and cultural mix that was to become the United States.

This mixture of peoples, combined with the varying conditions of soil and climate in the new world, led the thirteen colonies to develop in quite different ways. The rocky soil of Massachusetts was suitable only for small-scale farming; the lands of Virginia and the Carolinas were well-suited to the development of large estates. Many of those who settled in the southern colonies were well-to-do people of aristocratic background; many of those in the northern colonies were of merchant or craftsman traditions. Some colonies were populated by religious dissenters seeking religious freedom; others were members of the established church, quite content with the religious status quo.

The result was a population divided into thirteen distinct colonies, each with its own priorities, problems, and prospects, and thus a colonial legal system that was divided and differentiated. The tradition of British common law shared by most of the colonists was an important heritage that shaped legal ideas, but each colony developed laws that reflected the special problems and interests of its people, as well as their particular ideologies (Friedman 1984).

The element of diversity was important in shaping the basic legal system when the colonies joined to form the central government. The chief problem faced by the Constitutional Convention in 1787 "was to form a strong union without obliterating the states as constituent, in some respects autonomous, parts of the system" (Farnsworth 1963, 3).

The solution was to develop a government based on the ideas that the people are sovereign and that government has only those powers granted to it by the people—all other powers are reserved to the constituent states.

Those ideas, given shape and expression in the Constitution, have shaped the further development of law in the United States. Each state has developed its own body of law, reflecting the state's particular problems and interests as well as its historic development. But all have been influenced by the Constitution's careful delineation of civil rights and by the U.S. Supreme Court's actions as the arbiter of that constitution.

Legal culture in the United States thus becomes influenced by *con-stitutionalism*—the recognition that in the United States a sovereign people have delegated certain powers to the central government but have allowed the individual states to retain all other power. This is reflected in the fact that while there is a federal criminal code pertaining to federal concerns, each state has the power to define, under the provisions of the Constitution, its own laws governing criminal behavior.

Americans prize the diversity, the idea of local control, that this decentralized system of criminal law provides. This is an important element in American legal culture. But, as Farnsworth (1963) points out, the constitutional system has also aided in developing respect for law and belief in its supremacy, which is reflected in the fact that even the state is subject to judicial review under the Constitution.

Individual Rights   The second major element in the legal culture of the United States grows out of the Constitution's guarantees of individual rights. Although the Constitution adopted in 1787 did not specify individual rights, passage of the Bill of Rights in 1789 incorporated the basic rights central to our understanding of the concept of freedom or liberty.

One of the central features of the Constitution is that all these rights are conferred upon people as individuals by right of citizenship. Further, most of these rights are offered to all persons, whether they are citizens or not. The rights they enjoy are not theirs by virtue of their socioeconomic class, religion, or ethnicity. They are rights that the Constitution declares to be inherent to the individual.

The notion of civil rights is a major key to our understanding of both legal culture and criminal law. For most people in the United States, the idea of freedom and the notion of civil rights are virtually synonymous. Because we prize freedom, we value highly those rights that are guaranteed by the Constitution. Much of what has occurred in the area of criminal law in the past few decades has centered around varying interpretations of constitutionally guaranteed rights. The landmark decisions of *Gideon, Escobedo,* and *Miranda,* for example, all focus on civil rights issues. These decisions illustrate how the values of freedom and of liberty—a basic respect for civil rights—have helped shape the context of criminal law and its administration in the United States. It is interesting that, when one adds up all the separate rights guaranteed in the first eight amendments, well over half deal strictly with the rights of criminal defendants.

An Objective Approach to Law   Perhaps the centrality of civil rights issues in the legal system of the United States is necessary because of the objective approach taken in its criminal law. By an objective approach, we refer to the use of an adversarial approach to criminal law in which the objective elements of guilt or innocence leave little room for subjective considerations to influence the judicial process. Farnsworth (1963, 13) suggests that this approach comes from the heritage of British common law, in which a trial is "a contentious proceeding, a contest, in which the adversary parties take the initiative and in which the role of the judge is that of umpire rather than inquisitor."

The U.S. system of criminal law operates with a concept of *mens rea*—criminal intent—that really does not ask questions of motivation. The objective approach does not concern itself with the subjective issues of why the crime was committed. It asks only if the intent to commit the crime was present and focuses on the objective guilt or innocence of the accused.

This approach seems to reflect the pragmatic quality of U.S. society. Concern with crime is not usually focused on the questions of why but on efforts to combat crime. Further, just as Americans believe that success resulting from individual effort should be rewarded, so most are willing to accept the idea that the individual responsible for the crime should pay the penalty the law demands. This leads to the last element in U.S. legal culture as it affects criminal law.

The Punitive Character of Legal Culture in the United States   Social conditions always affect how criminal law is used. As Ronald Kramer (1982) has clearly shown, when crime rates increase, approaches to criminal law and the use of criminal sanctions tend to become harsher and more punitive. There have been periods of time when members of the justice community in the United States strongly believed that legal sanctions should be used to rehabilitate criminals and restore them to society. However, in keeping with the objective approach to crime, U.S. legal culture has generally been more punitive than restorative in character. Francis Allen (1964) has observed that even efforts that were intended to be rehabilitative have at times led to harsher sentences.

Our values, which focus on the individual rather than the group, do not place a great deal of importance on restoring the individual to the family or the community. As a consequence, our responses to crime—a significant aspect of legal culture—have been relatively harsh and punitive. This may be seen in the fact that the United States imprisons people at a rate much higher than most modern industrialized nations (Snarr and Wolford 1985), despite the use of probation and relatively easy treatment of first offenders.

The effect of legal culture on criminal law reflects the central values of society. Because we prize individual freedom and liberty, legal culture stresses civil rights. Because we distrust centralized forms of power, we prize the Constitution—which limits that power, provides for review of state legislative action, and works with decentralized laws that reflect local interests and concerns. Our belief in individualism and pragmatic orientation supports an objective view of criminal law and a punitive approach toward criminal offenders.

Development of Japanese Law

To understand contemporary Japanese legal culture, it is necessary to look at the historical development of law in Japan. Henderson (1968b) points out that after 1600, law in Japan developed through three stages: Rule by Status—1600 to 1868; Rule by Law—1868 to 1945; and Rule of Law—after 1945.

Rule by Status: The Tokugawa Period   As we have seen, the most lasting form of political structure in Japan before the seventeenth century was decentralized feudalism. During this period, law in Japan was influenced strongly by Chinese law developed during the T'ang period (Henderson 1968b). Japanese law was very limited and was applicable only in the domain of the daimyo who proclaimed it. In this decentralized system, the notion of corporate responsibility—a theme developed from Confucian teachings—led to exercising control and discipline through the family and the local community (Takayanagi 1963). Central to this control was the structure known as *gonin-gumi*, the five-family unit responsible for the behavior of the individual. Hirano (1963) argues that this system of control precluded the need for elaboration of the criminal law. Close supervision and immediate oversight of inferiors by community and feudal leaders were important elements in control (Varley 1984).

What made this system work was the acceptance of an informal code of correct conduct that "centered around the five Confucian relationships . . . [and] provided a fabric of detailed and fixed rules to handle most situations of daily life" (Henderson 1968b, 41). A part of this code is what Noda (1976b) refers to as the "rules of *giri*"—an informal system of rules that specified how persons in differing role relationships should behave toward each other. Noda (1976b) suggests that these rules deeply penetrated Japanese life and are still factors in Japanese society.

Early in the seventeenth century the Tokugawa family began to consolidate power very rapidly in a series of military and political maneuvers that resulted in the development of the Tokugawa (Edo) shogunate and a period of centralized political control that was to last for nearly three hundred years. In this period, lands not directly controlled by the Tokugawa clan were given as fiefdoms to daimyos who pledged loyalty and obedience to the Edo government, thus linking the society into a form of centralized feudalism (Reischauer 1956).

Under the Tokugawa regime, little written law was produced (Henderson 1968b). Tokugawa statesmen, influenced by Confucian ideals concerning the state, perceived their duty to be teaching rather than legislating moral behavior (Minear 1970; Takayanagi 1963; Wren 1968). Their concept of law was that of natural law—an immutable given that was "neither made by men, nor dependent upon human institutions for its validity or enforcements" (Henderson 1968b, 206). As a result, most law that developed in Tokugawa Japan was unwritten law, or custom. However, in 1742, a code of criminal laws, the *Kujigata Osadamegaki,* was promulgated by the central Edo government (Supreme Court of Japan 1982). This code consisted of two volumes, the first regulating a full range of legal proceedings from law enforcement to criminal adjudication, the second dealing primarily with substantive criminal law. The *Kujigata Osadamegaki* signifies the first attempt in Japanese history to base the practice of law on a unified code that formally established penal law and legal procedures. Although criminal cases could now be adjudicated in Edo by a supreme court, in actual practice, because judicial and administrative functions were still located in the local daimyo, local feudal lords continued to control the administration of justice (Supreme Court of Japan 1982).

Despite this code, law was seen as a given flowing from nature to govern a social order structured into a series of ranked social positions. The Confucian definition of the natural hierarchy, *Shi–No–Ko–Sho* (Warrior–Farmer–Artisan–Merchant), became the status structure on which the Tokugawa system was based. In this system it was essential that inferiors recognize the higher power and absolute authority of status superiors. Criminal law developed in the Tokugawa period to enforce this natural order of status inequality (Henderson 1968b).

While not extensive, and often intended for only a single fiefdom, Tokugawa criminal law was extremely harsh and punitive. The Tosa Code, for example, provides for cutting off the nose and ears of those who assist a runaway serf; the runaway would be put to death if caught (Jansen 1967b). The code in many places specified that, under the oriental principle that criminal responsibility be expanded to include the family or the community, not only the prisoner but the entire family be punished for specific crimes.

The intent of the law was to preserve both the status quo and the status system. In this system of rule by status, only those in positions of power could use the law. Common people had no access to the law or any rights against a superior before the law (Varley 1984). In fact, inferiors were forbidden by law to petition about grievances without the approval of their superiors. As Henderson (1968b, 222–223) notes:

> Transcendent petitions . . . wherein the inferior petitioned over the head of his superior were severely punished, even by crucifixion if the petition was false. . . . It is well known that a regulated schedule of torture was an institutionalized part of the conviction proceedings.

Rule by Law: The Meiji Era   In chapter 1 we pointed out that the Tokugawa system of government and law began to collapse as the second half of the nineteenth century approached. Reischauer (1956) observes that the considerable autonomy given feudal villages and commercial towns encouraged entrepreneurial and commercial activities that were contrary to the feudal spirit. In addition, Western industrialism and the ensuing hunger for new markets brought great pressure upon the Tokugawa regime, which had successfully kept Japan isolated from outside influences. When the "Black Ships" of Matthew Perry's fleet entered Japanese waters, the end of the Tokugawa period was in sight. Within twenty years, feudalism ended, and the period known as the Meiji Restoration began (Reischauer 1988).

Led by a number of men of middle samurai rank, a revolution replaced the Tokugawa shogunate with a central government dedicated to restoring the emperor to a central, though symbolic, position. The feudal estates were disbanded and the samurai class divested of its status, power, and privilege (Varley 1984). Central to this was the adoption in 1889 of a constitution, proclaimed as a gift to his people from the divine emperor (Reischauer 1988). This constitution, while vesting sovereignty in the emperor, provided for a bicameral legislature, proclaimed civil rights "under reservation of the law," and established an independent judiciary (Takayanagi 1963). Known as the Meiji Constitution, the document was developed in considerable haste.

Treaties that were harmful to Japan caused some of this haste. Following Perry, other Western nations sought to establish trade relationships with Japan. Because the Japanese were unacquainted with international law, the original treaties they signed with Western powers often placed Japan at a decided disadvantage. For example, the first commercial treaty between Japan and the United States contained a set of stipulations that became known as "the unequal treaty provisions." Among these was the "extra-territoriality" provision, or the right that American citizens could not be tried in Japanese courts for crimes they committed in Japanese lands (Varley 1984). In order to revise the treaties, Japan was forced to modify its entire legal system (Noda 1976a).

In its haste, Japan reached out to Europe and developed codes of law following the European tradition. The 1889 constitution, for example, was modeled after the Prussian constitution (Hashimoto 1963). As Tanabe (1963, 77) explains:

> One may ask why the Meiji government adopted the continental procedure pattern. It was no accident. With the dramatic mission of changing a country with a deeply rooted feudalism into a modern industrialized nation, the leaders of the Meiji revolution understandably took the fast and efficient way of more or less completely borrowing the systematized codes and statutes of the continental countries, particularly Germany, rather than the Anglo-American patterns found so largely in an enormous and complicated mass of common law.

The Meiji Constitution can be seen as modern because it provided for the separation of powers and guaranteed the rights of individuals (Ito 1963). However, the Japanese tradition operated on radically different principles than the Western law it had borrowed. As Minear (1970, 6) points out, one very strong political element in Japan

> emphasized the divinity of the emperor and rejected a secular approach to the state. In it, traditional biases against the conception of law in general and against the implications of Western law in particular remained strong.

Although there were those who believed in and desired a secular approach to government and law, the Meiji Constitution reflects

> a compromise between absolute monarchy and modern democracy. The constitution granted certain rights to the people, but those rights were each subject to restraints enacted by law, and were thus only nominally guaranteed (Hashimoto 1963, 239).

The result was a system that allowed for "rule by law" but not "rule of law." Under the constitution, "a law enacted by the Diet [legislative body] could abridge any freedom or right. . . . The Meiji constitution did not place the government under the law, and, therefore the principle of rule of law . . . was neglected" (Ito 1963, 206).

This became very evident after 1930 when militarism in Japan began to gain ascendancy, and Japan entered a period called *kurai tanima*—the dark valley. At this time, civil rights were again and again denied on the basis of the "common good," as judged by the military and legitimated by the emperor (Takayanagi 1963).

The Meiji era is the formative period for Japanese criminal law. A penal code—virtually a translation of the French code—was adopted in 1880. In that same year, the Code of Criminal Instruction was enacted. These documents established the European procedures of codified law and a semi-inquisitorial approach to the adjudication process. A new penal code, written under the influence of German legal scholarship, was adopted in 1907. This code, in essence, remains in force to the present time. In 1923, a revised Code of Criminal Procedure was enacted which remained in effect until the adoption of the new code in 1948 (Hirano 1963; Takayanagi 1963).

The Meiji period brought radically different methods of criminal justice to Japan. The older, more punitive methods typical of Tokugawa society were scrapped. For example, torture as a means of gathering evidence was forbidden under the new rules of procedure. The semi-inquisitorial approach, combined with the Japanese legal emphasis on moral blameworthiness, stressed the subjective elements in criminal procedures.

Rule of Law: The Constitution of 1947   In 1947, following its disastrous defeat in World War II, Japan adopted a new constitution. The Japanese and Americans who wrote the document shared a number of concerns. First, they perceived that the militarism that had led to Japan's disastrous defeat stemmed from the position and role of the emperor prescribed by the Meiji Constitution. To avoid any repetition of militarist control, they wanted to reform the political structure by making the people, rather than the emperor, the sovereign source of power. Second, conscious that the individual rights outlined in the Meiji Constitution were often denied the people because the government was not really under the control of law, the writers of the new constitution sought to guarantee rule of law. In the Constitution of 1947, legislative supremacy replaced the executive supremacy allowed in the old constitution.

To further guarantee rule of law, the role and power of the judiciary were increased. Under the present constitution, even a law enacted by the Diet has no legal force if it goes contrary to constitutionally guaranteed freedoms and rights. Following the American model, review by an independent judiciary is used as a guarantee of individual civil rights (Ito 1963; Takayanagi 1963; Itoh and Beer 1978).

The Constitution of 1947 is a brief document that replicates the basic form of the Meiji Constitution. However, the contents of the new constitution are distinctly more democratic. The position of the emperor is retained, but his role is limited to that of a symbol of the state and the unity of the Japanese people (Takayanagi 1963). Chapter 3 of the constitution contains thirty-one articles outlining the rights and duties of citizens. Interestingly, only four articles, which are exhortative in character and without real legal force, have to do with duties. The remainder outline civil and individual rights. Ito (1963) classifies these rights into four categories: rights of existence, economic rights, freedom of expression, and rights of intellectual freedom.

Takayanagi (1963, 23) points out that the new constitution "contains no less than nine articles directly affecting criminal procedure." These articles include such basic rights as no criminal penalty except according to law; the right of access to the courts; no arrest without a warrant except if caught in the commission of a criminal act; protection from unwarranted search and seizure; protection from cruel or inhumane treatment; the right to a speedy trial; protection from self-incrimination; and the right to sue the state for redress (Supreme Court of Japan 1972).

Because these civil rights represent a significant change from the rights guaranteed under the Meiji Constitution, a new Code of Criminal Procedure was adopted in 1948. Although the Penal Code of 1907 remains in effect and provides the fundamental framework for criminal law in Japan, numerous amendments have been enacted over the past eighty years. Many of these amendments, in keeping with the spirit of the postwar years, restrain the power of the government. However, revisions to the penal code are "relatively few in number as well as minor in importance. The main reason for the code's longevity is in its flexibility both in the definition of offenses and in the disposition of convicted offenders" (Suzuki 1977, 86).

While the 1948 Code of Criminal Procedure allowed the accusatory procedure to replace the semi-inquisitorial procedure of the Meiji era, the Japanese found that this does not work well for them, and as a result, the older system, somewhat modified, remains. In dealing with criminal cases, the Japanese system still uses the subjective approach. Japanese criminal law operates with what Suzuki (1977, 88) describes as the culpability principle:

> Under this principle it is imperative that punishment be imposed only upon those who acted with a guilty mind or at least negligently and only to the extent which is warranted by the degree of the actor's culpability. . . . Thus, only acts committed intentionally or negligently are punishable.

Japanese criminal law, in passing through these three stages, has shifted one-hundred-eighty degrees in its direction and emphasis. From the Tokugawa period, where the common people had no rights under law and where the death penalty in some circumstances could be applied not only to the criminal but to his or her entire family as well, to the present, where the presence of a "guilty mind" is required before a sentence may be imposed, is a journey of epic proportions.

Legal Culture in Japan

As in this country, legal culture in Japan is the product of the nation's social and legal history. Japanese attitudes toward and use of the law differ sharply from American perspectives on law because the history and cultural development of the societies are different.

Legal Consciousness   In the United States, people have a strong sense of constitutionalism—an awareness of their civil and legal rights and a confidence in the judicial process. We are a people who have lived under rule of law for two centuries. If Japanese have a much weaker awareness of and confidence in their constitutional system, the review of their legal history provides an explanation. Despite its long history, Japan has known democracy and true rule of law for less than a half-century. Instead, what it has known is the failure of the legal system in the late Meiji period to provide for equity and justice.

This experience combines with the Japanese value of group-relatedness and the desire for harmony to make the Japanese hesitant to use the law. Yosiyuku Noda (1976b) has suggested that the limited use of litigation in Japan derives from the desire to avoid the harmony-destroying bitterness that might develop in a black-white type of adjudication. The result is that Japanese seek alternative means of resolving disputes:

> We would rather pay a small price, if such a price rounds off the edges, and let by-gones be by-gones. This explains why a large majority of cases that are brought to the court are settled through compromise. This is very indicative of the Japanese (Noda 1976b, 307).

Although Japan's values and social structure have changed a good deal since the Tokugawa period, "the traditional reluctance to file a lawsuit and to resort to a lawyer continues strong" (Tanabe 1963, 85). The 1947 Constitution provides for new perspectives on the law, but those values and ideas require time to filter down to the consciousness of the individual (Krauss, Rohlen, and Steinhoff 1984). Further, as will be seen in the chapter on adjudication, Japan has developed a highly structured system of dispute resolution that provides a number of alternatives to the courts and formal litigation.

One of the more subtle factors shaping Japanese legal culture is that although Japanese legal codes and statutes are Western in content and form, Japan is an oriental society, and hence the law does not operate as it does in Western societies (Takayanagi 1963). In *The Japanese and the Jews,* Bendansan (1972, 294) argues that in the Japanese world view, the demands of human life and experience have created a "law beyond the law," which has flexibility as its chief characteristic. As it conforms to prevailing circumstance and influences Japanese thought and behavior toward law, law tends to lose its sacred and absolutist character. What becomes important is not the letter of the law but the demands of life that people face every day. This then leads to two other elements in Japanese legal culture: attitudes toward civil rights and subjective approaches to the adjudication process.

Attitudes toward Civil Rights   If Bendansan is correct, the "law beyond the law" may be manifested in Japanese attitudes toward civil rights. Civil rights consciousness has grown slowly in Japan since 1946. The older values of group-relatedness have produced attitudes in which the welfare of the group supersedes the rights of the individual. Although the individual is protected by the law, the needs of the larger social body appeal to some higher order of priority.

Ito (1963, 221) has observed that in its judicial review process, the Japanese Supreme Court "has consistently held that restrictions may be imposed [on civil rights] to protect the public welfare." Whereas in the United States, Supreme Court Justices Holmes and Brandeis have argued that suspension of certain individual rights could occur if there was a "clear and present danger" to society's public safety, the Japanese Court's ruling appears to be much more general.

Richard Minear (1970, 33) suggests that this attitude may spring from the traditional Japanese concept that sovereignty resides in the state, not the people:

> Japanese political thought has been consistent in favoring the community over the individual, acknowledging the freedom of the individual only insofar as the interests of the group are not affected.

As a consequence, Japanese tend to be less conscious of civil rights and less willing to use litigation to secure them. In general, however, Japanese courts, while "oriented more toward community tranquility than individual assertion in many civil liberties cases . . . [have shown] special concern for persons accused of crime" (Itoh and Beer 1978, 19–20).

Subjective Approaches to Criminal Law   The "special concern" Itoh and Beer mention can be seen in the criminal adjudication process in Japan. Perhaps the sheer volume of criminal proceedings demands the objective approach that characterizes criminal law in the United States and fixes concern on establishing who committed the crime and what the appropriate legal response is. As a result, "in American criminal law substantive criminal proscriptions embody objective elements which are relatively easy to prove" (Hirano 1963, 275). The goal in Japanese courts is as much to determine why the individual committed the act as it is to establish guilt or innocence.

One element of this subjectivity is that in Japan, criminal procedures follow an inquisitorial rather than a semi-adversarial process. In Japan there are no jury trials. Criminal procedures are carried out before a judge whose role is primarily to seek truth. Instead of playing the role of umpire over an adversarial prosecutor and defense attorney, the judge is active in determining the motive and intent of the accused (Hirano 1963).

This determination is necessary, for law in Japan operates with different standards of guilt or innocence than does law in the United States. In Japan, the objective fact of the accused's act may be mitigated by circumstance and motive. Even where actual harm has been done, the action may not be punished "unless the intent to do harm can be established." As Hirano (1963, 282–283) outlines it:

> In the Japanese view . . . in order to impose punishment, a certain state of mind—the intent to infringe upon a particular legal interest—is . . . required. In the United States criminal intent or negligence is not required in so-called public-welfare offenses. Such absolute liability is not recognizable in Japan. At a minimum, negligence is necessary, and in most cases criminal intent is required . . . [The basic principle of the Penal Code is that] unintentional acts are not punished.

Further, Japanese criminal law punishes attempted crimes only in certain instances. As Hirano (1963, 276) states, "In many other countries, all attempts are punished except those pertaining to certain minor offenses."

One consequence of this subjective approach is that Japanese procurators operate with considerable discretionary power. Walter Ames (1979, 99) has observed that "the criminal justice system in Japan is premised on the expectation that most suspects will confess early on in the investigative process, and indeed most actually do." If a Japanese accused of a crime is willing to admit guilt, ask for forgiveness, and agree to make some form of restitution, the prosecutor is empowered to respond in a variety of ways, including dropping the charge entirely (Nagashima 1963).

Use of Criminal Sanctions   Finally, legal culture in Japan differs from legal culture in the United States in that it appears to be far less punitive in its approach to penal sentencing. Again, procurators may drop a case if they think the accused is penitent and, as will be pointed out in the chapters on adjudication and corrections, the sentences handed down by Japanese judges tend to be much more lenient than those given for comparable crimes in the United States (Citizens Crime Commission of Philadelphia 1975). There may be a number of reasons for this, but certainly the cultural emphasis on the integrity of the group and the desire to preserve harmony are strong factors.

Japanese legal culture, shaped by the history of legal development, reflects the society's general cultural values. A willingness to place the interest of the group before personal concerns leads to a weakened civil rights consciousness, which is reinforced by the court's concern for "the public welfare." The importance of the group and the desire for harmony are reflected in the hesitancy to use the law in civil and criminal litigation. These values also lead to a subjective approach to law and a restorative rather than a retributive approach to penal sanctions.

STRUCTURE OF THE LAW

The second major component of law, according to Friedman (1984), is *legal structure*. As might be expected from the preceding discussion, there are major differences in the structure of Japanese and American criminal law. These differences can be described in terms of two major contrasts.

Common Law versus Code Law

Criminal law in the United States, reflecting its British heritage, is primarily common law. It has developed slowly, case by case, as a body of opinions written by judges as they have reached decisions. Criminal law, however, is also influenced by the development of the statutes defining criminal acts. Nonetheless, it is a structure in which precedent plays an important role in defining both what the law is and how the law is to be used (Friedman 1984).

Common law is inherently complex and inconsistent. Because it deals with issues in scattershot fashion, it lacks the order and consistent approach of codified law. In the United States criminal law is even more complex than in other common law countries because criminal law is mainly the creature of the fifty states.

Recognizing the need to bring some order to this chaotic situation, the American Law Institute drafted the Model Penal Code in 1962. Since then, thirty states have used this code in attempts to achieve some national consensus (Gibbons 1987; Friedman 1984).

Despite this model code, criminal law in the U.S. remains diverse, differentiated state by state. It is united only in that it operates within the guidelines provided by the Constitution and shares the common structural elements of *stare decisis* (precedent), procedural due process, the jury trial, and the semiaccusatorial adjudicatory procedure.

Japanese criminal law, on the other hand, is code law. The Penal Code of 1907, although frequently amended, remains the basic body of criminal law. This code, adapted from French and German penal codes, operates in conjunction with the Code of Criminal Procedure enacted in 1948.

Code law differs from common law in that it is an attempt to develop law rationally into an integrated system. Here, precedent is of limited importance. Instead, the Code of Criminal Procedure instructs on how the Penal Code is to be used or administered. Its use is subject to review by the Supreme Court, which has been given the power to determine the constitutionality of any judicial act. However, "the Supreme Court of Japan is not a 'constitutional court' and decides issues of constitutionality only in the context of concrete controversies" (Itoh and Beer 1978, 8).

In keeping with other societies that use code law, Japan does not use a jury system. As we will see, its more subjective approach to adjudication gives the judiciary a great deal of discretion.

Federal and State versus National Law Systems

"The most obvious, striking fact about the American legal system is that it is organized on a *federal* basis" (Friedman 1984, 123). However, it must be kept in mind that while the United States is basically a social and economic union, it is not a legal union. State laws tend to be similar because conditions within the states are generally similar and because all states share in the limitations imposed upon them by the Constitution. Nonetheless, states are free to vary within their own territories. Further, criminal law was one of the areas reserved as a state rather than federal power.

As a consequence, "American criminal law does not exist: rather a large number of state penal codes bear some loose relationship to one another" (Gibbons 1987, 53). While in many ways the states echo the structures of the federal government, each having executive, legislative, and judicial branches, each state has its own peculiar pattern of criminal law.

The diversity in criminal law is amplified by the fact that judges and attorneys are organized locally. There are no national networks of judicial positions in which a judge from one state might transfer to another. Membership before the bar operates on a state to state level. The result is that the United States is not legally unified except at the federal level (Friedman 1984).

The colonial heritage and the value placed on decentralization of authority and local control created this situation. The need for decentralization declined over time as our society became more unified in its technology, and the value of local control remained important, yet the independence of the state legal systems has eroded to some degree. As crime in America expanded and began to take on interstate character, federal regulation and federal law enforcement have taken on added significance. As Friedman (1984, 137) points out, legislation such as "the *Law Enforcement Assistance Act* (1965) and the *Omnibus Crime Control and Safe Streets Act* (1968) pumped money into state and local government." The argument that crime was a threat to the welfare of the nation justified federal support for local programs, and this support has helped to increase the similarities among local criminal justice agencies.

In Japan, a democratic unitary state, there is no federal structure: "All laws (*horitsu*) are national laws legislated by the Diet" (Itoh and Beer 1978, 7). While the Japanese have courts of special or limited jurisdiction (Family and Summary Courts), the courts and the single national code of law present a unified model of jurisprudence.

The Japanese system seems to reflect the centrism that is a part of the nation's heritage. Japan has never needed a strong regional structure. Although prefectural officials perform some administrative functions and have limited power to pass local ordinances, to all intents, Japan operates in terms of a single criminal code.

SUBSTANCE OF THE LAW

Friedman (1984) suggests that the major substantive feature of criminal law is its operating rules. What kinds of behavior does the system try to control? What does it define as crime? How does it treat criminal acts?

Substance of Criminal Law in the United States

Perhaps the first and most prominent substantive characteristic of criminal law in the United States is its diversity. Because criminal law was an area left to state control, criminal law varies from state to state. There are some obvious universals—laws about criminal violence, for example, are almost alike everywhere. However, "there are many regulatory or economic offenses [in some states] which are unknown to most people. . . . These are crimes only because the state so defines them" (Friedman 1984, 155). Laws about cattle rustling that are still important in western states such as Wyoming and Montana would have little meaning in eastern states like New York or Rhode Island.

A second major characteristic of our criminal law is how it defines and responds to differing kinds of social behavior. As alluded above, there are virtually uniform notions about crimes against persons or major crimes against property. However, there is wide divergence, in both time and place, about that class of behavior we call "morality."

In the United States, definitions of what constitutes "crimes against morality" have been very sensitive to shifts in public opinion. In colonial times, the Puritan ethic reflected deep concern with morality, and law in that day used harsh sanctions to control such "sins" as fornication, gambling, and drunkenness. In the colonies influenced by Puritanism, crime was synonymous with sin. By the nineteenth century the moral climate had shifted, as new migrants with different values changed the balance of public opinion. The laws remained on the books, but there was no strong concern to enforce them. In 1873, however, the Comstock Law, which made interstate shipment of obscene material a federal offense, ushered in a whole new era. The passage of the Mann Act (1910), which made it a crime to transport a woman across state lines for "immoral purpose," the Harrison Act (1914), which made illegal the selling or buying of narcotics without a prescription, and finally the "Noble Experiment" of the Eighteenth Amendment (1919), represent that period when Americans strongly believed that morality could be legislated (Friedman 1984).

By the 1940s this trend had run its course and a movement to liberalize the laws governing morality slowly began to develop. Attempts to decriminalize the so-called "victimless crimes" have been a part of the U.S. scene for the past four or five decades (Kadish 1967).

However, despite these movements, many people in the United States believe that the increased permissiveness of the past few decades has led to moral decline that seriously threatens society. The growth of the Moral Majority and its political strength reflect that belief. In the ebb and flow of social movements, even the strong sentiments about liberty and individualism may be less important than older moral values and beliefs (Friedman 1984).

The third major characteristic of criminal law in the United States is the increasingly important role that regulatory agencies play in the creation of administrative criminal law. Within the past fifty years, the number of federal regulatory agencies has proliferated. As agencies such as the Interstate Commerce Commission, the Federal Drug Administration, the Federal Trade Commission, and the Federal Communications Commission have come into being, the body of federal criminal law has expanded rapidly. As a result of increasing technical, industrial, and economic complexity and changes in transportation and communication, the regulatory agencies have spawned a vast amount of law. This is reflected in the growth of the federal law enforcement agencies and their activities.

Criminal law in the United States is a very complex system of state and federal law. Historically it has been characterized by both its decentralized, local character, and the belief that law can be used to define and promote moral behavior.

Substance of Criminal Law in Japan

Anyone studying the history of legal development in Japan cannot help but be impressed with the amazing differences in the criminal law of the Tokugawa era and modern Japanese criminal law. Most impressive is the change in the nature and character of criminal sanctions. The Tokugawa, seeking to preserve the status quo, used harsh and inhumane forms of punishment to deter criminal behavior. A review of contemporary criminal practice in Japan reveals a complete reversal of this pattern. Yoshio Suzuki (1978a, 24) describes current Japanese approaches:

> The criminal law should define crimes as narrowly as possible. Those who contravene the criminal law should not be subjected to the formal criminal processes and punishment unless the invocation of the criminal justice mechanism is called for by exceptional circumstances. Non-penal measure for social control or social welfare services should be utilized instead of punishment wherever possible. Even when punishment is necessary on a variety of reasons, community-based treatment measures should be preferred to imprisonment and other forms of custodial treatment, and terms of incarceration should be as short as possible.

Although there have been vast changes in Japanese attitudes toward most crime and punishment, there has been one constant in Japanese thinking about crime: the concept of morality and crimes against morality. Ideas of morality in the United States are based upon the Judeo-Christian religious tradition and the Puritan ethic that grows from it. As we have seen, Japan has operated with an entirely different ethical system, based on three major influences—Shintoism, Confucianism, and Buddhism—which differ from the Judeo-Christian tradition in their definition of what constitutes a moral or immoral act. Further, they influence the society's belief in the purposes of law. Japanese do not believe in legislating morality.

The result, as Hirano (1963, 280–282) points out, is that:

> a large number of acts, particularly those involving sexual crimes and crimes against the family, fall outside the bounds of criminality in Japan. . . . Homosexuality, incest, and sodomy are not punishable. The crime of adultery was abolished after the war. . . . Abortion is punishable under the Penal Code, but the Eugenic Protection Law promulgated after the war legalized [it] within broad limits. . . . Maintenance of houses of prostitution was prohibited in 1957, but the act of prostitution itself is not treated as a crime. . . . Obscene literature is not strictly controlled. . . . The scope of criminal law as actually applied is even more limited.

Suzuki (1978a) indicates that there has been a continued interest in decriminalization. He suggests that there are both practical and moral reasons for this. First, although the number of arrests in Japan remains very low in comparison to the United States, the courts and penal facilities are overcrowded. Second, in keeping with Japan's belief in informal control, there is increasing skepticism about the effectiveness of prison in rehabilitating offenders. Perhaps even more important are the moral considerations. Suzuki (1978a, 29) outlines these with some eloquence:

> Of the utmost importance among moral considerations . . . is humanitarian solicitude even for those who have violated the norms of society. . . . Society itself has contributed in a significant degree to its members' deviant behaviors through its failure to improve social conditions exerting obnoxious influences upon the life of individuals. . . . Sometimes the pain and loss suffered by an imprisoned offender and his family far outweighs what he himself has inflicted on the victim and society. It is the responsibility of a civilized society to alleviate . . . the plight of offenders subjected to the criminal process and to penal sanctions.

As industry and technology developed, however, Japan also increased the number and scope of its regulatory mechanisms. Just how the resulting regulatory agencies will influence the shape of Japanese law remains to be seen.

Criminal law in Japan, while sharing the same general outlook on the serious crimes against property or person, varies widely from law in the U.S. in the area of crimes against morality. Japan's definition of morality, stemming from a vastly different religious and ethical tradition, is reflected in its decriminalization of many forms of behavior defined as criminal in America.

5 ENFORCING THE LAW: POLICING

The differences in the core values of the United States and Japan profoundly affect the systems of law enforcement each has developed. As Clifford (1976, 73) notes, "No police force works in a vacuum." The police in any society are a social control agency that responds to the ways people keep or break the law. We have argued that values shape behavior. If this is true, then differences in societal values produce quite different forms of behavior and quite different needs for the style and character of the formal social controls the police represent. This can be seen clearly in the police in Japan and the United States.

To understand these differences in policing, a number of areas must be explored. Because police organization and practice are outgrowths of specific historical developments, we begin this chapter by reviewing the history of policing in each of these nations. That historical development has helped shape the relationship between the police and the publics they serve. We will examine these relationships and look at how they impact both the legitimacy that these societies give the police and the role the police play. How police and community define that role influences the structure of policing including both management and law enforcement operations. We will explore this area by looking at how police in the United States and Japan have developed similar yet very different structures and styles of management. We will then look at police work—the role police play in the larger society—and how that role has influenced the police subculture. Finally, we will briefly review differences in the way police recruits are trained in Japan and the U.S.

HISTORY OF POLICING

History of Policing in the United States

The history of policing in the United States has been the subject of much interest and study. Greenberg (1976), Fogelson (1977), Walker (1977), Reppetto (1975), Monkkonen (1981), Johnson (1981), Moore and Kelling (1983), and others have looked at various aspects of how the police developed. The approach we use follows the basic outline developed by Moore and Kelling (1983) but augments their approach with a brief discussion of policing in colonial America.

The Colonial Period   Just as law in America was influenced strongly by America's ties to Britain, policing in America—at least in its early development—also reflects the British heritage. The three principal law enforcement institutions imported from Great Britain were the watch, the constable, and the sheriff.

The *watch* was composed of men, sometimes drafted, employed on a part-time, fee-for-serve basis. Their task was to patrol the streets between sunset and sunrise to watch for fires or other disturbances. Usually these men were poorly paid and often were not fit to do much more than raise an alarm. Boston organized its first watch in 1638, and New York created its Rattle Watch in 1652 (Wrobleski and Hess 1986; Walker 1983).

Of greater importance was the office of *constable*. In colonial America the constable was an elected official—in some instances serving only part-time—who was paid from fees collected by the court or the justice of the peace (Monkkonen 1981). The constable was essentially an officer of the court with responsibility for both civil and criminal matters. Charged with keeping the peace, the constable was responsible in many communities for supervising the night watch activities as well as carrying out the municipal court orders.

The *sheriff* was appointed by the governor of the colony and soon "became the principal government official of the colony" (Walker 1983, 4). Although his role was originally that of a court officer, by the beginning of the nineteenth century the sheriff's office had begun to assume more and more law enforcement functions, in some communities taking on the role of town marshal. Although the sheriff and his deputies seldom had a patrol function, the office of the sheriff was gradually perceived as the primary law enforcement position within the county.

This combination of policing roles served the developing nation quite well. Duties were broadly defined and certainly were not seen as being centered in crime control or crime prevention activities. However, as population increased, especially after 1800, the constable–watch system of city policing began to prove inadequate for the task. Monkkonen (1981) points out that the system failed in two ways. First, because the early forms of policing were not focused on crime prevention, the system was unable to protect property in any adequate way. Second, as cities began to swell and grow with the flood of European immigrants, law enforcement was unable to prevent the relatively frequent outbursts of mass disturbance and riot.

Three observations can be made about policing in the colonial and immediate postcolonial period. First, law enforcement was carried out by what Lewett (1975) has called "entrepreneurial police." In most communities the police role was filled by part-time persons on a fee-for-service basis. Second, policing during this period, especially in the office of the sheriff, was not really a part of city government. Instead, law enforcement was perceived as an activity directed by the courts, which were a part of state and county governmental authority. Third, policing in this era was considered civil in character, an extension of the basic responsibility of each citizen to maintain order.

Policing during this period was consistent with several of the central values we have described. Distrust of centralized authority led the colonists to develop a policing system that operated at the local level. The decentralization of policing was given strong support in the Constitution, which delegated responsibility for law enforcement to the state and local level. The emphasis on individual freedom inspired a policing system in which officers were not uniformed or organized in any sort of military fashion. People were afraid that police might become too powerful a force of central control. Further, rather than focusing on crime control or prevention, the function of the police was largely service oriented. Policing was seen as a civic duty, the responsibility of each citizen.

The Political Era: 1840–1920   In the early 1800s cities began to grow rapidly as larger numbers of European immigrants arrived in the U.S. By 1840 nearly two million people lived in the nation's major cities. By 1860 New York had a population of about 800,000, while Philadelphia numbered 112,000 and Boston 178,000. Throughout the 1800s and early 1900s, a growing tide of immigrants continued to flow to America. Between 1820 and 1830, 152,000 migrants entered the United States. That number swelled to 8.8 million in the decade between 1900 and 1910 (Golden 1981).

As U.S. cities grew, the older style of policing was no longer effective. Many of the immigrants arrived both impoverished and uneducated or illiterate. For a great many, there were neither jobs nor prospects of decent employment. The result was that many of the new migrants, their way of life seen as a threat to "the American way," were forced to live in poverty-stricken ghettos. As has always been the case among peoples who are kept out of the mainstream economic institutions, some of these disenfranchised people developed alternative lifestyles that involved either illegal or deviant activities. Others continued to follow ethnic practices that were seen as immoral or indecent by the majority of people in the United States. These factors combined to produce a situation in which people living in the ethnic ghettos were seen as a threat that needed to be controlled (Fogelson 1977).

As fear and concern about "the criminal class" continued to grow, municipal leaders began to search for alternative forms of policing. They found a ready model in Sir Robert Peel's London Metropolitan Police. However, the idea of developing a uniformed police force did not meet with instant approval. Proponents of the idea argued that the development of an efficiently organized and managed police force was needed to provide competent personnel able to control the masses and maintain order. Opponents feared that a uniformed police force would become a standing army that would threaten civil liberties (Monkkonen 1981).

Despite strong protest—including dissent from within the police themselves— New York City started a uniformed police force in 1853. Boston, Cincinnati, Denver, Chicago, and other cities were quick to make a similar transition. Within a forty-year period of time, the older system of constable and watch, which had served for more than 200 years, was replaced by uniformed city police. As Monkkonen (1981) notes, U.S. cities first looked to London's police as the model, but they began very quickly to refer to one another for advice and example.

Perhaps the major reason for this was that in U.S. cities police were authorized and legitimated by local authorities. The Constitution left law enforcement power in the hands of the states and local communities. As a result,

> unlike their British counterparts, American police departments lacked the powerful, central authority of the authority of the crown to establish a legitimate, unifying mandate

for their enterprise. Instead, American police derived both their authorization and resources from local political leaders, often ward politicians (Kelling and Moore 1988, 3).

In this setting, the police soon became sharply politicized and, in most major cities, corrupt. Fear and distrust of centralized authority not only kept police a decentralized, municipally controlled agency, it allowed local politicians—aldermen and ward bosses—to exercise control over the police. Because jobs in the police department were patronage positions, ward leaders determined who would wear the uniform. More importantly, ward politicians controlled who would be appointed precinct captain, the official who shaped the character of law enforcement in the neighborhood. Fogelson (1977, 24) points out that:

> Although the chiefs had the authority, the captains had the power. . . . Thus it was they, along with the ward leaders, who decided which laws to enforce, whose peace to keep, and which public to serve.

Thus, despite the attempt to create an effective law enforcement presence, police in urban areas at the turn of the century did not eradicate crime—they regulated it (Fogelson 1977). Proponents of the uniformed police had won their battle on the basis of a new idea—crime prevention. They convinced the community that a uniformed force, making regular patrols, would be able to detect offenders and hence deter crime (Monkkonen 1981). This did not occur. Instead, the police in most cities became a decentralized organization, controlled by corrupt politicians who used the police both as a source of patronage power and as a means of extracting bribes and payoffs from illicit enterprises. It is small wonder that by the end of the nineteenth century and in the first decades of the twentieth century a strong movement for police reform had developed.

Despite the failures of urban policing in this era, one important development occurred: The role of the police became more sharply focused. While police were involved in a broad variety of social services, the ideas of crime prevention and order maintenance began to be emphasized. Foot patrol and rudimentary criminal investigation became established techniques and tactics (Kelling and Moore 1988). Monkkonen argues that this development in policing was a part of the general growth of urban service bureaucracies (Monkkonen 1981).

The Reform Era: 1920–1960   Early attempts to reform the police came from outside the police organization. The Progressive Movement of the late 1800s inspired great concern over political corruption in general and sought reform in urban government. Spurred by civic leaders and public protest over police corruption, state legislatures and governors appointed committees or commissions—such as the Lexau Committee in New York—to investigate the police:

> By the end of the century . . . a series of similar investigations in Atlanta, Kansas City, Baltimore, Chicago, Los Angeles, San Francisco, and other cities made it clear that most police departments carried on in much the same way everywhere in urban America (Fogelson 1977, 6).

Despite these investigations, not much changed. Although commission recommendations resulted in the firing of some police officials, the police bureaucracy—

and more important, the local political leaders who controlled it—did not support reform, and the previous situation soon returned. It was not until the 1920s and 1930s, when the reform movements were linked to people within the police organization itself, that major changes began to take place in U.S. policing. Perhaps the first clear voice for reform from within policing was that of August Vollmer, whose vision of an educated, professional police began its influence in the 1920s. The report of the influential Wickersham Committee in 1929 extended many of Vollmer's ideas and reinforced the desire for reform among influential law enforcement leaders.

Vollmer's protege, O. W. Wilson, "became the principal administrative architect of the police reform organizational strategy" (Kelling and Moore 1988, 5). The keystone of that strategy was the development of a police organization, removed from the political machine's domination, whose legitimation would be based on law and police professionalism (Wilson 1950).

In order to accomplish this, police were to become civil service employees whose jobs were not dependent on political patronage. Professionalism was to be enhanced by increased education and specialization, which then legitimated increased use of discretion in enforcing the law. Stress was to be placed on the idea that the police were highly trained specialists. The emphasis on policing resulted in the narrowing of the police function. If the goals of the police were to be crime control, criminal apprehension, and order maintenance, then other public service activities had to be deemphasized or discarded (Kelling and Moore 1988).

Much of the support given police reform reflects the characteristic value of pragmatism. Policing in the political era simply had not accomplished what the community wanted. Because that style of policing was not successful, the community was willing to give support to a new approach that offered promise of greater success in establishing and maintaining peace and order.

Many of the features of contemporary policing developed during this period:

• Police management became more hierarchical in character—developing what Lewett (1975) has called "bureaucratic policing." Despite the emphasis on professionalism, police management became structured in ways that enabled police leaders to maintain control over the rank and file. An emphasis on uniform standards of police conduct removed much of the flexibility present in an earlier era. Professionalism became defined in terms of specialization and technical proficiency and was controlled by bureaucratic organization.

• Relationships between police and public became redefined, with the police portrayed as the "Thin Blue Line" that protected the lives and property of a passive and dependent public.

• The primary modes of policing became preventive motorized patrol and rapid response to public demand. The introduction of the automobile and the radio in the 1930s enabled departments to eliminate foot patrol, to place officers in cars, and to supervise them via radio communication.

• Developments in criminalistics became emphasized as police sought to reinforce their image as a specialized profession (Kelling and Moore 1988; Johnson 1981; Fogelson 1977; Walker 1977).

• The need to control the quality of law enforcement practice led to a concern for keeping accurate statistical records of crime and police performance. This concern led to the development of statistical indices such as the Uniform Crime Report and an emphasis upon the quantitative evaluation of police performance.

The net result of all this was that by the end of the Reform Era, policing had become oriented to and was defined by professional crime-fighting, which was characterized by its use of three basic tactics: motorized patrol, rapid response to emergency calls, and the retroactive investigation of crime (Moore, Trojanowicz, and Kelling 1988). This, in turn, led to the development of a police force that had a highly centralized control structure and was essentially isolated from the community it had sworn to "serve and protect."

Time of Crisis: 1960–1980   As impressive as the efforts of police reform were, by the 1960s and 1970s the Reform Era had become a time of crisis for police. At least three separate crises can be identified. The first is the crisis of performance. When crime rates began to soar in the 1960s, the police justified their requests for additional funds by declaring they would "win the war on crime" (Manning 1974). Yet, despite this self-declared mandate and despite the influx of federal dollars it generated, the police were not successful in stemming the rise of crime.

Further, the late 1960s and early 1970s were a time of civil unrest in the United States. The civil rights movement, opposition to the war in Vietnam, and the whole counterculture movement presented a major challenge to police. In confrontation after confrontation the police were charged with inappropriate behavior as they attempted to deal with minorities or with civil disobedience. Because the reform movement had deemphasized order maintenance as a major police role, police were ill-equipped to deal with the disorder of the period.

This led to the crisis of credibility and legitimation. Because the police appeared to be losing the war on crime and because a large minority of people saw the local police as an oppressive force, isolated from the community and the neighborhoods, a significant portion of the public questioned both the credibility and the legitimacy of the police.

Research conducted in the 1960s and 1970s began to raise major questions about the cherished ideas of motorized patrol and rapid response. Studies such as "The Kansas City Preventive Patrol Experiment" strongly suggested that motorized patrol—originally developed to deter crime—had little influence on crime rates, satisfaction with the police, or levels of fear in the community (Kelling, Pate, Dieckman, and Brown 1974). Research in New York showed that increasing police numbers did not substantially reduce crime rates or solve crime (Chaiken 1975). Some research showed that increasing patrols in one area simply displaces crime to other areas. Data from Kansas City showed that the doctrine of rapid response was not based on fact—unless the police were virtually on the scene, rapid response had little impact on arrests, citizen confidence in police, or fear of crime (Kelling 1988). Serious questions were also raised about the effectiveness of retroactive crime investigation. As Skolnick and Bayley (1988b) point out, most crimes are solved because of information gained from the community. When community and police relationships are poor, little information is likely to be offered.

At the same time, the police were confronted internally by a third crisis—the crisis of police management. Despite the reformers' emphasis on police professionalism, police managers continued to deal with the rank and file in ways that were antithetical to professionalization:

> . . . patrol officers continued to have low status, their work was treated as if it was routinized and standardized; and petty rules governed issues such as hair length and off-duty behavior. Meanwhile, line officers received little guidance in use of discretion and were given few if any opportunities to make suggestions about their work (Kelling and Moore 1988, 9).

This management style weakened morale, increased militant police unionism, and created an embattled police force that believed itself to be misunderstood by the public and misused by its own management.

Policing in the United States Today   Policing in the United States has been in transition since the 1970s. Various research studies have raised many questions about the role and function of the police as well as about the techniques they use. Slowly, a new style of policing has begun to emerge. Called *community policing,* it recognizes that police need to establish new working relationships with the community, relationships that enlist civilian support and assistance in both the planning and the execution of the policing task. We will examine this style of policing in greater detail in the final chapter.

History of Policing in Japan

The history of the Japanese police is closely tied to the developing political structures in Japanese society. As the political system in Japan changed, so also did the form and character of Japanese policing. While this relationship between political form and police structure probably holds true for all societies, the relationship seems to be especially apparent in Japan. One reason might be that police have been used more openly and directly as an expression of political power in Japan than in other societies.

The Pre-Tokugawa Period   Prior to the Tokugawa shogunate, Japan had a relatively weak centralized government. As described earlier, economic and political consolidation began in about the seventh century. Borrowing from the Chinese, the Japanese began to develop a centralized state with the country divided into provinces under the administration of appointed governors. During the Yamato period, police and judicial functions were performed under the direction of the imperial ministries of war, justice, and popular affairs. In 794, under the so-called Taika Reform, the office of Imperial Police was formed.

The actual task of policing was, however, carried out at the local level by civilian action. The Taika Code called for the development of the *go-no-na-sei,* groups of five households charged with the maintenance of peace and order. The local village headman was given responsibility for supervising these groups. If needed, the army could be called upon to enforce the law (Ames 1976).

Gradually, as more powerful families began to acquire larger tracts of land, power began to shift away from the imperial family and the central government, and between the ninth and twelfth centuries a feudal system developed. Although the system was once again given limited reunification during the Kamakura shogunate, a war broke out in 1467 that lasted for a century. A centralized government did not reappear until 1600 when the consolidations made by Hideyoshi resulted in the establishment of the Tokugawa shogunate (Reischauer 1988).

The political structures of early Japan were fractured and decentralized, and so was policing. Relying upon the five-household group to provide basic social control, policing was largely reactive. If the five-household group failed to keep the peace, or failed to restrain and turn offenders over to the feudal master, the military would then be called upon to catch the offender and to punish both the miscreant and the family group that had failed in its duties (Ames 1976).

The Tokugawa Period   A protege of Hideyoshi, Tokugawa Ieyasu assumed the shogunate in 1603 and developed a system of centralized feudalism that lasted 250 years. He divided the country into domains held by his vassals and saved for himself the major and most valuable portions of the land. In order to control more than 250 vassals, he developed a central bureaucracy, staffed by samurai, that kept close control over the feudal lords (Reischauer 1988).

The stability of this period gave rise to unprecedented economic growth and development. These conditions influenced population growth and, along with the growth of specialized manufacture, encouraged the development of cities. This in turn affected the ability of the older system of social control to maintain order. The five-family grouping was restructured and became known as the *gonin-gumi*. Given both broader and more specific areas of responsibility than the *go-no-na-sei*, the *gonin-gumi* remained the central apparatus for social control. However, because it was no longer completely adequate, new forms of order maintenance had to be developed.

To provide for law enforcement, the Tokugawa leadership directed that a local magistrate *(machi-bugyo)* be appointed in each city. Acting as chief of police, prosecutor, and judge, the magistrate appointed samurai to carry out the police function. They, in turn, employed lower status persons—often thieves or outcasts *(Burakumin)*—to do the "dirty work" of policing: to carry out interrogations and to mete out punishment to convicted persons (Leavell 1975).

In addition, the Tokugawa leadership developed a secret police system, the *metsuke,* to keep the various daimyo under surveillance. This type of administrative police function was a part of Japanese policing for the next three hundred years.

As cities grew during the Tokugawa period, order was maintained by several types of watch posts—usually at major street intersections—where traffic into and through the city could be watched and controlled (Ames 1976). These posts appear to be the predecessors of today's *koban* (police box).

While policing in the Tokugawa period became better ordered, it remained largely decentralized. There was no national criminal code at this point in time, and each local daimyo was responsible for maintaining order in his own domain. The function of the police was largely reactive. Relying heavily upon the ability of the *gonin-gumi* to maintain peace and order, the police organization of the Tokugawa era was limited. Tokugawa police were neither uniformed nor standardized in structure or practice. Their basic role was to catch and punish lawbreakers. The major emphasis in social control was upon informal surveillance and deterrence and upon communal responsibility for the individual citizen's behavior (Ames 1976).

The Meiji Restoration   The Tokugawa rulers brought 250 years of peace and prosperity to Japan—but at the cost of isolation from the rest of the world. As we have seen, to prevent change the Tokugawa leadership cut off all contact with the outside world. While Japan did not stagnate culturally, this was the time when science and commerce were developing rapidly in the Western nations. In its splendid isolation Tokugawa Japan fell far behind both technologically and industrially.

Had Japan been able to remain secluded from the rest of the world, its way of life might have continued for a much longer period of time. However, Western commerce had expanded and now demanded that Japan open its doors. Perry's historic visit to Japan and the subsequent treaty of 1858 forced Japan into the modern world (Reischauer 1988).

Because Japan's feudal system simply was not equipped to deal with the rapid changes forced upon the country, a coalition of samurai seized control of the imperial court and declared that they were restoring the emperor Meiji to political power. It is important to understand that this restoration of the emperor meant complete and total break with the Tokugawa past. The need to industrialize, to compete with the Western nations, made it essential that Japan quickly develop a unified society with new systems of operation and control. As Verba and his associates (1987) point out, Japan needed to forge a nation-state capable of withstanding Western imperialism.

To do this, the Meiji leaders used law to create a unified society. By developing a unified system of law—largely borrowed from France and Germany—the reformers were able to replace the many local codes with a single legal system. As a result, the Japanese people were united with the emperor who gave that law its legitimacy (Leavell 1975).

This all had to be done at a time when there was much turmoil in Japan. Ames (1976) notes that immediately following the overthrow of the Tokugawa shogunate, Tokyo and most of the other Japanese cities were faced with chaos and lawlessness. Part of the problem stemmed from the samurai class, especially those samurai who had served the Tokugawa as bureaucratic officials, who had been cut off from the positions they had held. The magistrates appointed to keep the peace were powerless to do so. To remedy this situation, the central government recruited samurai who had proven loyal to the imperial cause and appointed them as police militia (Leavell 1977).

While this was occurring, Japanese scholars and officials were in Europe looking for models that Japan could use in developing its new political system. As we have noted, this search provided materials for both the legal codes and the constitution that Japan adopted. It also provided an outline for the development of the Japanese police. Yukichi Fukuzawa, who had studied continental police systems, recommended that a specialized police department, separate from the military, be established, and in 1871 the militia was abolished. The first professional police *(rasotsu)* were appointed in Tokyo (Nakahara 1955). At the same time, a Local Administration Act was issued to standardize the organization of the prefectural police (Leavell 1975).

Leavell (1975, 72) suggests that "more than any other single individual, Kawaji Toshiyoshi can be credited with designing the modern Japanese police system." In 1872 Kawaji was sent to Europe to study police organization. Upon his return he presented a number of recommendations (Ames 1976; Leavell 1975), which included the following:

- The police should be a national organization controlled by a home ministry.
- Tokyo, the capital, should have a separate police department operated by the home ministry.
- Police functions should include both judicial and administrative activities administered by separate agencies.
- Police should be armed and prepared to handle emergencies without having to use the army.
- Supervision of local police functions should be the responsibility of a prefectural governor.
- The police should administer the fire departments.

Following Kawaji's recommendations, in 1873 a Home Ministry was established, and fire departments were placed under police supervision. In 1874, the responsibility for local police was turned over to the Home Ministry and assigned to the local prefecture.

By 1875 police throughout Japan were wearing a standard, Western-style police uniform. As Leavell (1975, 97) observes:

> The unusual style of police uniform served as a statement by the government that a radical change in Japanese politics had occurred. The policeman was no longer the employee of the neighborhood association or even the retainer of the local lord. The unique uniform which carried no associations with previously known arrangements of political power in Japan served to distinguish servants of the new regime.

Thus, by 1877 the transition to the early-modern form of Japanese policing had been completed. In less than a decade, a uniformed police agency, centrally controlled and following standardized organizational structures and procedures, had become an instrument of the national government.

It was a police agency whose role was far broader than reactive policing. Influenced by Kawaji's belief that police should have an administrative function, a set of regulations known as the *Gyosei keisatsu kisekei* was declared in 1875 which described the role of the new police. It was a role which emphasized "crime prevention rather than simply apprehension of criminals" (Leavell 1975, 106). In addition to the supervision of the fire-fighting groups, the police soon gained responsibility for a wide range of duties—from licensing tea houses and brothels to serving as public health agents in the control of contagious diseases.

By 1876 police substations and patrol boxes had been established in all the prefectures. The dispersion of these policemen throughout the major communities brought the police into increasing contact with the people. When police were finally assigned to duty in the rural areas,

> it represented a radical departure from the Tokugawa period law enforcement system. Rather than depend upon the continued strength of traditional values and institutions in the countryside, the government in Tokyo directed its prefectural governors to break with the arrangements of pre-Restoration Japan. With the deployment of police stations and patrol boxes beyond the urban centers, the framework for substantial surveillance and supervision of the population was set in place (Leavell 1975, 118–119).

This system of policing, clearly foreshadowing the modern Japanese police, underwent only minor changes during the next sixty-five years. Some of these changes were influenced by people like Heinrich F. W. Hohn, a consultant to the Japanese police from 1885 to 1891. At his recommendation the police force was enlarged and the system of residential police boxes—*chuzaisho* and *koban*—was established (Ames 1976).

About this time civil service examinations were put into place, and training programs were initiated. Perhaps of greater importance was the expansion of police activity. Ames (1976, 49) notes that the police force held responsibilities

> far beyond the three essential police duties of crime prevention and the arrest of criminals, protection of life and property, and the maintenance of public peace. It regulated public health, factories, construction, social insurance *(shokai hoken)* and businesses, and issued permits, licenses, and orders mandated by law to achieve these functions. When the stringencies of war increased after the outbreak of fighting in China in 1937, the police were given the added responsibilities of regulating the economy, mobilizing labor and controlling transportation.

Tipton (1977, 79–80), in discussing the expansion of police responsibilities, lists "sanitation and health, traffic, firefighting, public morals, (and) peace preservation." Japan had opted to use the continental model for its police, and as state functions increased, they were assigned to the police. As time passed, the police became more and more important as an instrument of state policy.

This became even more evident as Japan moved closer to war. The *Tokko,* or special higher police, first organized in Tokyo in 1911, grew in its importance as an agency to maintain state political authority (Tipton 1977). As political police, the Tokko became involved in the surveillance of organizations and meetings, in the censorship of books and papers, and in election control. As the military came to dominate the government, the police were increasingly used to suppress ideas the military perceived as deviant. As Tipton (1977, 4–5) notes:

> Central to the image of prewar Japan is the brooding sense of menace inspired by the Special Higher Police . . . commonly known as the *Tokko. . . .* The *Tokko* is often made the supreme example of that "dark valley" which is supposed to characterize Japanese history in the 1930s and 1940s.

Police in the Postwar Era   Japan's defeat in World War II was acutely traumatic. Japanese industry had been destroyed, its cities had suffered severe damage, nearly 700,000 of its civilian population had been killed in air raids, and its economy had been completely disrupted. In addition to the physical damage, the psychological trauma was also intense. For the Japanese people the war had been a disaster, and it resulted in an abhorrence of war and revulsion for the leadership that had promised their sacrifices would result in victory (Reischauer 1988).

These attitudes helped make the U.S. military occupation of Japan effective in creating change. While the first concern of the occupation was to ensure that Japan would no longer be a military threat, the concerns went far beyond simple de-militarization in restructuring much of Japanese society. One major element of change came with the imposition of the new constitution that grafted the U.S. ideal of civil rights onto a parliamentary form of government (Burks 1984). It was something that the Japanese people, by and large, accepted with enthusiasm. While the prewar system of policing continued to operate during the first two years of the occupation, it too became the target of reform. The occupation authorities invited U.S. police specialists to study the Japanese police system and to make recom-mendations for revisions. These recommendations were conveyed to the prime minister of Japan and, at the urging of the occupation forces, were incorporated into the Police Law of 1947.

This law sought to achieve a number of things. First, police power and responsibility were curtailed by assigning administrative functions, such as fire protection, to other government agencies. Police functions were limited to criminal concerns, and all judicial and legislative functions were stripped away. Second, an attempt was made to decentralize the police by organizing independent police departments in every community with a population of 5,000 or more. Rural areas and very small communities were to be policed by a rural police force organized by each prefecture. Third, control of the police was placed in the hands of prefectural public safety commissions composed of citizens (Ames 1976; Nakahara 1955; Sugai 1957).

The new law went into effect in 1948, but in the following years unrest and civil disturbances created such problems that the effectiveness of the decentralized police was questioned (Sugai 1957). Some of the smaller communities simply could not afford the costs of operating an independent department, and, in general, police morale became quite low (Ames 1976). When disturbances reached such pro-portions that local police could not cope with the situation, leaders and populace insisted upon a return to centralized policing.

This pressure led to the adoption of the Reform Police Law in 1954. This law provided for a return to a national police system operated under the National Public Safety Commission and a National Police Agency (NPA). In this system police are organized on a prefectural basis. Because chiefs and ranking officers are officials of the NPA, the system maintains a national character. While each prefecture has a public safety commission, it is largely advisory. Basic policy is directed and regulated by the national body (Sugai 1957; Nakahara 1955).

While some administrative changes have occurred over the years, this basic structure of policing remains in force today. Because of its national character, the Japanese police remain independent of local political control. The Japanese police force has a somewhat broader role than its counterpart in the U.S., but its function remains considerably smaller in scope than during prewar times. Finally, the restrictions on police infringement of civil rights appear to be strongly in place.

POLICE–COMMUNITY RELATIONS: LEGITIMACY OF THE POLICE

As outlined in the preceding chapter, the forms of informal social control that characterize Japanese society create a social climate in which the crime rates are much lower than those in the United States. This presents a very different challenge for the Japanese police than the one faced by their American counterparts, and it results in a quite different structuring of the police role.

Another important factor that influences the police role and operations is the character of police–citizen relationships. The literature on policing in the United States portrays the police as an embattled minority whose tactics and strategies have failed and who are feared, misunderstood, and mistrusted by the people they serve (Reiser 1977; Moore 1977; Manning 1974; Bittner 1980).

In Japan quite the opposite is true. Smith (1983, 5) reports that:

> In the post-war years there has been a transformation of the public's perception of the police from that of occasionally harsh figures accorded respect largely out of fear, to one of a very different kind. It is today the assumption of the vast majority of Japanese that public and police alike are on the same side in the unremitting effort to maintain order and to minimize the dangers encountered by ordinary people in the conduct of their daily lives.

That assumption—along with the Japanese tradition of the citizen's responsibility for community order—leads to the active cooperation and participation of community members that was described in chapter 3. Clifford (1976, 101), in discussing police–citizen relationships, describes Japan's Crime Prevention Association as a volunteer citizen group whose objectives are to cooperate "spiritually and practically with the various activities of the police." Involved in crime prevention, the members carry out many activities in direct support of the police. Clifford also notes similar organizations which focus on aiding police in their work with delinquent youth, prevention of traffic accidents, and the like (Clifford 1976; Bayley 1976c).

While there is some organized support for the police in the United States, it seems clear that the quality of police–public relationships in the two countries differs significantly. Perhaps the basic reason for this is that the core values of the two societies provide quite different forms of legitimation for the police. As Samuel Walker (1983, 4) has observed:

> The heart of the law enforcement function . . . is one of legitimacy. To carry out effectively any of their various assignments, the authority of the police must generally be accepted by the public as legitimate. The crux of the American police problem has been the fact that the legitimacy of the police is so often challenged rather than accepted. From this issue alone stems some of the most long-standing and serious problems in American policing.

Japanese police gain their legitimacy from some of the basic characteristics of Japanese culture. First, as Smith (1983) notes, the Japanese ideal of harmony supports both a police presence and police activity. Police in Japan are not perceived as busybodies, interfering with citizens' rights. Instead they are public servants performing a desired service. Second, the Japanese sense of hierarchy, which ranks government service very highly, accords the police a position of respect. Third, traditional respect for authority is deeply ingrained in Japanese history and philosophy. Police represent the authority of the larger community. Historically the Japanese police have been respected as persons of relatively high status. Ames (1976) notes that the first policemen in modern Japan were recruited from the samurai rank and were accorded great respect. Since the police agency in Japan is national in design, police carry with them the legitimating influence of the national government. The Japanese police are a fundamental part of the nation–family, in which government employment commands respect.

Further, the role of the police in Japan, and the way the police perform that role, reinforces their legitimacy. As will be discussed below, police in the U.S. define their role as law enforcement. They are present to prevent crime and to force compliance with the laws. Japanese police perceive themselves as public servants, whose tasks include crime prevention and law enforcement but who are primarily engaged in aiding citizens in the preservation of order. Instead of being viewed as a repressive agency of control, they are perceived to be a moral force whose role and its performance are in keeping with the society's central values (Bayley 1976a).

By contrast, both the police role and the core values of U.S. society tend to diminish the legitimacy of U.S. police. First, distrust of centralized power has led to decentralization of authority. Because policing is a function of local government, and local government is often seen as operating inefficiently at low levels of integrity, a great many people tend not to trust the police. The history of police misconduct has further eroded public respect. Despite the flag they wear on their uniforms, police in the United States do not enjoy the legitimacy of being agents of the national will. Instead, they represent a nonnegotiable force (Bittner 1980), one that must be legitimated by the officers themselves as they operate in each specific situation. The officer may represent the community, but the citizen is part of that community. We pay the officer's salary. Therefore we can command the officer's respect, not vice versa.

Second, the police are caught up in the tension between the desire for individual freedom and the need for corporate constraint. People in the United States prize their freedoms and resist any action they feel impinges upon their rights. Because the police role is perceived as repressive, they tend to mistrust the police and deny legitimacy to many police actions. While the citizen wants the security and protection of the police, he or she also resents the discipline and authority inherent in the police role. By narrowing their role to "enforcer of the law" and by using strategies that limit their relationships with the public to crisis situations, the police have further eroded the basis of public acceptance (Moore 1977).

In addition, the diversity of U.S. society influences the legitimation and public support of the police in at least two ways. First, the diverse publics create a situation of conflicting demands and expectations which makes uniformity of policing operations, or standardization of the police role, virtually impossible. Second, the diverse mixture of people and ideas precludes any strong national consensus on a moral tradition. As a consequence, standards for behavior change very rapidly. What was seen as unacceptable behavior a short decade ago may now be given general approval. When police, operating within the structure of legal codes, attempt to enforce unpopular laws, they tend to lose legitimacy. The public response to the Volstead Act illustrates what occurs when police must enforce laws not supported by the public (Moore 1977). Because many people in the United States did not believe the use of alcohol was wrong, they resented police interference in their "right" to drink. When police attempted to enforce this unpopular law, many people withdrew their police support.

Finally, American pragmatism tends to support whatever works. When the crime fighter image and tactics the police adopted in their "war on crime" failed to produce the promised results, a withering of confidence and a withdrawal of legitimation occurred (Manning 1974).

THE STRUCTURE AND OPERATIONS OF LAW ENFORCEMENT

National versus Local Law Enforcement

Cultural values shape the social climate within which the police must operate, but the level of criminal activity and public attitudes toward both the law and law enforcement agencies help shape the policing operations within a society. As might be expected, the cultural variations between Japan and the United States have produced sharp differences in the structure, organization, and operations of the police in these two nations.

The first, and in some ways most obvious, difference is that Japanese police are a national police force. Attached to the office of the prime minister but relatively well insulated from political pressure, the National Police Agency (NPA) of Japan is divided into 47 prefectural headquarters and 1,220 police stations. As General Sadatoshi Suzuki (1983, 40), then the deputy commissioner of the NPA, explained, the Japanese police system has both national and local organization, with hierarchical and uniform order established through the authority of the national agency:

> The NPA is responsible for police operations and activities pertaining to national safety and for coordination of the activities of the prefectural police, police training, police communications, criminal identification, criminal statistics, and police equipment. It also sets standards concerning force size, organizational structure, police rank and appropriate behavior. Furthermore, because all high ranking officers of the prefectural police are, by law, national public servants, the NPA is authorized to appoint and dismiss them.

At the prefectural level, police are organized around six internal bureaus, which are also found at the national level: the Secretariat and the Bureaus of Administration, Criminal Investigation, Traffic, Security, and Communications. "Police stations are responsible to local headquarters, and the jurisdiction of each police station is divided into small areas for each of which there is an established police box to which police officers are assigned" (Clifford 1976, 78). (See Figures 5.1 and 5.2.)

Japanese police are thus a bureaucratically structured organization, using a traditional, paramilitary ranking structure similar to that used in the United States. However, under reforms brought into effect following World War II, the role of the

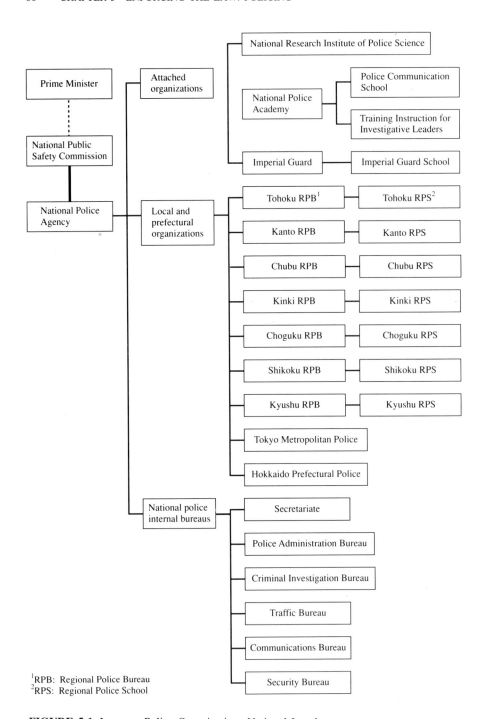

FIGURE 5.1 Japanese Police Organization, National Level
SOURCE: National Police Agency, Japan, 1982

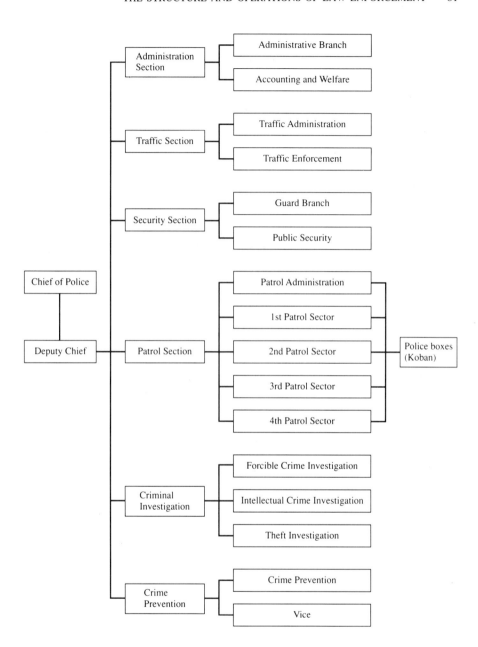

FIGURE 5.2 Organization of a Large Japanese Metropolitan Police Station
Source: Tokyo Metropolitan Police, *Keishicho*, Tokyo (1982), p. 9.

police was limited, and the control of the police, at both national and prefectural levels, was placed in the hands of civilian public safety commissions. Prefectural police maintain a degree of autonomy, but they must operate under the general supervision of the NPA (Clifford 1976; Ames 1979a).

This system contrasts sharply with the decentralized structure of American police. By constitutional law, police powers in the United States have been reserved to the individual states, and, through legislative action, that power has been delegated to the various municipalities and counties. The consequence is that there were about 15,000 state and local general law enforcement agencies operating in the United States during 1987. Of these, 11,989 (79.3 percent) were local or municipal police departments, 3,080 (20.4 percent) were sheriffs' departments, and 49 (.3 percent) were state police agencies (Reaves 1989).

The distrust of centralized power in the U.S. has resulted in a policing effort in which there is little standardization of policy, procedure, training, or equipment. Further, because policing authority has been delegated to local authorities, it is subject to the pressures of local politics (Bittner 1977; Bordua and Reiss 1977). The structure of local police agencies, however, is heavily bureaucratic and often characterized as "quasi-military" (Walker 1983). The organization chart of a typical large metropolitan police department in figure 5.3 reflects clearly such bureaucratic organization.

Bureaucratic Structures and Management Styles

Within larger departments, the same type of bureaucratic structure prevails in both the United States and Japan. There is, however, one major difference—the management model used in each system. In police organization in the U.S., a "top–down" model of management prevails. The need for supervision and control (which arises because of both the style of policing used and a management philosophy that places little trust in the individual officer) has led to the development of an organizational structure in which line officers receive orders from supervisory staff with little opportunity to participate in the decision-making process (Bittner 1977; Bordua and Reiss 1977). Although police have attempted to promote professionalism in policing, the hierarchical structure suggests that police leadership fears the independence of the individual officer.

Japan uses the same paramilitary model in structuring police organization, but Japanese culture stresses consensus and consultation in the decision-making process. This appears to influence the administration of the Japanese police (Archambeault and Fenwick 1983, 1985). It is not that police officials consult with line officers before decisions are made. It is, rather, that police leaders are very much aware of what the rank and file think and expect. Middle management police administrators spend much more time with line officers than do their counterparts in the United States. One of the management techniques used by the Japanese is the frequent social gathering that allows a licensed opportunity for management and workers to relax and to exchange ideas. Management decisions are made with a keen awareness of the policing situation (Bayley 1976a). As will be discussed later in this chapter, the relationship between managers and line officers is very different

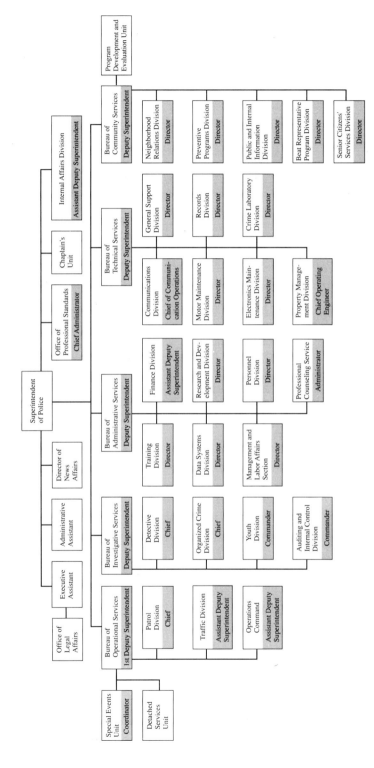

FIGURE 5.3 Organization of a Large U.S. Metropolitan Police Department

SOURCE: Chicago Police Department (1983)

in the Japanese police subculture. This is not to say that supervision is less strict in Japan. As a matter of fact, Bayley (1976a) points out that Japanese line officers are subject to much closer supervision than their American counterparts. Yet the relationship between superior and subordinate appears to cause little strain.

Certainly one strong evidence that speaks to the considerable difference in management is the fact of U.S. police unions. Ames (1981, 200) reports that "there are no labor unions, policemen's benevolent associations, or any other type of organizations to represent the police officers to police management in Japan." In the United States, police unions and collective bargaining continue to be major issues of concern to city administrators.

It should be pointed out that, in general, the labor movement in Japan is different from that in the United States. Most union activity in Japan is centered in what Reischauer (1988) has called "enterprise-wide unions," which enroll both blue-collar and white-collar workers as well as members of lower management. Yet Japanese labor unions are independent of management and have been aggressive in seeking benefits for their members. Although the labor union movement in Japan did not develop strongly until the U.S. occupation, it today involves a higher proportion of workers than its equivalent in the United States. But in spite of the strength of the labor movement in Japan, there is no police union.

Perhaps one reason for the lack of Japanese police unions is that because the police are not under the direct control of politicians, there is less need for police to use the defensive tactics of union organization (Bayley 1976a). It should be noted that in other public service areas, where the separation between political office and bureaucratic control is not as clear, aggressive union development has occurred (Reischauer 1988). Further, the style of consultative management used by police leadership in Japan has helped to forestall the need for union organization.

During the past thirty years, there have been sharp increases in police union membership in the United States and increasingly aggressive attempts by police unions to secure increased wages and benefits. Samuel Walker (1983) has argued that one of the major reasons police unions have flourished is that police officers were discontented with autocratic management practices that provided officers with little protection from disciplinary procedures that were often arbitrary and punitive. Robert Kliesmet, president of the International Union of Police Associations, has put it succinctly: "Stupid management made unions" (quoted in Kelling 1988, 4). Police in the United States have traditionally been under the direct control of local political forces, who often have been more responsive to civilian complaint than to the problems inherent in policing. As Bayley (1976a, 194) notes, "Local control and [police] professionalism are not compatible." The consequence has been the development of organizations designed to protect the interests of those who "protect and serve."

POLICE WORK

The Police Role in the Larger Society

Another difference in police operations is the role police play in the larger society. In the United States the role of the police is currently a matter of intense debate. As

Manning (1974) suggests, the police role has seen major revision as police have attempted to deal with rising rates of crime and disorder. Wilson and Kelling (1982), Manning (1974), Moore (1977), and others (Angell 1977) have discussed various models of the police role. While all agree on the basic components of that role, there is disagreement on what the specific content of the role should be.

The discussion indicates, however, that in the recent past American police have exercised what Moore (1977) refers to as a "law enforcement" model of the police role. Although police spend a very small proportion of their time in criminal apprehension, they see themselves as crime fighters and crook catchers. Their training is oriented to the detection of crime and to the legalistic application of the rule of law. Fishman and Dinitz (1989) argue that they have followed what Packer (1968) has called the "Crime Control" model of policing. Although there is growing sentiment for a peace-keeping or order-maintenance role that emphasizes a "watchman" style (Cole 1989), there is little evidence that American police are willing to accept that role definition. Although they spend little of their time dealing with crime and criminals (Goldstein 1977a; Scott 1981; Lundman 1980), the service component of the police role—which occupies the bulk of their time—is deprecated as not being "real police work."

Japanese police perceive their role in a very different way. First, because of lower crime rates, the Japanese police do not focus on criminal apprehension. Bayley (1976c) and Ames (1981) describe the role of Japanese police as strongly service oriented. The largest part of the officers' time is spent in providing a broad range of services to the public. Second, the Japanese police place great importance on crime prevention. Much of their time is spent in educating businesspersons and private citizens about property protection. A third emphasis is on order-maintenance and peacekeeping. Resolving disputes and exerting a moral influence by example and teaching are important elements in the activities of the Japanese police. Finally, and low on the list in importance, is the detection and apprehension of criminals. It can be low in priority because of both the relatively small amount of criminal behavior and the extraordinary willingness on the part of the general public to aid the police in the apprehension of offenders.

These differences in police roles become illuminated when the styles of policing in the two countries are compared. The basic strategy used by U.S. police is motorized patrol. In part because of the structure of our cities, and in part because of the emphasis given to criminal apprehension, police have accepted the doctrine of rapid response as an article of faith and have adopted its logical methodology: mobile patrol. As Sherman (1989, 53) suggests, "maintaining this rapid response, 'dial a cop' capacity can only be accomplished by assigning most patrol officers to stay in their cars most of the time waiting for a call to come in." Unfortunately, this strategy of patrol has several negative consequences. First, it is a great time waster, for the premise of rapid response demands that police hold in abeyance other activities. Second, motorized patrol keeps police and citizen isolated from each other. Police lose touch with the community, and citizen perception of the police as "them," rather than a part of "us," is heightened. Third, the role of the police as crime fighters becomes enhanced and reinforced (Sherman 1989).

Japan's basic patrol strategy is based upon the urban koban and the rural chuzaizo. This discussion, based on the descriptions given by Bayley (1976a,

1976c) and Ames (1981), will focus on the urban setting. There are nearly six thousand kobans in urban areas in Japan. Scattered throughout the cities in relatively small neighborhood settings, the kobans are the focal point of urban Japanese policing. The koban itself is a small structure, a house or a storefront, which provides an office and working space for the officers assigned to it. Staffed around the clock, the kobans provide a broad range of services to the people of the community. Since Japanese do not number their houses sequentially along the street but in the order in which they were built, it is almost impossible for a stranger to locate an address. One of the functions of the koban is to provide that information. Twice each year the patrol officers conduct a house-to-house visitation in their district, gathering information about who lives in the area and offering information about crime prevention and safety measures. The data they gather enable them to provide information to those who need to find someone in the community as well as to keep themselves apprised of what is taking place in their patrol area.

The koban also becomes a place where people in trouble can seek assistance. Most kobans keep a petty cash fund so that the police can loan carfare to someone who is stranded and without funds. They may provide a place for the temporary homeless to spend the night. Many kobans are designated as counseling centers and provide specially trained officers to aid in resolving family quarrels or to provide advice. They also serve as referral centers, directing people to various social service agencies.

Each day police leave the koban to make foot patrols through their assigned areas. The purpose of the patrol is to maintain a police presence and to foster good citizen–police relationships. Because assignments keep an officer attached to the same koban for a considerable period of time, police tend to become well acquainted with the citizens they serve. As Clifford (1976) reports, 46 percent of a national sample of Japanese citizens indicated that they had spoken to a police officer within the year.

Should a crime occur in their area, the role of the koban officers is that of securing the crime scene. Investigation of the crime and apprehension of the offender are the work of the criminal investigation bureau, which relies heavily upon the local officer's knowledge of the area. Koban officers do not perceive themselves as crime fighters. Despite representing the authority of the state and holding the power to apprehend those who break the law, their role is far broader than that of "law enforcement."

The result of this strategy is the integration of the police into the community. Instead of a feared and resented intrusive presence, police in Japan become an important agency of community service. As Bayley (1976a, 91) describes it:

> Police penetration of the community in Japan is more routine and personal than in the United States and it is more active in ways unrelated to law enforcement. Deployment in kobans forces police officers in Japan to play a role in the community as known persons, not like American policemen who are often seen as anonymous faces flickering by behind a facade of steel. A koban is an active force in community life; it is not simply a passive source of police assistance. In the United States the justification for contact between police and citizen, apart from criminal activity, is overwhelming need, and initiative belongs to the citizen. An American policeman is like a fireman; he responds

when he must. A Japanese policeman is like a mailman; he has a daily round of low-key activities that relate him to the lives of the people among whom he works.

Japanese police today are concerned that the growing use of motorized patrol may threaten a system of police that dates back to 1628, when the ruling shogun established the forerunners of today's kobans in Edo (Tokyo) (Clifford 1976).

It should be obvious that the koban system of policing could never be translated to the United States. Apart from the physical differences in population density and geographic structure, people would probably never tolerate the continuous presence of the police. The cherished values of privacy and individual freedom, as well as the distrust of governmental authority, conflict with a method of policing that assumes respect, acceptance, and cooperation with the police.

Police Subculture West and East

Perhaps an even greater barrier to this style of policing is the U.S. police subculture. First described by William Westly (1953), the idea of a "subculture of policing" has received much attention. Skolnick (1975). Bordua and Reiss (1977), Niederhoffer (1985), VanMaanen (1985b), Brown (1985), and others have attempted to describe and analyze the effects of this subculture on policing.

Skolnick (1975) has argued that American police have developed a distinct "style of life"—a subculture—in response to their relationship with the public and the basic structuring of what he calls the "constabulary role." Manning (1974) suggests that these relationships grow out of the "mandate" that the police have developed for themselves: "Based on their legal monopoly of violence, they have staked out a mandate that claims to include efficient, apolitical, and professional enforcement of the law" (Manning 1974, 16).

However, this mandate involves conflicting and contradictory ends: the protection of both public order and individual civil rights. In their attempts to control crime, the police have found themselves criticized by a public that often feels police have failed in both aspects of that mandate. The public points to a perceived increase in crime rates and expresses outrage at instances of police misconduct, especially the infringement of civil rights (Bittner 1980).

The result is that police in the U.S. operate with a set of assumptions about the public they serve: People cannot be trusted; you must make people respect you; everyone hates a cop; police officers make the best decisions about who is guilty or innocent; people will break the law if they are not controlled (Manning 1974; VanMaanen 1985a).

These assumptions grow out of the police subculture and also help shape it. They serve as lenses through which the police officer sees the world; experience in the world helps tint or shade the lenses. In an interactive relationship, these assumptions and the police subculture develop to influence how police perceive and perform the police role.

Blumberg and Niederhoffer (1985, 141) present a summary description of the values the police subculture develops and supports. They include:

• Respect for power and authority

- Secrecy, especially in matters possibly affecting colleagues and organization
- Loyalty to the organization even when it may mean compromise of all kinds
- A sense of minority group status and all that implies
- Political conservatism
- A broad cynicism that is rationalized in terms of knowing the real world and "what the score is"
- Unquestioned belief in and loyalty to country, flag, family, and religion
- An unswerving conviction that police do an exemplary job in combating crime but are hamstrung by judges, courts, and corrections officials
- A belief that the cause of crime and related social problems is widespread permissiveness

Given their self-declared mandate, the resulting social relationships with the public, and the consequent subculture, police in the U.S. develop a style of policing that contrasts sharply with the Japanese model.

What must be kept in mind is that this situation comes about as a consequence of the cultural environment. Police are confronted with the existential realities of a highly independent populace that insists upon its rights and that is deeply suspicious of attempts to impose controls upon what they, rightly or wrongly, perceive to be their basic rights. Police are caught in a conflict that is inherent in any democratic society: the emphasis upon individual freedom and the need for corporate control.

One reason police in the U.S. declared their mandate to be a "war on crime" was because they operate in a society whose social and economic structures have provided conditions in which crime has flourished. Police adopted the crime-fighter image with the approval of a society that felt itself vulnerable to criminal attack. And when police were perceived to be losing that battle, despite the huge influx of funds provided by government programs such as the Law Enforcement Assistance Administration (LEAA), that approval was withdrawn. The public's response was that the police had failed to do the job, that the police were both inefficient and corrupt. If police are suspicious of people, it is because the people they serve have become cynical and suspicious of the police.

The net result is a police force that is alienated from the public. Its members become more inward oriented, developing a sense of loyalty to the organization and its members that outweighs loyalties to abstract principles of justice. Because the role demands it, they are trained to be suspicious. Because people outside the profession cannot understand, police tend to become socially isolated, developing a clannishness that becomes a barrier to understanding and encourages feelings of hostility (Skolnick 1975).

Japanese police also operate within the context of an occupational subculture. However, the basic differences in the cultural environment of the two societies result in police subcultures that are, at best, only superficially similar.

Perhaps most important in shaping the difference in police subcultures is that Japanese police have a distinctly different mandate. Because Japan does not have a high crime rate, the police do not see themselves as engaged in a war on crime. Their mandate is to be a service organization, charged with maintaining peace and order. It is a mandate that includes a moral component. In some ways Japanese police are a part of the national conscience, charged with instructing as well as enforcing what is perceived to be acceptable conduct (Bayley 1976a, 155). It is a mandate that Japanese police have carried out with a great deal of success. While not every citizen is enamored of the police, in general the public has accepted the police role and is supportive of police actions (Smith 1983). This can be seen in the numerous voluntary organizations that have developed to aid the police in their task (Suzuki 1983). As a result, Japanese police are not forced into a defensive posture that breeds suspicion and mistrust (Bayley 1976a, 11–12).

Further, Japanese values of hierarchy and respect for authority influence the police subculture. Japanese police are respected as persons of relatively high status because they are agents of the government. They are seen as legitimate instruments of the national will. Because they represent legitimate authority, they receive a measure of deference not experienced by their counterparts. Since Japanese appear to be motivated more by a sense of duty than by an insistence on rights, there is an entirely different climate for policing. What Japanese police request citizens to do is not interpreted as an infringement of personal rights. Instead, police requests are honored as something that is necessary to maintain the highly valued harmony of Japanese society (Suzuki 1983).

Because the structure of Japanese policing places the officer into the relational network of the community, there is less of the divisive "we–they" framework that greatly informs policing in the United States. In Japan, citizens and police see themselves linked in a common cause (Clifford 1976).

Another factor influencing Japanese police subculture is the nature and character of violence in Japan. To be sure, Japanese culture is not without elements of violence. The fact that the Japanese riot police are one of the best organized and equipped forces of its kind anywhere in the world is evidence that violence exists. But much of the violence in Japan follows institutionalized or ritualized patterns, and it is seldom directed against the police per se. Riot police may confront an angry group of protesters, but there are understood rules which keep the violence in check (Ames 1981).

It is also important to note that Japanese gun control laws have effectively limited the number of firearms. An estimated 150,000 firearms are owned by civilians in Japan, as compared to the estimated 150,000,000 privately owned weapons in the United States. Japanese police officers are not faced with the same dangers that confront American police, and, as a result, they do not need to operate at the same level of suspicion (Bayley 1976a; Ames 1981).

While not all Japanese police are happy and contented in their work, their system of police administration seems to foster a higher level of confidence in and support of police supervision. Because police in Japan are not subject to the same political pressures as police in the United States, there seems to be less cynicism and a great deal more idealism (Suzuki 1983).

Drawing primarily from the work of Bayley (1976a) and Ames (1981), we see that Japanese police subculture includes the following concepts:

• Policing is an honorable profession that merits the support and approval it receives from the public.

- "Real police work" is service to the public, not simply apprehending criminals and fighting crime.
- The police have a moral mandate to teach proper civil conduct by precept and example.
- The public's respect for authority is reciprocated by respect for the citizen's rights and dignity.
- Intense loyalty to the group is based not on the group's isolation from the community but upon tradition and the principles for which the group stands.
- Group solidarity, conditioned by the cultural value of group-relatedness, provides a sense of identity to the individual and exercises control over misconduct.
- Police are not an embattled minority—they are a part of mainstream society and important spokespersons for the Japanese way of life.

The effects of this subculture on the behavior of the Japanese police have been described extensively by Bayley (1976a) and Ames (1981). For the purposes of this study, two areas need brief mention: the relationship between line officers and their superiors, and the Japanese police work group.

Relationships between Officers and Supervisors   One of the perplexing problems confronting police in the U.S. is the relationship between line officers and supervisory staff (Reuss-Ianni 1983). The paramilitary structure of the U.S. police—its sharp demarcations of authority and its narrow definition of professionalism that sharply limits discretion—requires that the work of the line officer be closely supervised. Paradoxically, the style of policing used in the United States demands that individual police officers exercise discretion in situations where supervision is usually improbable, if not impossible. As a consequence, supervision of the police in the United States places heavy emphasis upon rules and regulations, paper work, and "spit and polish" activities that have little to do with fighting crime. Police officers resent supervisors who enforce "Mickey Mouse" regulations considered to have little to do with "what really counts" (Bittner 1977). Further, the hierarchical structure tends to isolate supervisors from the rank and file. A common complaint among line officers is that the supervisor has been "behind a desk too long" (Tifft 1977).

While Japanese police also use a paramilitary structure, their style of policing allows for a great deal of direct supervision. The koban system places the police officer in a position where superiors may observe what he does almost at all times. In addition, Japanese superiors are expected to spend time in the field with line officers. Superiors from police headquarters visit the koban each day. While Japanese police also exercise a great deal of discretion, most decisions are made in the koban, and discretion is exercised under the watchful eye of a supervisor who understands what the policeman is doing because he has firsthand knowledge of the situation (Bayley 1976c; Schembri 1985).

Even more important is the *oyabun-kobun* relationship between superior and inferior, older and younger, police. This is a "father–son" or "mentor–protege" relationship, in which the superior is treated with honor, respect, and deference. In turn, the superior sees his relationship to the younger officer as entailing responsibility and interested concern. In the not-too-distant past, the superior officer was so strong a father figure that his approval was required before a young officer could be married. Even today a superior may check the suitability of a young officer's fiancée to make sure she will make a good police wife. The supervisor feels a sense of responsibility for the line officer's performance, and if an inferior makes a serious mistake, the superior is expected to share in the blame (Bayley 1976a).

This kind of relationship extends beyond the koban and the tour of duty. Supervisors are expected to know their subordinates as individuals and to be aware of what is happening in their personal lives. Frequent social gatherings are encouraged and provide opportunity for interpersonal relations to develop. While the administrative system is bureaucratic and hierarchical, the *oyabun-kobun* relationship, with its emphasis on shared responsibility and personal loyalty, relieves much of the stress the formal relationship may produce (Bayley 1976a; Clifford 1976).

The Police Work Group   Relationships between superior and inferior are best understood in the context of the Japanese police as a *work group*. As was discussed in chapter 2, Japanese culture stresses group-relatedness. The work group becomes the source of the individual's self-identity, the most important factor in determining status in society, social relationships, and behavior. While this is true of all Japanese, it is especially true of the Japanese police. As Bayley (1976a, 72) describes it, "The organization is more than just an instrument for accomplishing tasks; it is a community. Being a policeman is not just a job; it is a way of life."

Because of the koban structure, policing is a group activity in Japan. The extremely long hours in a noncyclical shift system separate police officers from the rest of the society. It makes friendships outside of the work group difficult. Officers work, eat, and sleep together in a way of life that is somewhat reminiscent of a college fraternity. During the year of cadet training, all officers live in dormitories, and dormitories are provided for single officers after they complete police school. Often many of the officers assigned to a given koban not only work together, they live together as well. Even married officers may live in police apartment buildings, where the person next door may work the same shift in the same koban (Bayley 1976a; Ames 1981).

Police solidarity is further enhanced by athletics. Sports teams, complete with cheerleaders and team songs, compete in hotly contested league play. An annual *kendo* tournament arouses strong competitive spirit and draws police throughout the nation into a sense of unity (Bayley 1976a).

While police in the U.S. are also conscious of belonging to a distinct group, that group identity is based on rejection. American police perceive themselves to be a minority, confronted by hostility and suspicion, whose role is misunderstood and whose work is deprecated. The Japanese police community has been deliberately constructed and serves to enhance police officers' sense of pride in their community and in their work. The work group provides them with a sense of attachment and place, and the larger community's acceptance of their group assures them of an honorable place in their world.

THE MAKING OF POLICE OFFICERS: TRAINING

One final element helps to shape differences in policing in Japan and the United States—the police training programs used by each society. Once again, the effects of cultural difference play a significant role.

Because police in the United States are decentralized, no national standards for police training are in effect. Efforts to provide training are scattered and vary widely in curriculum, quality, and duration. Although many large cities operate their own police academies, smaller communities generally send their recruits to state-run training facilities (Walker 1983).

Formal training tends to be heavily weighted toward the technical aspects of police work, and is usually structured like a military boot camp. Because most police departments in the United States do not require that recruits have more than a high school education, instruction tends to be at that level (VanMaanen, 1985).

Critics of police training in the United States acknowledge that there has been an increase in the amount of training. But they also point out that most programs are deficient in critical areas, especially in the use of discretion. For education in such areas, police rely on "on the street" training supervised by a Field Training Officer (FTO) (Walker 1983). Unfortunately, recruits are often told to forget everything they've been taught at the academy, that they will learn all they need to know about real police work out on the streets. John Van Maanen's (1985, 96–97) perceptive examination of police training points out that:

> This traditional feature of police work—patrolmen training patrolmen—ensures continuity from class to class of police officers, regardless of the content of academic instruction. In large measure the flow of influence from one generation to the next accounts for the remarkable stability of police behavior.

This also partially accounts for the difficulty administrators face in attempting to create change.

Although attempts are being made to formalize field training and to use specially selected and trained Field Training Officers, relatively few departments have instituted the highly developed and structured programs that were recommended by the Commission on Accreditation for Law Enforcement Agencies in 1983. One study suggests that a substantial number of field training programs continue to use only on-the-job training with a senior officer who has neither been carefully screened and selected nor received special training in how to fill the role of the Field Training Officer (McCampbell 1986).

As a consequence of this type of training, police in the U.S. become socialized into a self-perpetuating pattern of policing. Attitudes and values of the police subculture are internalized and shape the behavior of the next generation of police officers. Further, the disparity in the quality and quantity of training also guarantees great variation, from place to place, in the quality of policing.

Japan's system of police training differs in a number of ways (Ueno 1979). First, Japan's national system of policing allows for uniformity of training. The National Police Agency operates eight training academies, which provide a common curriculum for all recruits. In addition, the academies provide special programs for officers who move up the promotion ladder: At each step, additional training is required.

Second, recruit training in Japan is extensive. Cadets are required to complete a full year of training in a curriculum which includes a variety of social, cultural, and psychological materials. After training, they enter a year-long period of apprenticeship and then return to the academy for an additional three months of reflection and training.

Third, instead of using Field Training Officers, Japanese police have developed a mentoring system to provide on-the-job training for recruits. Each apprentice police officer is assigned to a mentor—an older, experienced police officer who has been carefully selected and specifically trained for the mentor role. Mentors meet regularly to discuss what is required of them and how to handle problems in teaching the new recruits.

Japan's training program results in a greater probability that recruits will learn what the organization wants them to learn, rather than what the "old hands" decide is important. In addition, the recruit–mentor relationship prepares for and reinforces the *oyabun-kobun* relationship that is so important in the overall scheme of Japanese police administration. Finally, the extensive training the recruit receives not only better prepares him for the role he is to play, it also serves to incorporate him into the work group and to reinforce the values and attitudes of the group (Bayley 1976a).

CONCLUSION

Policing in Japan and the United States shares the commonalities of a professional, paramilitary, hierarchical structure. However, comparative analysis indicates that these similarities are, in large measure, superficial. The major differences in the history and the development of these two societies have created very dissimilar cultural environments. Japanese and American people are not the obverse of each other. They share many of the traits of modern, industrialized, urbanized societies all over the world. Yet they are distinct and different people. The values they hold lead to differences in social milieu which critically affect the structure and style of policing found in each society. As Clifford (1976, 73) reminds us, "No police force works in a vacuum." It is the unique culture of a society that shapes and forms the institutions it develops.

If American and Japanese police are different, it is because they are just that: American and Japanese. While they can be compared, that comparison can be meaningful only in the context of the cultures in which they have developed.

6 PURSUING JUSTICE: THE COURTS AND CRIMINAL ADJUDICATION

PERSPECTIVES TOWARD JUSTICE AND JUSTICE SYSTEMS

An adequate understanding of criminal adjudication in any society cannot be developed unless that society's definition and use of the idea of *justice* are considered. In most Western societies the idea of justice is tied to the courts and court proceedings. The courts, more than any other component of the criminal justice system, are agencies specifically designed to allocate justice—to discern guilt, ensure the rights of both victims and the accused, and dispense punishment when required. However, from a philosophical perspective, the concept of justice has a much broader meaning (Myren 1988; Voigt and Thornton 1984). Justice reflects a society's moral ideals about human relationships. It involves such notions as "equality, freedom, opportunity, fair treatment, and security" (Myren 1988, 27). The arena in which justice operates is all human interaction, both on an interpersonal and on an institutional level. It is manifest both in how people deal with each other and in how rights and resources are distributed.

Many people in the United States, however, use the term *justice* in a fairly debased way to refer to the everyday conduct of institutional systems of social control, most commonly the "justice system" (Jenkins 1984, 105). Thus justice as a moral and social ideal is often framed in terms of legal procedures rather than the day-to-day relations among people. This is why many people in the United States find it difficult to understand the Japanese concept of justice. To Americans, justice is equated with legal procedures; to Japanese, justice is an ideal in interpersonal relationships. There are culturally bound values and notions attached to the concept of justice, and as might be expected, there is wide variation in what "justice" is held to be in the United States as compared to Japan (Clifford 1976). This is especially true with regard to the meaning and practice of justice in the context of criminal adjudication.

The American concept of justice is influenced by at least two prominent ideas. First, the objective orientation that is such a central part of our legal culture insists that justice is achieved only by using impartial standards that guarantee both fairness and equality. This insistence, growing out of the values of freedom and individual worth, was given clear expression in the civil rights provisions of the Constitution. These civil rights have been extended through the evolution of procedural law, most notably during the "Due Process Revolution" of the 1960s. Second, most people in the United States believe that unlawful behavior deserves and requires punishment if moral order in society is to be maintained. The image of Lady Justice, blindfolded and with scale in hand, symbolizes a just legal system in which punishment is proportionate to the crime, evenly dispensed, and used to reestablish moral balance in society. The importance of this image is emphasized in a contemporary perspective on crime and justice called the "Just Desert Model" (see Siegel [1989] for a review of this perspective).

These perspectives on justice are clearly reflected in the strong tendency to use legal channels whenever wrongs are committed, whether civil or criminal in nature. Not only is the formal system of justice used heavily, but it is also seen as the most appropriate way to ensure that the rights of the parties involved are protected and secured. As such, the law and the judicial system are imbued with a nearly sacred character. Most people in the United States see the system of justice as dispensing an almost magical, legal remedy for the problems that people face (Jacob 1984).

The result has been an increasing amount of litigation that has caused serious congestion in many courts. While some observers (Daniels 1984, 1985; Sarat 1985; Galanter 1983) have argued that there has been no "litigation explosion" in the United States, others (Marvell 1985, 1987; Neubauer 1986; Flango and Ito 1984) have produced evidence that suggests there has been a steady increase in the number of civil and criminal cases brought before the courts, producing delays in the judicial process. This has led to experiments with Alternative Dispute Resolution (ADR) mechanisms. These include various forms of arbitration and mediation, malpractice screening, the "Rent-a-Judge" and "Mini-Trial" hearings, the "Multi-door Courtroom," and Dispute Resolution Centers. However, at this point in time, ADR mechanisms remain largely experimental. Because these programs are not well known, they have not yet gained either popularity or legitimacy with the U.S. public (Lowry 1987; McGillis 1986; Posner 1986; Sander 1982).

The Japanese view of justice, rooted in the values of harmony, group-relatedness, and hierarchy, is quite different. These values, so central to Japanese life, permeate virtually all aspects of their approach to adjudication. This is seen particularly in their limited use of the courts:

> When a dispute arises between two parties, not very many Japanese view the dispute in terms of rights and obligations. Nor does it occur to them when they fail to work out a solution between themselves that the best approach to the dispute is to take the matter to the court. Instead the traditional value of "harmony" *(wa)* prevails upon them. In their minds, settlement of disputes, without arguing their points of view in a reasoned way and without fighting out their cases to the finish in court, is of supreme value (Tanaka 1976d, 261).

In a society where harmony is so important, legal proceedings are perceived to signify a breakdown in human relations (Thompson 1986; Bolz 1980; Ishida 1971). As a result, the Japanese use litigation only as a last resort and show a persistent tendency toward nonjudicial methods of dispute resolution. The value of harmony does not preclude interpersonal disputes but encourages informal means of resolution (Rosch 1987). The importance of harmony is also seen in the reluctance of Japanese to assert the rights of one individual over another and their rejection of dispute resolution methods that require moral fault be assigned by delineating who is right or wrong (Noda 1976b).

People in the United States prefer to see their own interests secured by using independent legal standards, but the Japanese prefer to secure their interests through participation in the settlement process. In the Japanese view, justice has a subjective character, incorporating situational factors of the dispute itself, seeking concession and compromise by the parties involved, and ultimately ending in mutual agreement (Clifford 1976). Kawashima (1976, 277) captures nicely the Japanese perspective toward justice in the context of legal adjudication:

> Traditionally, the Japanese people prefer extra-judicial, informal means of settling a controversy. Litigation presupposes and admits the existence of a dispute and leads to a decision which makes clear who is right or wrong in accordance with standards independent of the wills of the disputants. Furthermore, judicial decisions emphasize the conflict between the parties, deprive them of participation in the settlement, and assign a moral fault which can be avoided in a compromise solution.

Thompson (1986, 30) points out that "traditional rules of conduct and ways of thinking formed over a long period of history do not change quickly, and continue to influence modern attitudes toward the law." This can be seen in the historical persistence of informal social control in Japan. Dating back well before the Tokugawa period, the Confucian emphasis on harmony and a natural social hierarchy led to the development of a traditional, nonlegal system of social rules which directed the daily lives of the Japanese. These informal rules continue to operate today, side-by-side with the formal legal system (Thompson 1986). Called *giri*, these rules of social obligation prescribe social relationships, especially within groups, based upon status differential in the social hierarchy. As we have noted, Japanese tradition dictates that people are naturally unequal at birth and deference and loyalty should be shown to those of higher status and authority. However, the rules of *giri* also require benevolence on the part of the superior to subordinates (Noda 1976a).

An important extension of these rules of *giri* is the expectation that disputes be settled informally, through the practice of conciliation. According to Henderson (1965, 183–187), the tradition of conciliation remains a cornerstone of Japanese justice. There are three distinct forms of conciliation. The first of these is *jidan*, a conciliation process originating in the Tokugawa period. This tradition involves a person of high status—historically, a family elder or village leader—acting as mediator to allow disputing parties to reach a compromise agreement where neither one is a clear winner or loser. The aim of such informal reconciliation is to restore harmony without troubling governmental officials or relying on legal recourse. This appears to be a carryover of feudal deference to authority (Thompson 1986; See 1982; Kawashima 1976).

The practice of *jidan* has been transposed to modern Japanese society. Within governmental bureaus, business organizations, and other workplaces, supervisors often mediate differences among employees. Similarly, policemen in neighborhood kobans are specifically trained and relied upon for counseling in marital and neighborhood disputes (Bayley 1976a). Furthermore, this informal conciliation process has been structured into Japanese society through a host of formal agencies set up to help individuals resolve disputes without using courts (Rosch 1987). Although they are formal institutions, these agencies provide informal conciliation services. Probably one of the most extensively used of these is the Civil Liberties Bureau (CLU). Initially created to promote individual rights, the CLU has evolved into an institution that, in 1984, heard over 375,000 disputes between private parties (Rosch 1987).

The second form of conciliation, *Chotei,* is a formal, prelitigation procedure which developed between the two world wars in an effort to reduce rising rates of litigation. A succession of legislative acts beginning in the 1920s mandated that courts at various levels develop conciliation committees as a preliminary, often compulsory, stage in the judicial process. These committees, composed of trusted laypersons, provide an opportunity for out-of-court settlement of disagreements (Thompson 1986; See 1982; Haley 1978).

The third form of conciliation, *wakai,* is a practice borrowed from the Germans in which the judge encourages a compromise settlement (Smith 1983). The adaptation of the European tradition of inquisitorial justice to Japanese society in the late 1800s meant not only that judges took an active role in the adjudication process but that they encouraged conciliation. The judicial tradition of encouraging conciliation persists today even though the structure and process of adjudication, adopted when the new constitution was written following World War II, allow for a more adversarial approach.

The thrust behind the Japanese reliance on informal, mediated settlement and their limited use of formal mechanisms of legal adjudication is a matter of much debate (Haley 1978; Ramseyer and Nakazato 1989; Upham 1989; Ramseyer 1988; Miyazawa 1987; Ramseyer 1983; Krauss, Rohlen, and Steinhoff 1984; Smith 1983, 1984). Some scholars have argued that the particular historical development of Japan and the unique cultural traits which emerged there have produced a society with an aversion to litigation (Kawashima 1976). The high value Japanese place on harmony in social relationships and the hierarchical social order of society seem consistent with the popular view that the Japanese are nonlitigious. Then, too, the undeniable fact that Japan's litigation rates are much lower than those of the United States, as well as the fact that Japan has far fewer lawyers, appears to support such a view (Haley 1978). This cultural model certainly is not inconsistent with our argument; however, it seems to emphasize nonlitigiousness to the extreme, almost to the point of making it part of a Japanese national character.

Haley (1978) suggests that this cultural model fails to acknowledge many of the structural aspects of the Japanese judicial system and governmental judicial policies which create barriers to litigation. Structural characteristics such as statutory limitation on the number of prosecutors and judges result in incredibly high court caseloads. This creates delays and undoubtedly accounts for some of the reluctance Japanese have in resorting to formal adjudication. It is also true, as previously described, that a variety of informal and formal conciliation processes provide alternatives to litigation. As Haley convincingly argues, it is not so much that the Japanese are characteristically nonlitigious, but that "the Japanese may be more successful in avoiding litigation because of social organization and values more conducive to informal dispute resolution" (Haley 1978, 379; see also Rosch 1987). Finally, Haley also argues that Japanese litigation rates are low for the relatively simple economic reason that "suing does not pay"—the courts have traditionally failed to provide adequate relief (Haley 1978; Ramseyer 1988). Such a lack of financial compensation undoubtedly discourages individuals from pursuing legal recourse in dispute settlement.

Miyazawa (1987) further points out that nonlitigiousness is probably not a Japanese cultural value. Instead, he argues that nonlitigiousness is a consequence of a "legal conception" among the Japanese which fails to emphasize individual rights in social relationships. Nevertheless, Miyazawa contends that the distinctive nature of Japanese legal consciousness cannot be quickly or easily dismissed. Instead, he argues that Japanese legal culture and whether or not it results in nonlitigiousness are matters deserving further empirical study.

While much of the consideration of litigiousness in Japan and the United States deals primarily with civil matters, the same perspectives toward justice in each society carry over to criminal adjudication. The structures and processes of both civil and criminal adjudication in Japan and the United States reflect in a striking manner how ideals of justice in each culture are translated into practice.

COURT STRUCTURES IN THE UNITED STATES AND JAPAN

It has already been noted that law and legal systems reflect not only the complexity of a society but also its cultural characteristics. As societies grow larger and more complex, there is a tendency for informal mechanisms of social control to be replaced by formal laws and legal institutions. A judicial system, composed of courts and court personnel, is a common institutional structure to emerge from this process of social change. Yet, as Abraham (1986) has observed, while the court systems of different societies may share similar features, no two are truly alike. For example, every known judicial system shares the common feature of separate trial and appellate courts; however, beyond such general structural similarities, each court system has unique features (Abraham, 1986).

Court Systems in the United States

The most striking feature of the U.S. court system is its "dual structure," in which a federal court system operates alongside state court systems (Jacob 1984, 161). Judicial power, however, was first and foremost delegated to the state court systems and even when the Judiciary Act of 1789 created a federal court structure, the supremacy of state courts was well established:

> From the time of the ratification of the Constitution until the Civil War, the primacy of the state courts was not seriously questioned. The Judiciary Act of 1789 affirmed the primary role of the state courts and narrowly confined the jurisdiction of the federal trial courts (Abadinsky 1988, 40).

The supremacy of state court systems arose, at least in part, as an ideological commitment of the framers of the Constitution to keep centralized, federal government to a minimum. The colonists' distrust of centralized power was a strong influence on the framers of the Constitution. While the idea of a national judiciary was widely accepted, primarily to protect fundamental civil rights and to promote uniformity of judgment, there was much debate on the necessity of creating a federal court system beyond a single appellate court (Abadinsky 1988). Those who opposed the idea of federal inferior courts argued that the supremacy clause of the Constitution (Article IV) required state judges to enforce the Constitution and, as a result, an extensive system of federal courts would be redundant (Abadinsky 1988, 92).

Judicial power was also decentralized due to geographic necessity. Colonial America was a vast nation with primitive transportation, making it necessary to bring the courts to the people. Then, too, early state and local courts assumed a wide range of responsibility because of the unspecialized nature of government during this period. The concepts of separation of power and governmental specialization did not develop immediately after the Revolutionary War (Abadinsky 1988). As a result, the courts served as the legislative, executive, and judicial branches of county government (Walker 1980).

The controversy over the size and extent of the federal court system resulted in a compromise evident in the wording of the third article of the Constitution, which created a single appellate court, the Supreme Court, but left the door open to a larger federal judicial system: "The judicial power of the United States, shall be vested in one Supreme Court and in such inferior Courts as the Congress may from time to time ordain and establish."

Just a year after the Constitution was ratified, the Judiciary Act of 1789 extended the federal court system to include three circuit courts and thirteen district courts (Abadinsky 1988). In recent years, the federal court system has expanded in size and jurisdiction because of congressional statutory action (Jacob 1984).

Despite significant differences, the state and federal court systems share similar structural features (Friedman 1984). The essential structure of the court systems is easier to describe and understand when distinctions in jurisdiction are kept in mind.

Jurisdiction refers to the power and authority of a court to hear and decide a case as delegated by state and federal law (Abadinsky 1988; Reid 1987). Weston and Wells (1987, 80) astutely point out that "[j]urisdiction is first a matter of law, then it is largely a matter of administration." Personnel and budgetary limitations place a practical reality on the number and type of cases a court will hear. Additionally, individual prosecutors and judges differ significantly on how they view and interpret their jurisdictional authority.

The federal and state court systems can be distinguished based upon differences in geographic (or venue) and subject jurisdiction. State courts, for the most part, rarely have jurisdiction beyond their borders. They deal with state criminal and civil code violations. A majority of all criminal law is *state* law, and as a result, state courts handle the bulk of all criminal cases. Federal courts primarily handle cases involving federal law. However, the subject jurisdiction of federal courts has expanded dramatically since their inception:

> Originally, state courts held exclusive jurisdiction over most cases, and Congress confined federal courts to admiralty, patent, and copyright matters; suits where citizens of two different states contested a claim ("diversity of citizenship matters"); and criminal charges resulting from a few federal statutes. Only in the last half of the nineteenth century, when the nation's expanding economy broke through state and regional barriers, was the jurisdiction of the federal court broadened. Congress then expanded federal court jurisdiction to all matters involving federal rights—a category of conflicts that previously had been tried in state courts and only occasionally appealed to the United States Supreme Court. Congress also greatly expanded the scope of federal statutory law involving commerce, civil rights, taxation, and criminal law (Jacob 1984, 162–163).

Courts within different judicial systems also vary in the extent of jurisdiction they have. Abadinsky (1988, 83) summarizes this structural distinction of courts within a system:

> *Original jurisdiction* refers to the authority to hear or act upon a case from the beginning to its conclusion. *Appellate jurisdiction* refers to the authority to review decisions made by a lower court, to hear cases on appeal. *Limited jurisdiction* means that the court has original jurisdiction in only a limited number of narrowly defined cases, for example, only misdemeanor or civil cases where the money in dispute is below a specified sum, or only traffic cases. *General jurisdiction* refers to the authority of a court to hear any type of case, civil or criminal, misdemeanor or felony, those involving small amounts of money and those involving unlimited amounts.

State Court Systems   The structure of most state court systems, despite name variations, follows a four-tiered pattern:

1. *Courts of limited jurisdiction* are profusely spread across the country, most often in municipalities. They are restricted in the types of cases they can hear— usually the least serious cases and the least serious claims. Many of these courts also handle at least part of the preliminary procedures in criminal cases. Other courts of limited jurisdiction deal only with specific matters, such as traffic, family, and juvenile. These are sometimes called *courts of special jurisdiction.*

2. *Courts of general trial jurisdiction* handle the bulk of major litigation under state law. These courts have jurisdiction over all kinds of criminal offenses, including felonies, and in some states handle appeals from courts of limited jurisdiction.

3. *Intermediate appellate courts:* In an adversarial system of justice, losers have the right to appeal the decision, but most do not. In states with small populations, appeals go directly from the courts of general jurisdiction to the state supreme court—the highest court in the state judicial system. States with larger populations have intermediate appellate courts that provide a first round of appeals. Appellate courts do not conduct a new hearing—they review the trial record of the lower court for judicial error.

4. *Courts of last resort* are appellate courts which serve as the final authority in cases involving issues of state law. A supreme court has discretionary power to

decide which cases it will hear. The court can issue a writ of certiorari which instructs the lower court to send up the record for review.

The Federal Court System   The federal court system follows this same basic structure but has a three-tiered hierarchy because it lacks courts of limited jurisdiction. However, a number of institutions in the federal judicial system are delegated limited or special jurisdiction in federal cases. U.S. Magistrates, judicial officers appointed by the district court, may have full jurisdiction over minor offenses and typically handle many of the pretrial steps in more serious offenses (Abadinsky 1988; Reid 1987). Additionally, a conglomeration of special courts and quasi-judicial agencies deal with noncriminal offenses of federal codes. The Court of International Trade, District Court in Patent Matters, Federal Tax Court, Federal Trade Commission, and Court of Military Appeals are just a few of these federal judicial institutions.

Courts of original trial jurisdiction in federal criminal cases are called *district courts*. Every state has at least one district court as do the U.S. territories. Today there are roughly one hundred federal district courts. The *courts of appeals* are the intermediate federal appellate courts. These courts are divided into judicial districts, or circuits. The number of federal judicial districts was recently increased from ten to eleven. The number of judges in each district varies with geographic size and population, from four in the First Circuit to twenty-three in the Ninth Circuit. Unlike the district courts and most of the state courts, federal courts of appeal are composed of panels of at least three judges and, if a case is serious enough, it will be heard by all or most of the judges sitting as a panel—"en banc" (Friedman 1984).

The *Supreme Court* is the court of last resort for cases involving federal law. It also hears appeals from state courts if they raise significant federal issues, most commonly issues related to the federal Constitution. As is true of state supreme courts, the United States Supreme Court has virtually complete control over its docket through the writ of certiorari. As a result, the Supreme Court hears few original cases, even though it has original jurisdiction in some cases (Friedman 1984). (See Figure 6.1.)

The Japanese Court System

It should be apparent by now that the Japanese have a long history of reliance on informal means of social control in which legal codes, while not uncommon, were peripheral to customary rules of conduct. As previously described, these customary rules, or *giri,* have played and continue to play a vital role in prescribing and controlling behavior. Although criminal codes were adopted in Japan as early as the eighth century, the Japanese belief in a higher law, based most heavily in Confucianism, emphasized harmony, a common good, and a natural hierarchical order that transcends human laws (See 1982). Interestingly, the oldest written code in Japan, the *Jushichijo Kempo* or Seventeen Maxims (A.D. 604), was essentially a code of ethics, establishing formal rules of conduct for people and their rulers, rather than a code establishing the fundamental laws of the land (Supreme Court of Japan 1982). The importance of these customary rules of propriety, together with

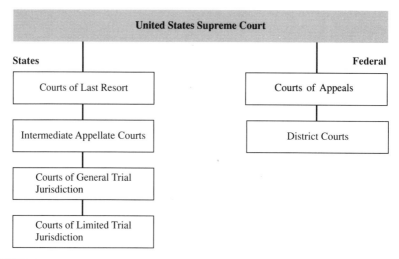

FIGURE 6.1 Diagram of the Court Systems in the United States

the tradition of conciliation, has led some legal scholars to suggest that there has been little inherent need for a formal system of justice in Japanese society (Mikazuki 1976).

Prior to the Meiji Restoration of 1868, there was no judicial system distinguishable from the administrative institutions of the local daimyo or the shogun's court (Allen 1984; Supreme Court of Japan 1983; See 1982). During the Feudal Period (1192–1867), judicial functions in criminal cases were handled predominantly by *Shugo,* the provincial military governors (Supreme Court of Japan 1982; Dando 1965). The governors exercised judicial power as a part of the broad range of authority held by these localized governments (See 1982). As a result, courts were more administrative than judicial in nature and this administrative character of the courts persisted into the Meiji era (Allen 1984; Supreme Court of Japan 1983). Criminal proceedings, called *Kendanzata,* allowed judges extensive discretion and inquisitorial authority. Judgments were based most often upon confessions, sometimes obtained through torture, and could rarely be appealed (Supreme Court of Japan 1982; Dando 1965). Nevertheless, judges were expected to shape the penalty to all the peculiar facets of the individual (Henderson 1952). Furthermore, according to Confucian doctrine, judges, as social superiors in the natural hierarchy, were expected to function as teachers, instructing people how to behave (See 1982).

Independent local adjudication within each daimyo's territory was the mainstay of the judicial system throughout the Feudal Era (Allen 1984). In fact, the judicial system was based upon systems of laws which were largely parochial in nature, codified and enforced only within the individual fiefs. As See (1982, 343) notes: "The bulk of the rules actually observed by the people in the country-side continued to be customary folk-ways [sic] which found their origins in communal life, not the will of the shogun." These local customary laws reached their zenith in the middle of the Feudal Era, during the *Sengoku,* or Civil War, period (1467–1573) (Supreme Court of Japan 1982). This reliance upon local laws and adjudication subjected the judicial system to the power dynamics between the shogun and local feudal lords (Supreme Court of Japan 1982).

Efforts to unify the judicial system and consolidate indigenous law began during the Tokugawa shogunate and resulted in the first unitary criminal law code, the *Kujigata Osadamegaki,* which was established in 1742 (Supreme Court of Japan 1982). However, because administrative and judicial functions still were not separate, the shogun and local feudal lords continued to control the administration of justice (Supreme Court of Japan 1982).

When the feudal age ended, the Meiji Restoration introduced gradual but wide-sweeping changes in the legal system, abolishing the indigenous judicial system and eventually replacing it with a national system (Allen 1984). It was not until 1871, however, that the Ministry of Justice under the new, centralized government assumed responsibility for adjudication and created the first comprehensive nationwide court system (Supreme Court of Japan 1982). The national character of the judicial system was firmly established early in the Meiji era, but the specific structure of the courts evolved over a twenty-year period (Supreme Court of Japan 1982). The character and structure of this national judicial system were heavily influenced by the same European models that inspired Japanese law. The court system emerged at the sole initiative of the central government, without political or public opposition or support. As a result, the Japanese judicial system achieved a simplicity and schematic consistency unlike that of most other nations (Mikazuki 1976). Passage of the Court Organization Law and the Code of Criminal Procedure in 1890 formalized this twenty-year transition in court structure and a similar evolution in criminal law (Supreme Court of Japan 1982; See 1982). These acts established a hierarchical court structure which included courts of original jurisdiction, intermediate appellate courts *(Kosoin),* and a court of last resort *(Taishinin),* which heard only cases involving legal issues. This structure remains essentially the same today.

In 1899, the central government enacted a constitution. It established a constitutional parliamentary monarchy and stipulated a separation of power between the national Diet (legislature), the emperor and cabinet (executive branch), and the courts (judiciary). However, the separation of power was incomplete because the emperor and cabinet held general supervisory power over the government (Supreme Court of Japan 1982). This was clearly evident in the administrative control that the minister of justice (a cabinet member) held over the judicial system (Allen 1984; Supreme Court of Japan 1982; Supreme Court of Japan 1983; Nomura 1981). Within its supervisory capacity, the cabinet could issue ordinances and establish administrative courts (Supreme Court of Japan 1983; See 1982). Not only did this power affect people's rights and duties, but the cabinet could effectively circumvent the legislative power of the Diet and the judicial power of the judiciary. This is what Henderson (1968b) has referred to as "Rule *by* Law," in contrast with "Rule *of* Law." The dominance of the executive branch was challenged as early as 1891 when the judiciary tried to establish the principle of judicial independence through a series of supreme court cases, but its efforts were not completely successful (See 1982).

Following World War II, a new constitution and Court Organization Law were simultaneously enacted. The new Constitution, still enforced today, reflects the influence of the United States' occupational forces (Allen 1984; See 1982). The judicial system was made independent of executive interference, and a full range of judicial power was vested in the Supreme Court (Supreme Court of Japan 1983). This included administrative power over the court system and court personnel, the authority to establish rules of practice and procedure, and internal discipline of the courts—powers formerly held by the Ministry of Justice (Allen 1984; Supreme Court of Japan 1982, 1983). In a radical departure from the previous government, the Supreme Court was also granted the power of judicial review—the authority to review the constitutionality of any law, order, regulation, or official act (Supreme Court of Japan 1983). Further, the Constitution stipulated that no special courts could be created nor could any executive agency be given final judicial powers (Supreme Court of Japan 1983).

The Court Organization Law created a multi-tiered court system, similar to court systems in the United States (Araki 1985). However, it is a national system alone, not a dual system as in the United States. The contemporary Japanese judicial system consists of five types of courts: the supreme court, high courts, district courts, family courts, and summary courts (Allen 1984; Supreme Court of Japan 1982, 1983; Nomura 1981; Lorenzo 1974; see also Figure 6.2):

1. *Supreme Court:* The Supreme Court is the highest court in the land and is composed of fifteen justices, including the chief justice. Appointed by the Cabinet, justices are subject to popular review. Generally, the Supreme Court exercises only appellate jurisdiction. In criminal cases, appeals are usually limited to constitutional questions or issues of precedent. The Supreme Court also handles a variety of administrative duties. These are dealt with through resolutions of the judicial assembly, a body made up of all Supreme Court justices and presided over by the chief justice (Supreme Court of Japan 1982, 10). The Supreme Court also oversees the training of attorneys at the court's Legal Training and Research Institute.

2. *High courts:* The high courts function primarily as intermediate appellate courts, hearing cases appealed from the district or family courts. Appeals can also come directly from the summary court when criminal cases originate there. Cases are usually heard by a panel of three judges. There are eight high courts throughout Japan, some of which have branch offices.

3. *District courts:* The district courts are primarily courts of general original jurisdiction, trying all cases in the first instance except those specifically coming under the original jurisdiction of other courts. Cases are heard either by a single judge or by a panel of three judges, depending on the nature of the case. There are fifty such courts in each of Japan's prefectural units except for Hokkaido which is divided into four judicial districts.

4. *Family courts:* Family courts are independent from but equal to the district courts. They were first created in 1949 to deal with family affairs of legal significance and juvenile matters (under age 20). After investigation into the nature and circumstances of a juvenile case, the family court can turn the matter over to the district or summary court for criminal action if the youth is over 16 years of age.

5. *Summary courts:* Summary courts are the most numerous in Japan—some

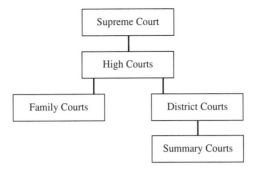

FIGURE 6.2 Diagram of Japan's Court System

575 courts. These courts have original jurisdiction on minor criminal and civil cases. In criminal cases, the sanctions are limited to fines or imprisonment of no longer than three years. It is important to note that summary courts utilize several types of special proceedings which facilitate prosecutorial and judicial discretion and offer defendants the option of not going through a courtroom trial. These summary procedures will be discussed later in the chapter.

The structure of Japan's judicial system reflects a long history of executive dominance, in which the sovereignty of the shogun or emperor, not the people, was preeminent (See 1982). Formal legal codes and judicial systems were not prominent structural characteristics of Japanese society until the Tokugawa period. Customary rules of conduct which emphasized a natural hierarchy and a respect for authority, together with a strong tradition of conciliation, indicate there was little need for a formal justice system in Japanese society.

THE LEGAL PROFESSION

Judicial systems in Japan and the United States are sharply differentiated in the practice of law. This differentiation begins with legal education. There really is no educational institution in Japan that is the equivalent of the American school of law (Matsuda 1958). First, over 170 schools of law are currently accredited by the American Bar Association (Gourman 1985). While there are law programs at a paraprofessional level at a number of Japanese colleges and universities, there is only a single institution preparing people for the bar in Japan—the Japanese Legal Training and Research Institute operated by the Supreme Court. Second, while competition for admission to law schools in the United States is keen, admission requirements and procedures in Japan are exceedingly rigorous, and the number of students admitted is restricted. In recent years as many as 35,000 candidates have applied, but only 2 or 3 percent of these were admitted—between 450 and 500 students per year for the entire nation (Allen 1984; Mayer 1984; Nomura 1981). Third, legal education in the United States occurs in the classroom, using the Socratic teaching style and the case-method approach. This promotes individual accountability and intense competition and teaches the skill of legal reasoning (Abadinsky 1988). Thus, American legal education broadly prepares people to become practicing attorneys without specialized training in a specific legal position. Japan's legal education is largely in the form of apprenticeships in each area of the legal profession: the judiciary, procuracy, and private defense. This system affords specialized field training in the practice of law via actual work experience (Shikita 1981).

The American legal profession reflects the diversity of its educational system. Just as there is no federal control of legal education and no national bar examination, the practice of law is chiefly organized into state bar associations. Each state bar association administers a bar exam that controls entrance into the legal profession of that state. As a result, lawyers in the United States generally practice within a single state jurisdiction. Traditionally, judges and prosecutors are selected (elected or appointed) from the ranks of experienced lawyers, and state law and local ordinances often have a residency requirement. There is a significant degree of mobility among the ranks of private practice, prosecution, and the judiciary.

By contrast, the Japanese Legal Training and Research Institute offers a final exam for law students in their last term. Graduates who pass the final exam—and very few fail—may either register as practicing lawyers anywhere in Japan or apply to join the judiciary or procuracy (application is made to the Supreme Court or Ministry of Justice respectively). The number of judges and prosecutors is set by law, and a few are unable to enter the field of their choice (Abe 1976). New members of the judiciary, because of their lack of experience, are appointed as assistant judges with limited power for a ten-year period and are provided extended training through the Institute (Shikita 1981). Entering a particular branch of the legal profession is usually a lifetime commitment, and transfers among the three tracks are rare, except when retired judges and prosecutors enter private practice (Nomura 1981; Shikita 1981). Tanaka (1976b, 549) argues that this limited career mobility within the legal profession results in a much weaker sense of professional unity than is found in the United States. However, Shikita (1981, 46) contends that the Institute's apprenticeship program and the creation of committees composed of legal professionals to deal with specific problems has fostered "a sense of unity, feelings of comradeship, and mutual understanding among legal professionals."

One of the most pronounced differences in the legal profession between Japan and the United States is the number of practicing attorneys. Friedman (1984, 249) states that "there are more than twenty times as many lawyers in the United States per 1,000 population" as there are in Japan. Japan, with a population about half that of the United States, has about 12,000 attorneys, or one attorney for every 10,000 people (Ramseyer 1983; Nomura 1981). By contrast, there are about 700,000 attorneys in the United States, or one attorney for every 360 people (Abadinsky 1988; see also Tanaka 1976d). There is a relatively small number of lawyers in Japan, despite the fact that it is a modern industrialized state with the full range of situations that in the United States would require the service of an attorney.

However, Japan does have a rather large number of paralegal professionals who perform important legal services but do not correspond exactly to the U.S. lawyer or paraprofessional. Smith (1984, 53 contends that, when the calculation of the number of "legal workers" is based on a broader definition that includes these paralegal professionals, the difference between Japan and the United States is not so extreme: 1,119 people per legal worker in Japan as compared with 505 people per legal worker in the United States. Nonetheless, the limited number of attorneys in Japan and the extensive use of paralegal professionals suggest that the role of the lawyer is defined quite differently in Japan than it is the United States.

The prestige of the legal profession also is dissimilar in Japan and the United States. In Japan, the legal profession was not fully formed until the Meiji Restoration, and the idea of looking upon lawyers as professionals failed to take root in the people's mind (Tanaka 1976d). In fact, until recently the Japanese held a jaundiced view of the new legal profession:

> Practicing lawyers were looked upon as intruders, meddling uninvited in disputes which otherwise could have been resolved in the traditional spirit of "harmony." Even in criminal cases, a practicing attorney was viewed not as an agent charged with the grave responsibility of protecting the civil rights of the accused but as an apologist begging for mercy, or even worse, as a schemer bent on thwarting the law (Tanaka 1976d, 265).

Much of this negative view reflects the Japanese reliance on conciliation. The Japanese value of *wa,* or harmony, would urge that disputing parties meet and actively participate in the settlement. Lawyers simply do not have a role in this sort of informal process.

The public image and status of the Japanese legal profession have improved markedly since the end of World War II when the new constitution and Court Organization Law created an independent judicial system and enhanced judicial power (Tanaka 1976d).

People in the United States have a somewhat mixed view of the legal profession. While some hold the profession in relatively high regard, others view the legal profession as a necessary evil in a complex and diverse society. Others have pointed to an apparent overproduction of lawyers and an associated proliferation of unnecessary legal work and litigation (Bok 1983; see also Curran 1986). Nevertheless, the prestige rankings of lawyers, their incomes, and the clamor to get into law school remain high in the United States (Blodgett 1986). Perhaps lawyers have the prestige they do in the United States because they are seen as persons whose role is to secure the rights the law guarantees. Popular myth portrays the Perry Masons and the Ben Matlocks as folk heroes struggling to guarantee the freedom of the individual from the tyranny of the law.

THE CRIMINAL ADJUDICATION PROCESS

Although the general procedures of criminal adjudication in Japan closely resemble those in the United States, there are significant differences (Araki 1985, 605). Criminal adjudication in both countries is an elaborate process that involves a great deal of prosecutorial and judicial discretion and a wide range of alternative actions. Nevertheless, the nature and character of each country's adjudication process are distinctive. Four areas of contrast will be discussed: adversarial justice, the decision to prosecute, the aversion to trial, and sentencing.

Adversarial Justice

Adversarial justice refers to a judicial process that seeks to uncover the "truth" and promote justice by having two adversaries—the prosecution and the defense—present evidence, testimony, and arguments following procedural rules. While the Constitutions and procedural codes of Japan and the United States allow for an adversarial process by establishing due process rights, neither country's adjudication process is truly adversarial in practice. However, there are major differences in the nonadversarial nature of adjudication in each country.

Judges in the United States, operating on the basis of the common law tradition, assume a role fairly consistent with the adversarial process. Because the common law tradition in most instances provides for a jury to render the judgment of guilt or innocence, the judge fills the role of umpire or referee, ruling on the appropriateness of courtroom conduct, the admissibility of evidence, the applicability of law and precedent, and, finally, pronouncing sentence when guilt has been established.

It should be recognized, however, that while this is the popular image of criminal court proceedings in the United States, only a very small proportion of all cases filed with the court result in a jury trial. As will be discussed later, a vast majority of criminal court cases are resolved by guilty pleas, often through plea bargaining between the prosecutor and defense attorney. Then, too, a sizable number of criminal trials are bench trials in which the defendant waives his or her right to a trial by jury and requests that the judge decide the case (Brosi 1979).

Japanese judges, operating in a civil law tradition, try cases without juries. Although the Meiji Constitution provided for trial by jury as an option, the Japanese did not find this suitable, and the jury system was dropped (Reischauer 1988). As a result, the role taken by Japanese judges differs significantly from that of their counterparts in this country. Japanese judges assume an inquisitorial role. Their task is to review all of the evidence, to seek information about the accused, to direct the prosecutor in his work, and to share in the questioning of the accused. In the absence of a jury, it is the judge's responsibility to arrive at a decision about guilt or innocence and to determine an appropriate sentence for the guilty—a sentence tailored to the offender (Reischauer 1988). Moreover, Japanese judges are expected to encourage and allow ample time for conciliation (See 1982). In many ways, then, the role of the Japanese judge is that of a benevolent truthfinder. The adjudication process in modern Japan retains much of the inquisitorial flavor found in Japanese courts prior to the Showa era (1912–1989).

An adversarial process is based upon procedural rules which make the process objective, impartial, and fair. As previously described, the concept of justice in the United States is based strongly upon the notion of individual civil rights. These rights, advanced in the Constitution, have been applied extensively to the judicial process through the due process revolution of the 1960s in which the Supreme Court took an advocacy role in extending constitutional rights to state criminal procedures.

The Japanese Constitution, modeled after that of the United States, advances a similar range of civil rights, many directly affecting criminal procedure (Takayanagi 1963). In fact, the Code of Criminal Procedure of 1890 had to be revised to take into account the fundamental civil rights provisions of the new Constitution (Clifford 1976). However, even though Japan's new Constitution created an independent judiciary and charged the Supreme Court with insuring civil rights in court proceedings through judicial review, the supreme court has been "remarkably reluctant" to guarantee these rights in judicial proceedings (Allen 1984; Nakayama 1981; Nomura 1981; Bolz 1980). Part of the court's reluctance stems from an ongoing debate over whether civil rights or public welfare and order should be emphasized. Although both sides of the issue find support in the Constitution, the Supreme Court has consistently held that civil rights should *not* be advanced at the expense of public welfare (Nakayama 1981; Ito 1963).[1] Bolz (1980, 94) comments that such judicial reluctance to guarantee civil rights is not "remarkable" when one considers that Japan's cultural heritage of social conformity and group loyalty stands in stark contrast to the individual rights so strongly reflected in the Constitution of 1947.

The Decision to Prosecute

Both Japan and the United States give prosecutors a broad range of discretion, and in both countries prosecutors exercise such discretion with vigor. An important dimension of prosecutorial discretion is the decision whether or not to prosecute. This decision is commonly exercised in two ways. First, a case is screened to see if charges should be filed with the court. Second, prosecution may be suspended after a case has been filed with the court *(nolle prosequi)*. The Japanese refer to the former as nonprosecution and the latter as suspension of prosecution. The prosecutor's decision on whether or not to pursue prosecution involves a number of considerations, including the seriousness of the offense, the sufficiency of evidence and testimony, due process issues, and factors related to system efficiency—primarily case processing time (Jacoby 1979, 1980).

   Japan and the United States do not appear to differ greatly in the number of cases dropped by the prosecutor (Feeney 1985). However, the reasons for dropping a case and the procedures for doing so are quite distinct in each country. Somewhere between one-third and one-half of all U.S. felony arrests are rejected at screening or dismissed after the case has been filed with the court (Boland et al. 1988, 5). While there is jurisdictional variation in when cases are dropped, a slightly greater proportion of cases are rejected during the screening process than after cases have been filed (Boland et al. 1988). Evidence and witness problems account for well over half of the rejections at screening (Boland and Sones 1986).

   Like their counterparts in the United States, Japanese prosecutors dismiss about one-third of all cases; however, substantially more are dropped through suspension of prosecution than through nonprosecution (Araki 1985, 617; Dando 1970). Moreover, the decision to suspend prosecution is markedly more discretionary in

---

[1]Article 12 of the Japanese constitution provides: "The freedoms and rights guaranteed to the people by this Constitution shall be maintained by the constant endeavors of the people, who shall refrain from any abuse of these freedoms and rights and shall always be responsible for utilizing them for the public welfare."

   Article 13 provides: "All people shall be respected as individuals. Their right to life, liberty, and pursuit of happiness shall, to the extent that it does not interfere with the public welfare, be the supreme consideration in legislation and in other governmental affairs."

Japan than it is in the United States. Reflecting the Japanese subjective approach to law, this decision involves considerations of the "appropriateness" and "desirability" of prosecution, even when sufficient evidence exists in the case (Satsumae 1978). Such deliberation is meant to promote individualized justice and provide an incentive for rehabilitation: "When properly utilized, the warning accompanying suspension will appeal to the heart of offenders" (Satsumae 1978, 103; see also Goodman 1986). Nagashima (1963) and Dando (1970), in commenting on the subjective character of Japanese justice, note that if the accused acknowledges guilt, asks for pardon, and appears willing to make some restitution to the victim, the prosecutor may suspend court action. "In short, the practice is very adaptable to reflect the individual circumstances of the cases" (Satsumae 1978, 103).

Central to the subjective nature of Japanese justice is the weighty consideration of expressions of remorse and apology by the offender. As Haley (1982, 269) describes it:

> Confession, repentance, and absolution provide the underlying theme of the Japanese criminal process. At every stage from initial police investigation through formal proceedings, an individual suspected of criminal conduct gains by confessing, apologizing, and throwing himself upon the mercies of the authorities.

Wagatsuma and Rosett (1986) offer a fascinating discussion of the legal aspects of apology in Japanese justice, including its role in the decision to prosecute.

The subjective nature of the decision to suspend prosecution has a long history in Japan, dating back to the mid-1880s, and it has been explicitly provided for by law since the 1922 Code of Criminal Procedure (Goodman 1986; Dando 1970, 1976). Article 248 of the 1948 Code of Criminal Procedure maintains this emphasis: "Prosecution need not be instituted if it appears unnecessary because of the character, age, and environment of the offender, the circumstances and gravity of the offense, or the circumstances following the offenses" (quoted in Dando 1970, 521).

Thus, unlike their counterparts in the United States, Japanese prosecutors often drop cases for reasons other than insufficient and faulty evidence. Factors subsequent to the offense, such as an offender's expression of remorse, apology, and repentance, settlement with the victim, and the possibility that leniency will promote an offender's rehabilitation, are more likely to lead the prosecutor to suspend court action than evidence problems (Araki 1985; Dando 1970). Even though there has been a gradual decrease in the use of suspended prosecution since World War II, its use is easily comparable to that of the United States and the benevolent and rehabilitative intent remains exceedingly strong (Dando 1970).

The Aversion to Trial

An interesting study of contrasts is the common aversion to trial that exists in both Japan and the United States. In both countries constitutional and statutory provisions allow for an adversarial process that culminates in a criminal trial; however, the day-to-day practice of criminal adjudication is far from adversarial. In both Japan and the United States, a vast majority of cases prosecuted never proceed to a criminal trial (Araki 1985; Boland et al. 1988). However, beyond this surface similarity, the mechanisms used to avert criminal trials are quite different in each country.

In the United States, about 90 percent of all felony convictions are a result of guilty pleas, not criminal trials (Boland et al. 1988; Boland and Forst 1984). These guilty pleas frequently result from plea bargaining, an informal process of plea negotiation between the prosecutor and defense attorneys. Such plea negotiation entails concessions by the prosecutor in the form of a reduced charge(s) or a more lenient sentence recommendation in return for the defendant's guilty plea. It is commonly held that about 90 percent of all guilty pleas are a result of plea bargaining; but as Boland and Forst (1984) are careful to point out, some guilty pleas are voluntarily entered by the defendant, without any plea bargaining (see also Reid 1987).[2]

The necessity of plea bargaining is most commonly attributed to the overload of cases confronting the courts. As such, plea bargaining represents a pragmatic solution to court overcrowding and, at the same time, lowers the cost of prosecution. In turn, defendants avoid extended trials and receive concessions in return for guilty pleas. Walker (1989), however, argues that there really is not much negotiation in plea bargaining; the process is characterized more by cooperation than conflict, and it is highly routinized. In other words, the heavy use of plea bargaining in the United States makes the adjudication process more administrative than adversarial.

Although plea bargaining is illegal in Japan (Reischauer 1988), two other shortcuts to criminal trials have been instituted in order to deal efficiently with uncontested cases: summary procedures and modified public trials. These procedures are used extensively in Japan because only a handful of cases are seriously contested—about 10 percent (Araki 1985).

We have already described the importance of summary courts in the Japanese court system. Like the lower courts in the United States, Japan's summary courts are limited to less serious offenses, but these courts frequently utilize a summary procedure that allows cases to never reach a formal hearing. Upon the prosecutor's request, minor offenses in which the fine upon conviction is not more than 200,000 yen (about $1,000 dollars) may be determined *in camera* by the judge, without the defendant, prosecutor, or complainant ever appearing in court. The prosecutor sends the judge the evidence in the case, a recommendation for penalty, and a suspect's signed consent form. Virtually all traffic offenses are handled in this way, as are some traditional crimes, such as public indecency, gambling and lottery violations, simple assaults, and possession of a dangerous weapon (Araki 1985).

A second procedure, a modified public trial, is utilized in summary and district courts for less serious offenses which are not disputed. About 12 percent of all district court trials (including a sizable number of larceny cases) and 63 percent of all summary court trials are heard in this manner (Araki 1985). When all parties agree to this procedure, evidence is submitted to the court without contest. Further-

---

[2]The exact proportion of guilty pleas which result from plea bargaining is obscure. Senna and Siegel (1990, 402) note that "[i]t has been estimated that more than 90 percent of criminal convictions result from negotiated pleas of guilty." Inciardi (1990, 375) argues that "this figure has been accepted as an article of faith with little empirical evidence to support it."

more, the prosecutor may present summaries of the evidence, and the judge is able to pass judgment without providing written reasons for his decision. Thus, the modified public trial simplifies such trial procedures as the in-court examination of evidence, and it eliminates the written justifications a judge must provide for sentences.

Araki (1985, 622) points out that Japanese judges must assume a significantly different role in the few cases which go to full trial than they would in cases handled through summary procedure or a modified public trial:

> In contrast with these short-cut procedures for fact-finding in cases without dispute, the judge of a case with dispute is expected to umpire a much more adversarial procedure rather than endorse the prosecutor's evidence. But when 90% of a judge's work involves endorsing the prosecutor's evidence, there is danger that the judge cannot shift to a more impartial mode in the 10% of the cases in which the facts are disputed.[3]

Thus, a vast majority of all criminal cases in Japan and the United States never reach a full public trial; however, the procedures used to avert trial are quite different in each country. The emphasis on individual rights and pragmatism in the United States has led to a process of informal, negotiated justice that is heavily based upon prosecutorial discretion and plea bargaining. The major consideration in such discretion and plea bargaining is the strength of the case, primarily in terms of evidence. The objective approach to law in the U.S. is sacrificed in order to promote individual freedom and system efficiency. The defendant seeks the best deal (in terms of freedom), and the prosecutor pursues high conviction rates while not adding to an already overburdened court docket.

The limited use of trials in Japan is based initially on the large number of uncontested cases. In turn, prosecutorial discretion and the reliance on summary procedure and modified public trial occur within a historical tradition in which judicial officials have dealt with most cases informally. For much of Japan's history, prosecutors and judges, relying on the defendant's admission of guilt, have operated as moral authorities where justice was to be dispensed in an individualized and benevolent manner.

The Purpose of Sentencing

Four distinct purposes of the criminal sanction are commonly advanced and form the rationale behind sentencing: retribution, deterrence, incapacitation, and rehabilitation. *Retribution* is the oldest justification for punishment. It centers on the notion that offenders deserve punishment because they violated the rights of others and upset the collective order: "Someone who infringes the rights of others . . . does wrong and deserves blame for his conduct" (von Hirsch 1976, 49). Punishment expresses social disapproval of criminal behavior, reestablishes moral balance by "righting the wrong," and reinforces the legitimacy of laws. Retribution focuses on the crime itself and the blameworthiness of the offender and has little concern with

---

[3]Both Japan and the United States have a small number of cases which ultimately go to trial, but they have significantly different acquittal rates. In Japan, only 3.1 percent of all trials end in acquittal (Araki 1985, 624). In the United States, 25 percent of all trials end in acquittal (Boland et al. 1988, 2).

the future acts of the offender or with utilitarian purposes such as deterrence or reform (Cole 1989; Meier 1989). Furthermore, retribution is grounded in the principle of equity: Punishment should be proportionate to the harm done, as expressed in the Old Testament standard of "an eye for an eye, a tooth for a tooth." Retribution is central to the contemporary concept of "just deserts" (von Hirsch 1976).

The idea that punishment may serve to deter crime was first advanced systematically by classical utilitarian philosophers beginning in the 18th century. The principle of *deterrence* asserts that crime can be prevented when people fear punishment for wrongs they might commit. Thus, criminal sanctions not only provide a formal response to criminal behavior but also serve as an example to the general public and the offender of the consequences for unlawful behavior, thereby discouraging future criminality.

Incapacitation seeks to render the offender incapable of committing further law violations. In contemporary societies this most commonly takes the form of incarceration, but other means have also been used to accomplish this goal, such as capital punishment, banishment, medical treatment (including castration, lobotomies, hormonal therapy), and intensive supervision in the community. Incapacitation focuses less on the crime the offender has done than on the fear of what the offender might do in the future (Siegel 1989).

When the emphasis is on *rehabilitation,* the aim of sentencing is to change the offender in such a way that the likelihood of future criminality is reduced. Grounded in the positive school of thought, the rehabilitation perspective asserts that criminal behavior, which results from negative social, psychological, or biological influences in a person's life, can be changed or eliminated. The rehabilitative ideal has traditionally been associated with the medical model, an approach to correctional intervention based upon the conviction that the causes of crime can be "identified, isolated, treated and cured" (Bartollas 1985, 26). Rehabilitation was the dominant purpose in sentencing and correctional practices in the United States from the early 1900s until the late 1970s. In fact, by the 1950s, the goal of rehabilitation became so widely adopted that Francis Allen (1959, 226) offered the following assessment: "It is almost assumed that matters of treatment and reform of the offender are the only questions worthy of serious attention in the whole field of criminal justice and corrections."

The goals and justifications of criminal sanctions can be discussed as if they were distinct, but the practice of sentencing reflects overlapping and often incompatible objectives (Cole 1989, 473). Additionally, the dominant justification for the criminal sanction varies over time and between cultures. Sentencing in the United States offers a classic example of the ebb and flow of justifications for criminal sanctions, and comparisons between the United States and Japan reveal the distinctive mix of rationales upon which the practice of sentencing is based.

In a constitutional democracy such as Japan or the United States, there is an inherent contradiction when a criminal sanction is imposed which suppresses or restricts civil liberties. However, this contradiction is exacerbated in the United States because of the changing purposes of sentencing. The value of utilitarianism has fueled a parade of justifications for the criminal sanction (Cole 1989; Meier

1989; Bartollas 1985). For much of this century, rehabilitation dominated sentencing practices in an effort to generate change in the offender and subsequently prevent crime. More recently, convinced that rehabilitation doesn't work, legislators, the public, and many criminal justice professionals have moved toward an emphasis on deterrence and incapacitation as means to protect society. Just as important today, however, is the goal of retribution. This justification calls for sanctions not because they facilitate change in the offender or prevent crime but because the offender deserves punishment. Thus, the full range of justifications is called forth in contemporary sentencing practices in the United States. As a result, there is no clear consensus on just what sentencing is supposed to accomplish (Cole 1989; President's Commission 1967).

The Sentencing Reform Act of 1984, a federal criminal code revision passed after years of debate, reflects this decisive shift away from rehabilitation in sentencing philosophy (Reid 1989). The act conspicuously maintains rehabilitation, but places it at the bottom of the list of sentencing purposes, which include:

- The need to reflect the seriousness of the offense, to promote respect for law, and to provide just punishment
- The need to afford adequate deterrence to criminal conduct
- The need to protect the public from further crimes of the defendant
- The need to provide the defendant with educational or vocational training, medical care, or correctional treatment in the most effective manner (U.S. Code, chapter 18, § 3553 [a][2][Supplement II 1984])

It should be noted also that, until recent changes in many state penal codes, most states did not specify the purpose of sentencing (Reid 1989, 459).

Coinciding with this philosophical shift in sentencing purposes is a dramatic change in the statutory provisions for sentencing in many jurisdictions of the United States (Reid 1989; Zawitz 1988). The predominant emphasis on rehabilitation which existed in the United States for much of the current century necessitated statutory provisions for shortening sentence length if the offender was rehabilitated. *Indeterminate sentencing* evolved as the dominant statutory provision because it provided judges and correctional officials wide latitude in determining sentence and sentence length. In the last twenty years, however, a number of states and the federal government have moved toward a new form of sentencing: *determinate sentencing* (Zawitz 1988). While a variety of mechanisms are used under the guise of determinate sentencing (Reid 1989), the general aim is to reduce sentencing disparity and judicial and parole discretion and thereby provide greater uniformity and predictability in the sentences imposed for specific offenses. This movement toward determinate sentencing is closely connected with the growing emphasis on the retributive and deterrent value of punishment.

Japan has much greater clarity of purpose in imposing a sentence as compared to the United States. Article 48 of the Japanese Draft Penal Code of 1974 establishes the dual purpose of retribution and rehabilitation (quoted in Suzuki 1979a, 186):

- Punishment shall be assessed commensurate with the culpability of the offender.
- Punishment shall be imposed for the purpose of repressing offenses and reforming and rehabilitating offenders, in light of the age, character and environment of the

offender, the motive, method, result and impact on society of the offense, and the attitude of the offender after the offense.

While this statement expresses a variety of justifications for punishment, the practice of sentencing in Japan emphasizes and closely links retribution and rehabilitation. Two basic principles appear to govern the imposition of punishment in Japan and reveal the blending of retributive and rehabilitative purposes. First, the tenet that punishment should be commensurate with the culpability of the offender establishes the ideal of proportionate and individualized justice. Sentencing in Japan considers a full range of offense and offender characteristics in order to determine culpability and, subsequently, punishment (Tanizawa 1979). Punishment is intended not simply to fit the crime, but to "be imposed only on those who acted with a guilty mind and only to the extent warranted by the degree of culpability" (Suzuki 1977, 89). Bendansan (1972, 293) further describes how the Japanese principle of culpability is individualized:

> When making judgments, courts must turn their attention to such questions as: Was the accused under unusual stress at the time of the crime? Had he suffered an especially embittering childhood? Is he now repentant? . . . If a court evaluates such factors, it is thought to have acted wisely or humanely. If it does not, no matter that its verdict follows the written law to the last letter, the Japanese consider it unfair.

Japanese courts extend the notion of culpability to circumstances after the offense (Dando 1976). There is a longstanding tradition, following the criteria for suspending prosecution (Article 248 of the 1948 Code of Criminal Procedure), which allows judges to consider factors subsequent to the offense, especially apology and repentance, in the sentence decision:

> A criminal who shows sincere repentance in court for his wrongful act in committing a crime has a much greater chance of receiving a less severe penalty and/or of obtaining a "suspension of execution of sentence" (*shikko yuyo*) (Tanaka 1976c, 316; see also Wagatsuma and Rosett 1986).

As Reischauer (1988, 146) notes: "In legal sentencing, the post-crime attitude of the culprit, that is, his degree of penitence, is considered as important as his pre-crime motives and, if felt sincere, will lead to judicial leniency."

A second principle governing the penal sanction in Japan is that sentencing is intended to prevent crime by rehabilitating offenders. The Japanese penal code specifically prescribes that, in the sentencing process, the offender's character be considered both in assessing culpability and in promoting individualized treatment. Suzuki (1979a) points out that while rehabilitation has fallen into disfavor in the United States, the purpose remains vital in Japan. In fact, the Japanese have made efforts to further strengthen rehabilitation as a goal of the criminal sanction.

Grounded in this rehabilitative ideal, Japanese judges have maintained a wide range of decision-making authority with regard to sentencing. The statutory provisions of Japanese criminal law provide for indeterminate sentencing where alternative sentences are identified in the criminal code, as well as minimum and maximum amounts of punishment for each offense. However, the penal code does not specify any clear standards for sentencing (Tanizawa 1979). Moreover, efforts to promote sentencing consistency have been kept within the control of judges and are based upon both the systematic training of apprentice judges and the in-service training of full-ranked judges. Such training focuses on educating judges to what the former chief of the training division called the "market price in sentencing"—the collective standard for sentencing in the judicial ranks, made evident by sentencing studies (Tanizawa 1979, 197). This includes information on the relative frequency of different types of sentences imposed for specific offenses and on offense and offender characteristics, which are frequently taken into consideration in sentencing different types of offenses (Tanizawa 1979; Suzuki 1979a).

Sentencing Practices

Comparison of data on sentencing practices in Japan and the United States is exceedingly difficult. It is not unlike the problem of comparing cross-cultural crime data. Japan's sentencing data are most commonly reported in a summary fashion, being based upon the total number of Penal Code violations. The numbers of Penal Code violations which result in sentences of death, life imprisonment, fixed-term imprisonment, and fines are commonly reported (Ministry of Justice 1989; Araki 1985; Holmberg–Okuba 1985). Based upon these summary data, it is frequently observed that Japanese judges are exceedingly lenient because about 95 percent of all Penal Code violations result in fines and only about 1 percent result in imprisonment (Ministry of Justice 1986; Japan Institute 1983–1984). However, what is not often pointed out is that a vast majority of these cases involve less serious offenses, predominantly traffic violations, which fall under the limited jurisdiction of the summary court, where fines are the most common sentencing alternative.[4] However, the inclusion of such a broad range of offenses and the predominance of less serious offenses obscure sentencing practices for more serious types of offenses. As a point of comparison, fines are also an exceedingly common disposition in the lower courts of the United States which deal with minor offenses (Hillsman et al. 1987; Hillsman, Sichel, and Mohoney 1984). In particular, fines are the dominant sanction for traffic offenses, which constitute the bulk of these minor offenses.

Japan's Supreme Court fortunately provides data on the sentencing of nontraffic, criminal offenses (Ministry of Justice 1989). Table 6.1 reports the relative frequency of different sentences imposed for convicted criminal offenses in 1987, which appears to be typical for this decade. The most widely imposed sentence by Japanese judges was a suspended sentence of imprisonment. Over half of all offenders convicted of criminal offenses (56 percent) received suspended sentences. In the United States, the imposition of suspended sentences is closely tied to probation, whereas in Japan this is not the case. Japanese judges rarely stipulate probation or supervision as a part of a suspended sentence. Parker (1986, 35) estimates that in recent years probation has been required of about 17 or 18 percent of the Japanese defendants granted a suspended sentence of imprisonment. In 1987 only 14 percent (4,718 out of 34,383) of those receiving suspended sentences were

---

[4]Araki (1985, 625) offers summary sentencing data in figure form which clearly depict the predominance of minor offenses relative to all penal offenses.

placed on probation. Imprisonment is also a fairly common outcome for criminal offenses, with 43 percent of all criminal convictions in 1987 resulting in imprisonment.[5] Despite the customary use of fines in minor offenses heard by the summary courts, fines were levied in less than 1 percent of all Japanese criminal cases. Finally, life imprisonment and the death penalty are rarely imposed. Despite the harshness of criminal sanctions in the pre-Meiji era, for the past century the Japanese have had a tradition of little or no use of capital punishment (Reischauer 1988). In 1987, only 6 convicted offenders were sentenced to death, and less than 1 percent of those given a sentence of imprisonment without suspension were given life sentences (65 out of 26,686) (Ministry of Justice 1989).

The image which emerges from sentencing data in the United States is vastly different. A surge of data has surfaced recently on the sentencing of felony offenders (Boland et al. 1989; Langan 1989; Boland et al. 1988; Cunniff 1985, 1987; Boland and Sones 1986; Boland and Forst 1984; see also Jamieson and Flanagan 1989). In contrast to Japanese sentencing data, U.S. data tend to focus on the serious felony offenses and rarely account for the sentencing of misdemeanor offenses. Table 6.2 indicates the relative frequency of different types of sentences in both U.S. district courts and in a nationally representative sample of state felony courts. The U.S. district court data cover a broad range of criminal offenses but include only violations of federal criminal law (Jamieson and Flanagan 1989). State courts handle the bulk of all criminal cases because a majority of all criminal offenses are violations of state law—about 95 percent of all felony convictions are in state courts (Langan 1989, 2). The felony sentencing data from state courts reported here focus on the felony offenses of homicide, rape, robbery, aggravated assault, burglary, larceny, and drug trafficking (Langan 1989).

TABLE 6.1 Sentences Imposed for Convicted Criminal Offenses* by Japanese Courts, 1987

	Number	Percent
Death	6	0%
Imprisonment	26,686	43%
Suspended Sentence of Imprisonment	34,383	56%
Fine	586	<1%
Other	157	0%

*Includes a variety of penal code and special law violations, including traditional street crimes, white-collar crimes, drug, and vice crimes

SOURCE: *Summary of The White Paper on Crime—1989*. Research and Training Institute, Ministry of Justice—Japan (1989), table 7, p.14.

[5]Japanese sentencing data typically report two general categories of incarceration: incarceration with forced labor and incarceration without forced labor. Suspended sentences of imprisonment are included in the total number of incarceration sentences but are also broken out as a subcategory together with a number of other types of prison sentences, such as life term, fixed term. Additionally, some reports of sentencing data use the term "probation" instead of suspended sentences of imprisonment (Ministry of Justice 1986; Statistics Bureau 1986; Japan Institute 1983–1984), but not all suspension of imprisonment involves probation as the term is used in other countries to include conditions (rules) of probation and supervision.

TABLE 6.2 Sentences Imposed for Convicted Offenses in U.S. District Courts and State Felony Courts

	U.S. District Courts, 1987[a]	State Felony Courts, 1986[b]
Incarceration	53%	67%
Probation	36%	31%
Fine Only	10%	N/A
Other	<1%	2%
Total Number of Cases	43,942	51,594*

*The 51,594 case records were drawn from a national representative sample which included 100 counties. The nationwide number of felony convictions is estimated to be 582,764 (Langan 1989, 2).

SOURCES: [a]Katharine M. Jamieson and Timothy J. Flanagan, *Sourcebook of Criminal Justice Statistics—1988*. Washington D.C.: U.S. Department of Justice, Bureau of Justice Statistics (1989), table 5.29, pp. 558–559.
[b]Patrick A. Langan, "Felony Sentences in State Courts, 1986." Washington, D.C.: U.S. Department of Justice, Bureau of Justice Statistics (1989), table 2, p. 2.

These data reveal that U.S. judges incarcerate anywhere from 53 to 67 percent of all convicted criminal offenders. The data from state felony courts indicate that over two-thirds of all felony convictions result in incarceration. An earlier study of state felony court sentencing distinguished different forms of incarceration: prison, jail alone, or jail and probation (Cunniff 1985, 1987). Prison sentences were found to be by far the most common form of incarceration, constituting about two-thirds of all incarceration sentences (Cunniff 1987, 5).

The slightly greater use of probation by U.S. district courts as compared to state courts is possibly a reflection of a wider variety of offenses included in the data. Nevertheless, probation is involved in about one-third of all dispositions. It should be kept in mind that these data deal only with serious offenses; when all types of offenses are considered, probation is one of the most common sentences. Similarly, while fines alone are a relatively infrequent sanction for felony offenses, the use of fines in conjunction with other forms of sentencing is not distinguished in the reported data but is likely a common practice. Furthermore, as mentioned earlier, fines may be the most commonly imposed sentence when all types of offenses are considered (Hillsman, Sichel, and Mohoney 1984; Hillsman et al. 1987).

When we compare these data on sentencing in Japan and the United States, one major question that quickly emerges is the comparability of the data. Are similar types of offenses included? While sentencing data from Japan incorporate a fairly broad range of offenses,[6] the range of offenses reported by U.S. district courts is

[6]Offenses included in the Japanese data include a variety of offenses classified as "Penal Code Offenses" or as "Special Law Offenses." Penal Code offenses include: homicide, robbery, bodily injury, extortion, larceny, fraud, rape, arson, gambling, violent acts, professional negligence, and an unspecified "other." Special Law offenses include: election law offenses, firearm and sword offenses, stimulant drug laws, horse race law, road traffic violation (more serious than the common traffic ticket), and an unspecified "other" category (Ministry of Justice 1988).

quite similar.[7] The types of offenses accounted for in the dispositional data from U.S. state courts are somewhat less broad but still provide a reasonably comparable range of offenses.[8] It must be noted, however, that sentence imposition will certainly vary with the type of offenses considered. Comparison of these data is quite tentative.

Variation in legal terminology raises another issue of comparability. For example, Japanese sentencing data point to the frequent use of suspended sentences, and, as we have said, the term "probation" is sometimes used synonymously with suspended sentence. However, the imposition of suspended sentences does not always include conditions of probation and supervision, as is common in the U.S. (Parker 1986). Subsequently, probation in Japan is different from probation in the United States. Still another problem relating to the comparability of sentencing data arises from differences in court jurisdiction from which the data are drawn. Even though the sentencing data from U.S. district courts encompass an array of offenses quite similar to the Japanese data, the U.S. district court data do not include violations of state criminal law, and the federal offenses differ in nature from the more general Japanese offenses even though the legal terminology may be the same. For example, the larceny–theft offenses which fall under the U.S. federal criminal code are of a specific type, centering on bank, postal, interstate, and transportation of stolen property violations. Further, in the United States, the more common forms of "street theft" fall under state criminal codes. Japan, however, has but one penal code that covers a full range of larceny–theft and other offenses. With these qualifications in mind, a few limited observations can be made. Table 6.3 combines the data from tables 6.1 and 6.2 to aid comparison.

These data suggest that Japanese judges are indeed more lenient in sentencing than are U.S. judges. Probably the clearest depiction of leniency is the liberal use of suspended sentences of imprisonment. Article 25 of the Japanese penal code allows for the suspension of imprisonment sentences under certain circumstances, often when the offender has no prior convictions or incarcerations or, as described earlier, the offender expresses "sincere" remorse (see Tanizawa [1979] for some interesting case illustrations). In 1987, 56 percent of all the sentences imposed for criminal offenses were suspended sentences of imprisonment. If we assume that sentences of probation in the United States involve such a suspended sentence, the comparative figures are 36 percent in U.S. district courts and 31 percent in state felony courts. Moreover, the rates of suspended sentences have shown a gradual increase in Japan from 45 percent of all criminal convictions in 1960 to 56 percent in 1975. Since then the rates of suspended sentences have been fairly constant (Statistics Bureau 1986, 723). In contrast, U.S. district courts have shown a declining tendency to use probation, which typically involves a suspended sentence. In 1975, 48 percent of all

[7]Offenses included in data from the district courts include: homicide, robbery, assault, burglary, larceny-theft, embezzlement, fraud, auto theft, forgery and counterfeiting, sex offenses, Drug Prevention and Control Act violations, and a variety of specified miscellaneous serious offenses (Jamieson and Flanagan 1989).

[8]Offenses included in the state court data include: murder, rape, robbery, aggravated assault, burglary, larceny, drug trafficking, and an unspecified "other" category (Langan 1989).

TABLE 6.3 Sentences Imposed for Convicted Offenses by U.S. District Courts, U.S. State
Felony Courts, and Japanese Courts

	U.S. District Courts, 1987	U.S. State Felony Courts, 1986	Japanese Courts, 1987
Incarceration	53%	67%[a]	43%
Probation or Suspended Sentence[b]	36%	31%	56%
Fine Only	10%	N/A	<1%
Other	<1%	2%	0%
Total Number	43,942	51,594[c]	61,818

[a]This figure includes sentences of imprisonment and sentences which encompass jail together with probation (a form of "split sentencing").
[b]In the United States, probation almost always includes a suspended sentence. The Japanese figure refers to suspended sentences which may or may not include probation.
[c]The 51,594 case records were drawn from a national representative sample which included 100 counties. The nationwide number of felony convictions is estimated to be 582,764 (Langan 1989, 2).

SOURCES: as identified in tables 6.1 and 6.2.

criminal convictions resulted in probation, whereas in 1985 this had reduced to 36 percent (Jamieson and Flanagan 1989, 554–555).

The use of suspended sentences by Japanese judges is extensive even for serious, violent offenses. A study by Tanizawa (1979) pointed clearly to the frequent use of suspended sentences for serious offenses. He found that in 1976, 30 percent of all homicide convictions, 45 percent of all rape convictions, 56 percent of all bodily injury convictions, and 29 percent of all robbery convictions resulted in a suspended sentence of imprisonment. Data from U.S. state felony courts—the courts that sentence a vast majority of all predatory street crime—were not available until 1985 (Cunniff 1985). Table 6.4 provides comparative figures for the use of suspended sentences for specific types of violent offenses (Langan 1989, 2). The difference in use of suspended sentences is most striking for the serious violent offenses of homicide and rape. In these cases, Japanese judges traditionally consid-

TABLE 6.4 Percent of Convicted Offenders Receiving Suspended Sentences by Type of
Violent Offense

	U.S. State Felony Courts, 1986	Japanese Courts, 1987
Homicide	4%	19%
Rape	10%	35%
Robbery	12%	13%
Assault*	26%	52%

*Classified by the Japanese Penal Code as "bodily injury."

SOURCES: as identified in tables 6.1 and 6.2.

er circumstances which are held to mitigate criminal responsibility: an act of passion, psychological disorders, and remorse and expressions of apology after the offense (Tanizawa 1979).

The Japanese also make limited use of imprisonment, compared to the United States (Araki 1985). Even though 43 percent of all criminal convictions in Japan result in incarceration (table 6.1), the rate is much lower than in the United States. Because incarceration is utilized in both countries more extensively for serious offenses and because a majority of the serious offenses in the United States are violations of state criminal codes and fall under the jurisdiction of state felony courts, the most comparable figure from the United States is the state felony court rate of 67 percent. This difference in the use of incarceration is more vivid when comparing its use for violent crime. Table 6.5 reports the percent of offenders convicted of specific types of violent crime who were sentenced without suspension to a period of incarceration. In each of the violent offenses, except robbery, incarceration was imposed less frequently by Japanese judges than by U.S. state felony court judges.

Furthermore, while longitudinal sentencing data are not available for state felony courts, several indicators suggest that in recent years the use of incarceration as a sentencing option is increasing dramatically in the United States and remaining relatively constant in Japan.

The number of persons serving prison sentences in Japan increased sharply after World War II, reaching a postwar high in the early 1950s. In the 1960s and 1970s the average daily number of inmates decreased and reached a low of 45,690 in 1975. In the early 1980s the number of persons serving sentences of incarceration increased slightly, mirroring a small increase in crime, but since 1984 the number of inmates has remained fairly stable. In 1987 there was a daily average of 55,210 inmates in Japan's prisons (Ministry of Justice 1988, 108; see also Statistics Bureau 1986, 727; Ministry of Justice 1986, 7; Japan Institute 1984–1985, 195).

The number of state and federal prisoners in the United States also increased following World War II but not as dramatically as in Japan. Then, beginning in the 1960s and into the early 1970s, the number of inmates in state and federal prisons declined. Since 1973 there has been a striking and steady increase in prison

TABLE 6.5 Percent of Convicted Offenders Receiving Sentences of Incarceration by Type of Violent Offense

	U.S. State Felony Courts, 1986	Japanese Courts, 1987
Homicide	95%	80%
Rape	88%	64%
Robbery	87%	88%
Assault*	71%	47%

*Classified by the Japanese penal code as "bodily injury."

SOURCES: as identified in tables 6.1 and 6.2.

population, reaching a high of 627,402 prisoners in 1988, an increase of over 90 percent since 1980 alone (Greenfeld 1989; Minor-Harper 1986). The tremendous increase in the number of prisoners in the last fifteen years is consistent with the trend in incarceration rate—the number of prisoners for each 100,000 residents. From the early 1960s until the early 1970s, the imprisonment rate declined to less than 100 per 100,000 population, but since then the rate has increased dramatically, reaching a rate of 244 per 100,000 population in 1988 (Greenfeld 1989; Minor-Harper 1986).

Much has been made of the "get tough" policies that now dominate criminal justice practices in the United States. The public strongly believes that the courts are too lenient (Jamieson and Flanagan 1987, 86–87), and legislators have moved toward reducing judicial discretion and disparity through a variety of determinate sentencing statutes (Reid 1989; Zawitz 1988). Sentencing practices appear to reflect such policy changes, most clearly through the increasing use of incarceration as a sentencing option.

In contrast, Japanese sentencing practices have tended toward greater leniency, especially through the increasing use of suspended sentences (Reischauer 1988, 258–259; Nakayama 1981, 139; Tanizawa 1979, 203). A judge of the Tokyo High Court explains that "judges think that mere severity in sentences does not meet the purpose of punishment" and that leniency serves as an incentive for rehabilitation by obligating the offender to the benevolence of the judge (Tanizawa 1979, 204). With the Japanese cultural emphasis on hierarchy and respect for authority, judges not only assume the position of superiors in the natural hierarchy, but they also take on the role of moral authorities who dispense benevolent justice to facilitate rehabilitation (See 1982). Furthermore, in Japan's traditional group orientation, social control is based upon shame—shame the convicted offender brings to his or her family, friends, or associates at work (Clifford 1976). In this context, the sentence is not the punishment, but the mere fact that an individual has been convicted of violating the law is punishment in and of itself. Nevertheless, a willingness to forgive has long been a part of Japanese custom (Terrill 1984; see also Clifford's [1976] notion of *tolerance*). This, combined with an understanding that offenders are less apt to succeed when cut off from group involvement, has led to a limited use of incarceration. Furthermore, an offender's sincere expression of remorse and/or a demonstration that he or she has been rehabilitated often allows an offender to be restored into the group.

SUMMARY

Criminal adjudication has acquired a significantly different form in Japan than in the United States. The cultural values that have developed in each society provide an underlying and recurrent theme reflected in the structures and processes of criminal adjudication.

A deep-seated suspicion of centralized power led the framers of the U.S. Constitution to decentralize governmental power. In terms of judicial authority, a dual court system was created in which the federal court system operates alongside state court systems. However, jurisdiction in criminal matters is delegated largely to state courts because most criminal law is state law. Subsequently, state courts handle a vast majority of all criminal adjudication.

People in the United States also hold jealously to the values of freedom and individuality. In fact, the federal court system was devised chiefly as a vehicle to promote and protect these values as expressed in the civil rights of the federal Constitution. Through a number of court decisions, the federal appellate courts gradually made these civil rights binding on state criminal court procedures. An extensive array of procedural requirements pertaining to criminal adjudication followed from these decisions and established an objective approach to law.

At the same time, valuing pragmatism has led to a nonadversarial approach to the adjudication process. In this context, guilty pleas have become the norm, many resulting from plea negotiations. Similarly, the contemporary movement toward determinate sentencing practices arose, in part, from a utilitarian belief that rehabilitation was an unobtainable goal in sentencing and, in part, from the view that the indeterminacy of rehabilitation violated fundamental civil rights.

In Japan, cultural values of group-relatedness, harmony, a natural hierarchy, and respect for authority led to less reliance on formal systems of justice than in the United States. These values are manifest in customary rules of interpersonal relations which the Japanese call *giri*. These informal rules extensively prescribe and control behavior. Additionally, conciliation, an informal mediation process for resolving disputes, is widely encouraged. In the last seventy-five years this process of conciliation has been structured into the Japanese justice system and has become more formal in nature.

As one might expect, the Japanese judicial system is much smaller than that in the United States and is centralized into a single, national system of courts. The adjudication process in Japan is characterized by a wide variety of informal processes ranging from suspended prosecution to suspended sentences in which benevolence and individualized justice are emphasized.

SANCTIONING OFFENDERS: CORRECTIONS

Japan and the United States, as we have seen, have very different crime rates and very different approaches to sentencing criminal offenders. As a result, corrections in Japan assumes very different proportions and requires very different strategies than corrections in the United States. However, it is not simply the volume or type of crime that creates this difference, but distinctive cultural contexts in each society have engendered different correctional approaches. Earlier we pointed out that American society depends heavily on formal means of social control but Japanese society depends more on informal means of control. As Ames (1981, 228) describes in his study of police and community in Japan: "Japanese society places emphasis on intertwining bonds of human relations to maintain the social fabric and to prevent crime and disorder." Given their cultural heritage, one would then expect the Japanese to be much less reliant upon a correctional system to generate conformity than people in the United States.

It is not that the Japanese and American correctional systems are all that different in basic structure. They are not. However, it should not be surprising that the demands each society makes of its correctional system have produced systems of different size, purpose, and procedures. Like the other parts of the criminal justice system, a country's corrections system is influenced in fundamental ways by the social, cultural, and political context in which it emerges and operates (Johnson and Hasegawa 1987).

In this chapter we will compare these two correctional systems, paying special attention to how differences in cultural values help explain the differences between the systems. We will begin with a historical sketch of the development of corrections in Japan and the United States, including the evolution of correctional thought and practice, and the structure of contemporary corrections in each society. Following this we will briefly compare correctional populations in Japan and the United States. Finally, three fundamental aspects of the practice of corrections will be addressed: rehabilitation, the rights of incarcerated offenders, and personnel practices in corrections.

THE HISTORY AND STRUCTURES OF CORRECTIONS IN JAPAN AND THE UNITED STATES

The Development of the Japanese Corrections System

Suzuki (1979b, 143) notes that "the history of Japan provides . . . many instances in which a sincere attempt to copy a foreign institution resulted in the development of a system not dissimilar in form but quite different in substance from the original." Japan's corrections system reflects clearly such a process of institutional appropriation and adaptation to Japanese culture. Thus, while the structure of Japanese corrections has been strongly influenced by Western nations, the nature and character of the correctional process are decidedly Japanese and must be viewed and understood within this social and cultural context.

History and Legal Foundations   *Corrections,* in the modern sense of the word, had its inception in Japan after the Meiji Restoration of 1868. The *Kangokusaku,* or Prison Rules, enacted in 1872 and the Penal Code of 1880 were the first wave of significant change in which Japan's corrections system was gradually Westernized (Corrections Bureau 1982). Prior to the Meiji period, there was no formal corrections system. As was common in many preindustrial societies, punishment in pre-Meiji Japan most frequently took the form of exile *(ento)* or corporal or capital punishment. Although prisons have a long history in Japan, dating back to the late 1500s, they were used predominantly for holding people for trial or pending execution of sentence. These prisons were known as the *roya* and were administered by the *shugoku,* an office passed along family lines that held no great status. Nevertheless, the *shugoku* was not required to pay homage to the shogun and could fill staff positions with family members and relatives (Clifford 1976).

It is interesting to note that the ranking and handling of prisoners that developed over time replicated the hierarchical system of Japanese society. Clifford (1976, 86) observes that:

> In the general penal administration of the day, samurai of high rank and priests were kept in the custody of the *daimyo* and not placed in the *roya.* Those of lower but still elevated rank were kept in a separate section of the *roya* and were given attendants from among the lower classes of prisoners. Commoners were kept in barracks more like a modern prison, but those with a registered address were separated from the homeless. Women were segregated from men, but they were not from each other according to status.

After the Meiji Restoration, Japanese corrections adopted a decidedly Western pattern, importing both penal codes and institutional forms. The Penal Code of 1880 relied heavily on the French Penal Code of 1810 and established a comprehensive system of penal sanctions, including capital punishment, six different kinds of imprisonment, and two kinds of fines (Suzuki 1979b, 141). The code also introduced conditional release from prison prior to the expiration of sentence, an antecedent of contemporary parole. In addition, it instituted two important alternatives to imprisonment: suspension of prosecution (discussed in chapter 6) and suspension of execution of sentence. The latter established the legal foundation for probation, even though the practice of probation was not instituted until the early 1950s (Rehabilitation Bureau 1981).

While the 1880 Penal Code provided for early release from prison, it was rarely used, probably due to the lack of support services. At this same time, however, philanthropists and religious organizations became concerned about the need for services for released prisoners who were dissociated from family and group relationships. As a result, private aftercare hostels were pioneered to provide shelter, employment, and guidance to discharged offenders. When an unusually large number of prisoners were granted amnesty and commutation by the imperial family in 1912 and 1914 (almost 37,000), the government urgently encouraged and supported the expansion of these private aftercare facilities. The development of Rehabilitation Aid Hostels, as they became known, represented the first involvement of private citizens and organizations in Japanese corrections and firmly established a vital role for volunteers.

The role of volunteers in correctional services was institutionalized by laws enacted in 1939 and 1950. These laws authorized the involvement of volunteers in probation (volunteer probation officers—VPOs) and in the prison aftercare programs of the Rehabilitation Aid Hostels. The newly found legitimacy of volunteers in corrections inspired the formal organization of a number of associations. These associations have had significant influence on correctional policy and practice because of the indispensable role volunteers have played in rehabilitative services (Parker 1986; Rehabilitation Bureau 1981; Suzuki 1979b).

Training programs for prison officers were instituted fairly early in Japan. In 1884 a training program was devised and implemented at a major prison, and in 1890 a national training institute was begun for prison personnel in Tokyo. Systematic training has been a key component of Japan's corrections system since that time (Corrections Bureau 1982).

The Penal Code of 1880 was replaced by a second penal code promulgated in 1908. This code is still in force today and, together with a number of amendments and supplemental statutes, provides the operating basis for contemporary corrections in Japan (Kaiser 1984; Nakayama 1981). Suzuki (1979b, 141) summarizes the changes in penal sanctions that arose from this penal code:

> The code of 1907 was drafted under the strong influence of the German penal code of 1871, and put into effect in 1908 along with the prison law enacted the same year to supersede older prison rules. Both the penal code and the prison law still keep their basic structures originated almost three quarters of a century ago. The code provides six kinds of punishment: death, imprisonment with forced labor, imprisonment without forced labor, fines, penal detention, and minor fines. Imprisonment without forced labor is a special sanction for crimes of negligence and offenses likely to be committed with political motives such as insurrection and riot. Penal detention and minor fines are lighter penalties for minor offenses.

A number of important reforms in Japan's corrections system occurred after the end of World War II when a new constitution was adopted. The Juvenile Law of 1948 created a separate juvenile justice system that included a corrections system solely for offenders under the age of twenty. Passage of the Offenders Rehabilitation Law of 1949 placed juveniles and adults conditionally released from prison under "protective supervision," thus creating Japan's parole system. Amendments to the Penal Code in 1953 and 1954 authorized the criminal courts to place under supervision those offenders granted suspension of execution of sentence. This created the adult probation system (Kaiser 1984; Nakayama 1981; Rehabilitation Bureau 1981; Suzuki 1979b).

Contemporary Correctional Structures in Japan   The organization of Japanese corrections is centralized under the control of the national government and is highly hierarchical. This structure reflects and reinforces the Japanese values of hierarchy and respect for authority and yields an extremely unified and coordinated corrections system (Suzuki 1979b, 143; Archambeault and Fenwick 1988; Johnson and Hasegawa 1987). Correctional programs are administered under two bureaus within the Ministry of Justice. The Corrections Bureau is responsible for all institutional corrections, including prisons, houses of detention, women's guidance homes, juvenile prisons and training schools, and juvenile classification homes. The Rehabilitation Bureau administers all noninstitutional rehabilitative services, including probation, parole, and other community-based programs. Figure 7.1 shows the explicit division of correctional administration between these two bureaus (Corrections Bureau 1982; Rehabilitation Bureau 1981; see also Terrill 1984; Nakayama 1981).

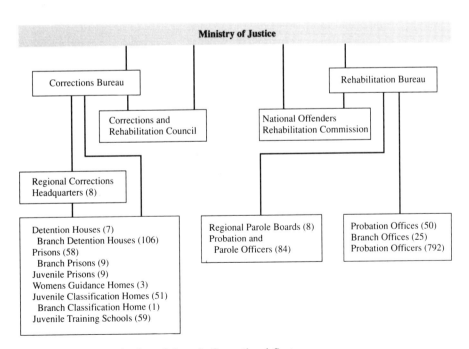

FIGURE 7.1 Organization of Japan's Correctional System

The Corrections Bureau, which operates all penal institutions in Japan, is advised by the Corrections and Rehabilitation Council, a consultative group made up of scholars and correctional officials which is responsible to the Ministry of Justice. To aid in management, the Corrections Bureau is administratively divided into eight regions, each with a Regional Corrections Headquarters. These administrative regions are highly structured, assigning particular correctional responsibility and authority to different divisions. All the Regional Corrections Headquarters operate a classification center used to orient new inmates to prison life and to assess appropriate placements based upon aptitude tests and social background information. Each region also has a Training Institute for Correctional Personnel, supervised by a central training institute in Tokyo. While initially established to train prison administrators, these institutes now provide extensive training for all correctional personnel in each region (Corrections Bureau 1982).

The Corrections Bureau operates a wide variety of prisons that are used for different purposes and different types of offenders. Adult correctional facilities include separate prisons for men and women, medical prisons offering treatment for prisoners with mental or physical disorders, and houses of detention. The latter are used primarily for unconvicted prisoners awaiting trial or investigation but also for detaining convicted offenders sentenced to "penal detention"—a short term of incarceration, usually less than thirty days (Corrections Bureau 1982, 16). Juvenile prisons were originally established as reformatories for offenders under age twenty; recently, however, they have been used to incarcerate young adult prisoners under twenty-six years of age. The three women's guidance homes are used predominantly for rehabilitating prostitutes (Corrections Bureau 1982; Terrill 1984).

Although early release from prison was institutionalized in the Penal Code of 1880, few provisions were made for its use. In fact, private rehabilitation hostels developed in the late 1800s as the first systematic attempt to provide aftercare services, but they served prisoners released at the expiration of their sentence (Rehabilitation Bureau 1981). The passage of the Offender Rehabilitation Law in 1949, however, instituted a number of provisions for the discretionary release of inmates on parole. This law, and subsequent statutory changes, had dramatic impact on Japanese corrections. Many of these changes, especially the institutionalization of probation and parole, were initiated in response to the tremendous overcrowding in Japanese prisons following World War II (Rehabilitation Bureau 1981).

The Rehabilitation Bureau was established in 1952 as a separate branch of the Ministry of Justice in order to integrate all parole, probation, and community-based correctional programs under the administrative supervision of one agency. The National Offenders Rehabilitation Commission, an independent committee attached to the Ministry of Justice, renders judgment on complaints regarding parole decisions of the eight regional parole boards. This administrative committee also makes recommendations to the cabinet via the Ministry of Justice regarding prison pardons, reductions and remissions of sentences, and restoration of an inmate's rights (Rehabilitation Bureau 1981).

Actual parole decisions, however, are made by the eight regional parole boards—sometimes called District Offender Prevention and Rehabilitation Commissions—each composed of a panel of three individuals who review applications for parole from the penal institutions. These boards also make decisions regarding revocation of parole, terminations of treatment, and extension of the parole period, based upon the recommendations of the local probation/parole officers. The regional parole boards are assisted by eighty-four probation/parole officers who have no supervisory responsibility (Rehabilitation Bureau 1981; Parker 1986).

Although administrative authority and control of probation and parole are maintained at the national level by the Rehabilitation Bureau, offender supervision and services have been decentralized through fifty local probation offices located throughout Japan—one in each prefecture and four on Hokkaido (Parker 1984). It is astounding that in all of Japan there are just 792 probation officers assigned responsibility for both probation and parole supervision (Rehabilitation Bureau 1981, 10). In comparison, the United States has almost 22,000 probation officers, twenty-eight times as many as in Japan (Flanagan and Jamieson 1988, 70–72, 476). In addition, there are a large number of parole officers in the United States who supervise offenders released from prison. In Japan, probation officers supervise both probationers and parolees. Easily as remarkable is the heavy involvement of Japanese volunteers in probation: There are about 47,000 volunteer probation officers (VPOs) in Japan (Rehabilitation Bureau 1981, 13). Interestingly, the passage of the Volunteer Probation Officer Law in 1950, which sanctioned and legitimated the role of volunteers in probation, actually preceded the amendments to the Penal Code in 1953 and 1954 that initiated Japan's probation system. It is clear that the relatively low number of probation officers in Japan is only possible because of such active involvement of volunteers in providing probation and parole services. In the early 1980s, each probation officer supervised 132 offenders but had the assistance of 81 volunteer probation officers (Rehabilitation Bureau 1981, 11).

The Development of Corrections Systems in the United States

The development of corrections in the United States is a virtual parade of approaches, programs, and structures, driven by the changing winds of correctional thought. What makes correctional thought and practice even more inconstant is the extremely decentralized and fragmented structure of corrections in the United States.

Historically, correctional thought and practice in the U.S. has gone through distinctive periods of fundamental transformation and change. The birth of the American republic occurred at a time of revolution in the conception of criminal punishment (Cole 1989, 508). This conceptual change, emerging from the work of classical utilitarian philosophers in the second half of the eighteenth century, was briefly discussed in chapter 6 in the context of sentencing rationales. Changes in correctional thought and practice were an indispensable element of the humanitarian reform of justice systems proposed by classical theorists. In particular, the use of incarceration was introduced as a more humane form of punishment than the arbitrary and harsh punishment administered prior to this time (Vold and Bernard 1986).

The creation in the late 1700s of a formal corrections system in the United States was fueled, to a large degree, by this revolution in penal philosophy. However, the influence of classical thought on corrections in the U.S. was augmented and accentuated by the ideals of individual freedom and human per-fectibility—two central themes of the American Revolution that have their roots in the Enlightenment (Rothman 1971). Cole (1989, 508) notes that the Declaration of Independence offers an "optimistic view of human nature" and an "implied belief in each person's perfectibility"—beliefs fundamentally incongruent with a penal sys-tem based upon retribution and arbitrary justice as was common in many societies before the development of classical thought. Subsequently, the penal reform advo-cated by classical theorists and the spirit of the American Revolution fostered a distinctive structure and purpose in the emerging system of corrections.

The Evolution of Correctional Thought and Practice in the United States   Al-though physical punishment and banishment were the main criminal sanctions during the colonial and early postrevolutionary years, the development of a formal corrections system, beginning in the late 1700s, initiated a steady succession of change in the structure and purpose of corrections in the United States (Cole 1989; Hawkins and Alpert 1989; Bartollas 1985).

While European classical theorists first advanced the idea that imprisonment could be an appropriate and effective punishment, the marriage of this notion to the American ideal of human perfectibility led to the creation of the penitentiary. In many respects, the idea of the penitentiary as "a place of penance," where prisoners could be isolated from society, engage in productive labor, reflect on their mis-deeds, repent, and be reformed, is an American invention (Clear and Cole 1990; Bartollas 1985). Penitentiaries were initiated to provide a controlled, yet humane environment intended to promote prisoner reform. It is important to note that the penitentiary and numerous subsequent correctional reforms in the United States were advocated by a number of influential private citizens and associations. The penitentiary, as a case in point, was championed by a Philadelphia group composed of a large number of Quakers who called themselves the Society for Alleviating the Miseries of Public Prisoners (Clear and Cole 1990).

Although much controversy surrounded the physical design of penitentiaries and what form incarceration was to take, the idea of the penitentiary caught on quickly in the United States, and numerous facilities were built in the mid-1800s (Clear and Cole 1990). However, the high ideals that led penal reformers to establish penitentiaries were quickly dimmed by implementation problems that yielded poor results. Clear and Cole (1990, 78–79) note that:

> In the post-Civil War period American reformers became disillusioned by the results of the penitentiary movement. . . . The failure of the penitentiaries, however, was seen as a problem of poor administration rather than an indictment of the concept of incarceration. Within forty years of their advocates' optimistic proclamation, penitentiaries were bulging, understaffed, and minimally financed. Discipline was neglected, administra-tors were viewed as corrupt, and the institutions were places of brutality . . . (see also Hawkins and Alpert 1989; McKelvey 1977).

After the Civil War, a new generation of prison reformers came on the scene. They questioned whether the highly disciplined and controlled environment of the penitentiary could generate reform in prisoners. The creation of the National Prison Association and its 1870 meeting in Cincinnati provided a national forum that embraced and promoted a new round of penal reform. While retaining the humanitarianism of earlier reformers and their emphasis on moral reform, followers of the "new penology" advocated the progressive classification of prisoners and the development of prison education programs. They also actively sought legislated provisions for indeterminate sentencing and parole. No longer was moral reform to be based upon strict discipline and hard work but upon rewarding prisoner reformation with early release from prison. Thus, this new generation of penal reformers actively sought to redesign the prison environment to facilitate inmate rehabilitation. The corresponding transformation of penal practices is referred to as the Reformatory Movement (Cole 1989; Clear and Cole 1990; Bartollas 1985).

Drawing from correctional innovations in England, Ireland, and Australia, the new penologists introduced a number of prison reforms that dramatically changed the nature of incarceration and the structure of corrections in the United States (Clear and Cole 1990). Progressive classification of prisoners and early release on parole were intended to motivate prisoner reformation, and the enactment of indeterminate sentencing laws provided the legal foundation for the discretionary release of prisoners. Parole decisions were to be based upon inmate reformation as indicated by character and behavioral change, productive labor, and educational advancement. Furthermore, parole release was conditional, incorporating rules and supervision that were intended to support an inmate's transition from prison to the community.

A new wave of optimism swept the country during the Progressive Era—the period from about 1900 to 1920 (Bartollas 1985, 7; Rothman 1980). Progressive reformers emphasized the intrinsic worth of people—including criminals—and the harsh social consequences of rapid industrialization and urbanization (Gibbons 1979). Increasingly, offenders were viewed as products of a poor environment or as sufferers from psychological dysfunctions or biological limitations. Confident that a scientific approach could be used to uncover the causes of criminality and to reform offenders *(positivism)*, progressive reformers initially sought societal change to alleviate the social conditions "known" to breed crime: broken homes, poverty, poor health and housing conditions, disorganized neighborhoods, inadequate schools. Gradually, however, progressive reformers turned their attention to individual pathologies thought to be rooted in biological and psychological impairments. It was assumed that these forces which caused an individual to engage in criminal behavior could be "identified, isolated, treated, and cured" (Bartollas 1985, 26). Consequently, greater and greater emphasis was placed on individualized treatment. In so doing, the notion of rehabilitation was transformed from an emphasis on moral reformation to an emphasis on treatment, analogous to that in medicine. As a result, the *medical model of corrections* emerged:

> Under the banner of the newly prestigious social and behavioral sciences, the emphasis of corrections shifted to treatment of criminals as persons whose social, intellectual, or biological deficiencies had caused them to engage in illegal activity (Clear and Cole 1990, 86).

Several of the reforms first instituted during the Reformatory Movement—most notably probation, indeterminate sentencing, and parole—were appropriated by progressive reformers and infused with the notion of individualized treatment and rehabilitation. Under the guise of the medical model, these correctional reforms acquired legitimacy, and only then were they adopted by a majority of the state correctional systems. Probation, for example, had its origin in the work of John Augustus, a Boston shoemaker, in the mid-1800s. It was first institutionalized by law in Massachusetts in 1878, but by 1900 only six states provided for it. However, in the thirty years which followed, probation became one of the key components of the medical model of corrections. The growing acceptance of probation is closely connected with the development of the juvenile court and the central role probation played in the early juvenile court. While probation initially involved services provided by volunteers seeking to morally reform offenders, it was increasingly dominated by social workers and social casework strategies, including case assessment and therapeutic counseling (Cromwell et al. 1985; Clear 1979). The "medicalization" of probation resulted in widespread acceptance: By 1930 all states had provisions for juvenile probation and thirty-six had adult probation laws.

Probation is just one of a wide range of correctional innovations implemented during the first half of the 1900s with the explicit goal of individualized treatment and rehabilitation. The implementation of the medical model resulted not only in the proliferation of correctional programs—many of them outside of prison—but also in a significant change in the practice of corrections. The medical model embraced a variety of methods, including the use of diagnostic and assessment instruments, systems of offender classification, a host of treatment modalities, and the professionalization of correctional personnel, now involving trained social workers, psychologists, and psychiatrists (Clear and Cole 1990; Bartollas 1985).

The medical model of corrections attracted an immensely strong following in the first half of the twentieth century. During its heyday, Francis Allen (1959, 226) observed, "It is almost assumed that matters of treatment and reform of the offender are the only questions worthy of serious attention in the whole field of criminal justice and corrections." However, in the late 1960s the medical model came under attack. A widely read report by the American Friends Service Committee (1971), entitled *Struggle for Justice*, characterized this attack. The report pointed to the lack of credible scientific data on either the causes or treatment of criminality. Subsequently, the committee objected strongly to the excessive amount of discretion wielded by correctional personnel in the name of treatment and rehabilitation. They reasoned that if individualized treatment rests on shaky evidence, then the medical model of corrections is paramount to "messing with people's lives." The result, the committee argued, is a corrections system that is ineffective, inequitable, and unjust. Additionally, numerous empirical studies of correctional effectiveness began to appear in the mid-1960s. These studies yielded limited evidence of success, and even though successful programs and implementation problems were sometimes acknowledged, the general conclusion was that nothing works (Lipton, Martinson, and Wilks 1975; Martinson 1974). The "nothing works" attitude toward rehabilitation was widely adopted by the public and criminal justice professionals; as the dominance of the medical model faded, a new era of correctional thought and practice was ushered in.

In the social climate of the 1960s, renewed attention was given to the importance of environmental factors in causing crime. Specifically, growing consideration was given to the community's role in generating and responding to crime.

A task force report on corrections by the President's Commission on Law Enforcement and the Administration of Justice (1967, 7) captures this change in outlook:

> crime and delinquency are symptoms of failures and disorganization of the community . . . .The task of corrections, therefore, includes building or rebuilding social ties, obtaining employment and education, securing in the larger sense a place for the offender in the routine functioning of society. This requires not only efforts directed toward changing the individual offender, which have been almost the exclusive focus of rehabilitation, but also mobilization and change of the community and its institutions.

The development of the *community corrections model* was associated with this change in perspective. Emphasizing reintegration, this model aspired "to keep offenders in the community and to help them reintegrate themselves into community life" (Bartollas 1981, 24). The goal of reintegration, however, was greeted with a fair amount of ambivalence. Although the importance of the community in causing and responding to crime was widely acknowledged and while a wide range of community correctional programs were developed, the rising crime rate and general social unrest of the 1960s and early 1970s dampened enthusiasm for the model. Additionally, its decidedly rehabilitative stature quickly put it under the attack of rehabilitation opponents (Bartollas 1985). Although a variety of community-based correctional programs, such as group homes, halfway houses, restitution centers, work release centers, and drug treatment centers, continue to play a vital role in corrections today, the community corrections model was fully adopted in only three states: Minnesota, Oregon, and Kansas (Clear and Cole 1990).

The increase in crime and widespread public fear of crime in the 1960s and 1970s, together with the attack on rehabilitation, spurred an emotional "get tough" reaction that dominates contemporary correctional thought and practice in the United States. Bartollas (1981, 25) observes that "[o]fficial crime statistics and the media have presented convincing evidence that crime has gotten out of control and that firm measures must be taken to restrain it." Referred to as the *crime control model,* this view has its roots in classical theory and emphasizes public safety and deterrence of crime through punishment. The crime control model has generated strong public support and has incited major changes in contemporary corrections. Many states have revised their criminal codes to restrict sentencing discretion (determinate sentencing). Parole decisions, which provide for early release from prison based upon rehabilitation success, have been reduced or eliminated in several states and in the federal system. Probably the most dramatic change, however, has been the increased use of incarceration in the United States. Prison and jail populations have swelled in the last fifteen years (Greenfeld 1989; Kline 1988), reflecting a more punitive approach to sentencing, more restrictive statutory provisions for sentencing, and elimination or limitation of parole discretion. Thus, the steady reduction in the use of correctional institutions, which characterized correctional thought and practice throughout much of the current century, has been abruptly reversed with recent correctional changes reflecting the crime control model.

Contemporary Correctional Structures in the United States   We have repeatedly observed that people in the United States have a long-standing distrust of centralized government. Fearing abuse of power, the framers of the Constitution established a decentralized government in which each level of government—federal, state, and local—operates under the principle of separation of power. Thus, political power in the United States is delegated first and foremost to state and local governments and is divided among the legislative, judicial, and executive branches.

The structure of corrections reflects this governmental organization. Like other parts of the criminal justice system, corrections in the United States is widely decentralized and fragmented among the various levels and branches of government (Clear and Cole 1990). The federal government, each of the fifty states, every county, and many municipalities operate correctional institutions and programs. Additionally, each branch of government exercises some jurisdiction over the correctional enterprise. The responsibility for corrections is heavily centered in the executive branch, but the legislative and judicial branches play significant roles. The legislature allocates funds and enacts criminal statutes and procedural laws that influence correctional structures and practices. The judiciary makes sentencing decisions which corrections agencies must carry out and establishes case law that dramatically influences correctional practices, such as interpretations of "cruel and unusual punishment." Additionally, the courts often have jurisdiction over probation services. Cole (1989, 518) notes that such fragmentation leads to a lack of coordination among correctional institutions and programs:

> Each level of government has some responsibility for corrections, and often one level exercises little supervision over another. The federal government has no formal control over corrections in the states. In most areas, maintaining prisons and parole is the responsibility of the state, while counties have some misdemeanant jails but no authority over the short-term jail operations of towns and cities. In addition, there is a division between juvenile and adult corrections. The fragmentation of corrections reminds us that within the physical boundaries of a state there are many correctional systems, each with its own special orientation.

Thus, the administration of corrections in the United States is a confusing array of decentralized and fragmented practice and responsibility. Although the federal government and every state have centralized executive branch departments that administer correctional programs and institutions, their administrative responsibility varies extensively. Additionally, while many people think of corrections only in terms of institutional incarceration, corrections includes a wide variety of programs and services, and the administrative responsibility for these programs is widely dispersed among different levels and branches of government. Jails are operated mainly by county sheriff's departments (local, executive branch), but in six states they are integrated within the state prison system (state, executive branch). Prisons are administered by state departments of corrections (state, executive branch).

Probation services are probably the most administratively varied form of corrections (Abadinsky 1987). Probation is often attached to the judiciary, as it is in seven states and the federal government. In other states it is the combined responsibility of the executive and judicial branches; and in still other states, probation is an executive responsibility, a division within the state department of corrections. Furthermore, probation is administered at the local, county, state, and federal levels of government (National Council of Crime and Delinquency 1981). Much controversy surrounds the administrative organization of parole boards and parole supervision. In most states and in the federal government, parole boards are an element of the executive branch but are administratively independent from the executive organization that administers prisons—most commonly a department of corrections at the state level and the Federal Bureau of Prisons at the federal level. At the same time, supervision of parolees is usually the responsibility of parole officers who are employed by state departments of corrections (Clear and Cole 1990; McCarthy and McCarthy 1984).

The federal government operates probably the most unified corrections system in the United States, but only about 5 percent of the correctional population is under the jurisdiction of federal authorities (Clear and Cole 1990). The Bureau of Prisons, a division of the Department of Justice (executive branch), administers federal prisons, detention centers, prison camps, halfway houses, and a single medical facility. These institutions are organized into five regions with regional administrative offices. Parole release decisions are made by the U.S. Parole Commission, an independent entity within the Department of Justice. Supervision of parolees is provided by federal probation officers who are appointed by the Administrative Office of the U.S. Courts (judicial branch). Thus, even at the federal level, correctional administration is divided between the executive and judicial branches. At the same time, Congress (legislative branch) has significant impact on corrections by controlling allocations of funds and by enacting statutory regulations apropos to correctional operations and procedures (Clear and Cole 1990; Cromwell et al. 1985).

A COMPARISON OF CORRECTIONAL POPULATIONS IN JAPAN AND THE UNITED STATES

A comparison of correctional populations in Japan and the United States yields interesting results that provide insight into the nature and character of each country's corrections system. Just as Japan's crime rate is dramatically lower than that of the United States, so is the size of its correctional population.

In chapter 3 we pointed to the difficulties of comparing the crime rates of Japan and the United States. Similarly, comparable data on correctional populations are difficult to assemble. Correctional data from Japan's Ministry of Justice are based primarily on the number of new cases in different correctional spheres. Official correctional data from the United States tend to center on the total number of cases in a given year; however, the number of new correctional cases can also be gleaned from the data. In deciding on what comparative data to use, there is lingering question of *who* gets counted and *how*. In the U.S. data, the average daily jail population is provided, but the average daily prison population is not. In Japan, the Corrections Bureau is responsible for both jail and prison facilities and provides combined data on the average daily population of those incarcerated. These data are reported separately in the U.S. because jails and prisons are operated by different levels and branches of government.

The number of adults placed under correctional supervision in a given year provides for relatively straightforward comparison. Table 7.1 reports on three of the most important elements of corrections: the numbers of adults placed on probation, admitted to prison, and granted parole in 1987. While offenders placed on parole are coming out of prison and are therefore not newly placed under correctional supervision, their placement on parole is a change in their supervision status. Clearly, the total number of new cases in probation, prison, and parole is so much lower in Japan than in the United States because of Japan's lower crime rates. Nevertheless, the number of individuals being placed under some form of correctional supervision is astoundingly different: In 1987, 1,841,623 individuals were placed under correctional supervision in the United States, as compared with 53,806 individuals in Japan.

This great difference could be attributed to a difference in population size, but even after controlling for the difference in population size by calculating the *rate* of correctional supervision per 100,000 population, the comparison between Japan and the United States is astounding. In the United States 756 individuals out of every 100,000 were placed under correctional supervision in 1987. In that same year, just 44 out of every 100,000 individuals were placed under correctional supervision in Japan.

It is probably more informative, however, to compare Japan and the United States in terms of the specific correctional practices of probation, imprisonment, and parole. Whereas the rates for these practices are all extraordinarily low in Japan as compared to the United States, the difference is greatest in the case of probation. Very few adults are placed on probation in Japan—only 6,477 in 1987 as compared to 1,376,244 in the United States. That's a rate of 5 per 100,000 in Japan and 565 in

TABLE 7.1 Number of Adults Placed under Correctional Supervision in 1987: Japan and the United States

	Japan	United States
Total Population, 1987[a]	122,264,000	243,400,000
Total Number Placed in Prison, on Probation, or on Parole	53,806	1,841,623
Rate per 100,000	44.0	756.6
New on Probation[b]	6,477	1,376,244
New on probation/100,000	5.3	565.4
Newly Admitted to Prison[c]	29,726	225,627
Admissions/100,000	24.3	92.7
New on Parole[d]	17,603	239,752
New on parole/100,000	14.4	98.5

SOURCES: [a]Population estimates: Japan—*Japanese Empire Statistical Yearbook,* 1984–85 (p. 193); U.S.—Census Bureau. [b]Probation data: Japan—Ministry of Justice (1988, 19); U.S.—Hester (1988, 2). [c]Prison data: Japan—Ministry of Justice (1988, 109); U.S.—Greenfeld (1989, 7). [d]Parole data: Japan—Ministry of Justice (1988, 19); U.S.—Hester (1988, 3).

the United States. You may recall from chapter 6 that in Japan a significant proportion of suspended sentences of incarceration do not involve probation, whereas it is exceedingly common for suspended sentences in the United States to involve probation. Moreover, in Japan, probation appears to be used mainly for juveniles. In 1987, 70,447 juveniles were newly placed on probation (Ministry of Justice 1988, 122).

It is also informative to consider the distribution of new correctional placements. Table 7.2 shows this distribution among probation, prison, and parole. Probation is by far the most common form of correctional supervision in the United States: three-fourths (75 percent) of all new correctional placements are on probation, whereas the remaining placements are almost equally divided between imprisonment and parole (Hester 1989). The distribution of new entrants into corrections is far different in Japan where only 12 percent are placed on probation, but 55 percent are admissions to prison and 33 percent are granted parole. Keep in mind that these figures have to do with the distribution of adults placed on correctional supervision and have no bearing on sentencing practices. It might be tempting to focus on the fact that over half of all new adult correctional placements in Japan are imprisonment, whereas in the U.S. over three-quarters are probation. However, these figures are indicators of the final step in a long series of discretionary decisions. In chapter 6 we saw that Japanese judges are far less likely than U.S. judges to place convicted offenders under correctional supervision and that they are far more likely to use suspended sentences. The present data reveal that *if* correctional supervision is ordered, it is more likely to take the form of imprisonment in Japan as compared to probation in the U.S.

TABLE 7.2 Distribution of Adults Placed on Correctional Supervision in 1987: Japan and the United States

	Japan	United States
Probation	12%	75%
	(6,477)	(1,376,244)
Prison	55%	12%
	(29,726)	(225,627)
Parole	33%	13%
	(17,603)	(239,752)

SOURCES: see table 7.1.

THE PRACTICE OF CORRECTIONS

Three areas of contrast in the practice of corrections graphically illustrate the distinctive approaches taken by Japan and the United States: the role of rehabilitation in corrections, the rights granted to prison inmates, and personnel practices.

Rehabilitation

It should be apparent by now that the structure of Japanese corrections is strikingly Western. An administrator of Japan's Corrections Bureau made the rather curt observation that "a Japanese prison has the progressive stage system of Irish origin in a Pennsylvanian radical-winged building, operated under German laws, regulations, and staff organisation. Recently these have been seasoned with a series of American ideas, of so-called 'scientific treatment'" (Yanagimoto 1970, 210).

Despite the Western structure of Japanese corrections, the practice of corrections is decidedly Japanese. A comparison of rehabilitation practices in Japan and the United States provides valuable insight into how the U.S. practice of rehabilitation was transposed into Japan's corrections system. Additionally, the evolution of rehabilitation in each country demonstrates how cultural values influence correctional practice.

We have already observed that the U.S. presence in Japan following the end of World War II dramatically influenced Japan's legal system. At that time, U.S. corrections was embedded deeply in the medical model. Consequently, the goal of rehabilitation was imported into Japanese corrections.

The tenets of the medical model—offender classification, a progressive level system, and parole release—have become central components of corrections in Japan. Moreover, Japan's centralized corrections system, administered by the Corrections and Rehabilitation Bureaus, produces consistency and standardization in rehabilitation policies and practices. For example, the Corrections Bureau operates prison admission and classification centers in each of its eight regions. These centers apply uniform offender classification standards, instruments, and procedures, all of which are intended to "provide scientific basis for more effective treatment and resocialization of convicted offenders" (Corrections Bureau 1982, 14).

The fragmented nature of corrections in the United States has never allowed for such uniformity in rehabilitation policy and practice. In terms of offender classification, each state and federal correctional system is left to its own devices to develop and implement a classification system. Proponents of the medical model contend it has yet to be tried because rehabilitation has been so poorly implemented in the United States (Cullen and Gilbert 1982; Halleck and Witte 1977). The fragmented nature of corrections certainly fails to produce a concerted and consistent application of rehabilitation policies and practices.

The American value of pragmatism continually elicits the question "What works?" As previously noted, the medical model of corrections was barraged with this question in the 1960s and 1970s. When the collective response was "nothing works," many people were more than ready to move on to another correctional approach. This response, intensified by an increase in crime and a growing fear of crime, is largely accountable for the rise of the crime control model in the late 1970s and the 1980s.

Japanese corrections has yet to abandon the medical model. Nevertheless, rehabilitation in contemporary Japanese corrections is conducted in a decisively Japanese manner. While there seems to be little question of the goal of rehabilitation (Nakayama 1981), what is really meant and put into practice in Japanese corrections is *resocialization* (Archambeault and Fenwick 1988; Kaiser 1984; Corrections Bureau 1982; Suzuki 1979b).

Work is the primary means of resocializing offenders in Japan. In fact, work is often designated as the Japanese corrections system's central activity (Kaiser 1984; Clifford 1976). Contrary to many modern justice systems, Japan maintains a sentence of "imprisonment with forced labor." More than 90 percent of all inmates work whether or not their sentence is one of forced labor (Corrections Bureau 1982). Additionally, prison industries are not nearly as controversial in Japan as in the United States (Suzuki 1979b). With a rigorous daily schedule, including a six-day work week, work engenders the explicit goal of resocialization in Japanese prisons:

> Its objective [work] is not only to give inmates vocational knowledge and skill, but also to strengthen their will-to-work, sense of self-help and spirit of cooperation through working together in well-regulated circumstances. Thus, prison industry contributes to the correctional aims of resocializing offenders (Corrections Bureau 1982, 26).

There appears to be widespread unanimity among Japanese prison officials that this work experience promotes rehabilitation through vocational training and enhanced employment opportunities. Equally as important, however, is the belief that work teaches prisoners the Japanese values of harmony, respect for authority, and group-relatedness. Such resocialization, Japanese correctional officials believe, allows offenders, when released, to have a better chance to reintegrate themselves into group life (Archambeault and Fenwick 1988).

Rehabilitation in Japanese corrections has never been based upon extensive psychological or therapeutic counseling, as was the case in the United States when the medical model prevailed. The rise of the crime control model, however, radically limited the role of counseling in American corrections. Counseling has never assumed a great deal of prominence or acceptance in Japanese corrections, but *Naikan* therapy, a unique form of psychotherapy, was introduced into juvenile and adult institutions in the early 1960s and continues to be used today despite widespread resistance to other forms of counseling therapy (Matsumoto et al. 1978). *Naikan* therapy was derived from Zen meditation and is based upon introspection. Inmates who volunteer for this therapy enter a period of self-imposed isolation in which they reflect upon their past deeds, the expectations of others, and their obligations to others. Thus, *Naikan* therapy stresses moral responsibility and is remarkably consistent with the prominent cultural values in Japan (Clifford 1976; Yanagimoto 1970).

Perhaps the most distinctive corrections feature in Japan is the extensive involvement of volunteers in rehabilitation (Parker 1986; Ochiai 1984). While volunteers have an extended history of involvement in both Japanese and American corrections, the extent to which they are utilized in Japan is probably unmatched anywhere in the world. Additionally, the national organization of volunteers, the extent to which the government authorizes and legitimizes volunteers, and the fact that their role and qualifications are established by law make the role of volunteers unique to Japanese corrections.

To a large degree, volunteers are the mainstay of rehabilitative services in Japan. As mentioned earlier, while there are only 797 professional probation officers in Japan, there are almost 47,000 volunteers, and the assistance of volunteers makes high probation and parole caseloads manageable (Rehabilitation Bureau

1981). These volunteers provide a wide range of rehabilitative services including individual and family assistance. Another explicit responsibility of volunteer probation officers in Japan is community organization. This entails the mobilization of community resources and opportunities in order to assist offenders, as well as efforts aimed at eliminating the environmental conditions which generate crime (Rehabilitation Bureau 1981, 14). In many ways, community organization is quite similar to the goals of the community corrections model in the United States. Thus, a large part of the volunteer's role in Japanese corrections is to facilitate the integration of the offender back into the community (Tanigawa 1982).

While volunteers in the U.S. were instrumental in instigating prison reform, probation, and the juvenile court, their role in contemporary corrections is limited. The numbers of volunteers and their level of involvement are difficult to ascertain because corrections in the U.S. is so fragmented and governmental authorization and support are so varied among jurisdictions. Additionally, there is no national organization of volunteers. Recent estimates suggest that there are more than 500,000 correctional volunteers involved in more than 3,000 jurisdictions (Allen et al. 1985, 224; see also National Council on Crime and Delinquency 1981). Although this number is large, there are indications that correctional programs are relatively passive in recruiting volunteers and that many volunteers quit after a very short period of involvement (McCarthy and McCarthy 1984). In looking at the involvement of volunteers in contemporary American corrections, one is left with the distinct impression that they fail to play a vital role and that they are virtually an untapped resource (McCarthy and McCarthy 1984; Allen et al. 1985).

Rights of Incarcerated Offenders

Although the civil rights of prisoners are acknowledged in both Japan and the United States, how these rights are construed is very different. Historically, both countries have maintained that a sentence of imprisonment is tantamount to the offender surrendering all civil rights. This notion of *civil death* for prisoners is not unique to Japan or the United States but draws from a tradition in English law (Cohen and Rivkin 1971; see also Hawkins and Alpert 1989). While prisoners in Japan continue to hold a "disengaged" status, with few civil rights explicitly guaranteed, the rights of prisoners in the United States have been extended considerably since the Due Process Revolution of the 1960s (Hawkins and Alpert 1989; Kaiser 1984; Krantz 1981; Jacobs 1980; Clifford 1976; Cohen and Rivkin 1971).

This difference in how prisoners' rights are interpreted and handled in the contemporary correctional systems of Japan and the United States can be characterized by distinguishing between the moral responsibility *of* prisoners and society's moral responsibility *to* prisoners (Clifford 1976; Kaiser 1984). In Japan, the civil rights of prisoners are qualified by an emphasis on collective order and public welfare. The Japanese values of harmony, a natural social hierarchy, and group-relatedness result in the status of prisoners being viewed not in terms of civil rights but in terms of the social responsibilities and obligations they are expected to fulfill and the need for them to be reintegrated back into society (Kaiser 1984; Clifford 1976). At the same time, prison officials are expected to deal with prisoners in a benevolent, yet authoritative, manner. Reflecting the social values of a natural hierarchy and respect for authority, both prisoners and prison officials are expected to fulfill their proper role (Clifford 1976). Archambeault and Fenwick (1988, 16) note that:

> In Japanese prisons, the goal of justice translates to a simple doctrine of fairness and equality in the context of collective responsibility. In this regard, it is important to note that the ideology of collective responsibility and the submission of individual desires in favor of group harmony and collective order are basic tenets of Japanese society. Collective responsibility is of greater import than self-assertion and the protection of individual rights. In short, justice, in terms of fairness and equality, is expressed in Japanese corrections as collective responsibility to the group, whereas in the United States it is expressed as protection of individual rights (references omitted).

Additionally, in Japan, order and security within the prison institution are seen as prerequisites for the effective implementation of resocialization programs, and this goal of resocialization is given priority over considerations of prisoner rights (Suzuki 1979b). In fact, Kaiser (1984, 138) claims that "*all interferences* with prisoner's rights are permissible to the extent that it is necessary to attain the correctional goal [of resocialization]" (emphasis added). Although a prospectus for amending Japan's Prison Law has been under discussion since 1976, the impetus for this amendment is not only to extend prisoner rights but also to enhance administrative efficiency and to facilitate resocialization of prisoners (Kaiser 1984; Corrections Bureau 1982; Suzuki 1979b).

The current constitutional and statutory provisions for prisoners' rights in Japan are modest at best, and prison authorities are vested with a wide range of discretion in restricting rights and withdrawing privileges (Kaiser 1984; Suzuki 1979a). Furthermore, Japanese courts have not demonstrated an interest in clarifying the status of prisoners or extending the civil rights of prisoners through judicial review (Kaiser 1984). In fact, judicial review is employed only for legal violations of prison officials toward prisoners (Kaiser 1984). The most widely used grievance mechanism in Japan's prisons is an administrative one in which prison officials exercise ultimate authority. Prisoners with grievances may file a complaint against the prison administration with the prison warden, the Minister of Justice, or with a visiting official appointed by the Ministry of Justice, whose primary responsibility is to inspect the prisons (Kaiser 1984; Corrections Bureau 1982). These complaints are handled either through a personal hearing or through administrative review. The number of complaints has risen rather dramatically in recent years, from 281 in 1976 to 616 in 1981, indicating that prisoners have a growing interest in civil rights (Corrections Bureau 1982). Nevertheless, this grievance mechanism tends to deal with complaints on a case-by-case basis rather than by extending the rights and privileges of all prisoners.

In contrast to the Japanese emphasis on the moral responsibility *of* prisoners, there has been growing recognition in the United States that the Constitution establishes a moral responsibility to provide fundamental civil rights *to* prisoners. Until the 1940s, however, inmates had very few rights. In fact, most states had civil death statutes that abolished the civil rights of inmates, including the right of access to the courts (Hawkins and Alpert 1989). An 1871 Virginia case decision, *Ruffin v.*

Commonwealth, provides an extreme rendition of civil death: "[A prisoner] has, as a consequence to his crime, not only forfeited his liberty, but all his personal rights except those which the law in its humanity accords to him. He is for the time being a slave to the state" (p. 796).[1]

Based upon this status of civil death, state and federal courts held that a consideration of prisoners' rights was outside their purview. Additionally, the judiciary maintained that intervention into the operations of prisons—an executive agency—violated the doctrine of separation of power. The resulting "hands-off doctrine" was followed widely until the Due Process Revolution of the 1960s. First challenged in 1941 *(ex parte Hull),*[2] a series of court decisions disavowed this policy of judicial noninterference and allowed prisoners unrestricted access to the courts, thereby providing them with a forum for complaints and a means to pursue civil rights. At this same time, most states abandoned their civil death statutes (Cole 1989; Hawkins and Alpert 1989; Krantz 1981).

A majority of all prisoners' rights suits have been filed under the Civil Rights Act of 1871—Title 42, Section 1983 of the U.S. Code (Thomas, Keeler, and Harris 1986). Section 1983 provides for various legal remedies when individuals have been deprived of their constitutional rights.

The landmark Supreme Court decision in *Cooper v. Pate* (1964)[3] ruled that prisoners are entitled to the provision of the Civil Rights Act. Cole (1989, 580) points to the significance of this case:

> Because of this decision, the federal courts now recognize that prisoners are *persons* whose rights are protected by the Constitution, and prisoners in both state and federal institutions may challenge the conditions of their confinement in the federal courts.

Although the Constitution has surprisingly little to say directly about the rights of prisoners—only a few brief phrases in four of the amendments—a tremendous number of suits have been filed by prisoners in recent years: twenty-six thousand in 1984 alone (Thomas, Keeler, and Harris 1986, 786; see also Hawkins and Alpert 1989; Clear and Cole 1990).

The controversy that has accompanied this flood of prisoners' rights suits is not so much a question of whether constitutional rights should be extended to prisoners as one of which rights should be granted to prisoners and what qualifications of those rights are necessary for the successful operation of prisons (Krantz 1981). Generally, prisoners have been granted a variety of constitutional rights, but the extension of rights has not been wholesale, and the courts have acknowledged that the status of prisoners and the practice of incarceration necessitate limitations on rights (Cole 1989; Hawkins and Alpert 1989; Jacobs 1980; Krantz 1981). James Jacobs (1983, 35) in summarizing this movement to grant civil rights to prisoners notes that it was a "broadscale effort to redefine the status (moral, political, as well as legal) of prisoners in a democratic society."

---

[1]*Ruffin v. Commonwealth,* 62 Va. 790 (1971).

[2]*Ex parte Hull,* 312 U.S. 546 (1941).

[3]*Cooper v. Pate,* 378 U.S. 546 (1964).

Personnel Practices

Earlier in this chapter we noted that Japan's national corrections system involves a centralized, uniform, and highly coordinated structure and administration. In contrast, the wide assortment of correctional systems in the United States are decentralized and fragmented, resulting in administrative structures and practices with little uniformity or coordination. As a result, there are clear differences in the personnel practices of the corrections systems in Japan and the United States. These differences involve recruitment, training, and management styles.

Recruitment   Corrections systems in the United States give limited attention to standards or qualifications when recruiting correctional personnel. By contrast, the Japanese corrections system is highly selective (Archambeault and Fenwick 1988; Johnson and Hasegawa 1987). The concentration of correctional administration in just two national bureaus—one for institutional corrections and one for community-based corrections—allows the Japanese to maintain standardized requirements for each correctional position throughout the nation. Because the structure and administration of corrections in the United States are so decentralized and fragmented, there is no standardization of employment requirements. Each unit of government—federal, state, local, judicial, and executive—establishes independently the employment requirements for correctional positions within its jurisdiction. The result is wide variation in requirements. For example, while the Federal Bureau of Prisons recently extended the educational requirement for a prison guard to a bachelor's degree, several state prison systems have no educational requirements at all for prison guards (*Corrections Compendium* 1984; Allen and Simonsen 1989).

Beyond the standardization of requirements, Japan also has more extensive requirements for various correctional positions. In Japan, individuals applying for various positions in corrections must first pass a special examination administered by the National Personnel Authority and meet physical requirements; then they must pass an extensive background check and a rigorous personal interview (Corrections Bureau 1982; Archambeault and Fenwick 1988; Johnson and Hasegawa 1987; Holmberg–Okuba 1985). Compared to the United States, the application requirements are significant, and the procedures are rigorous.

Another important characteristic of recruitment in Japan is the intense competition for positions. One clear illustration of this is that in recent years, two-thirds of the applicants for prison guards have been university graduates, and only one-fourth of the applicants were hired (Webb 1984; see also Johnson and Hasegawa 1987). Correctional employees are seen as government officials—employees of the Ministry of Justice—and because government service is highly respected in Japan, employment in corrections carries with it a good deal of prestige. As a result, it attracts talented applicants (Parker 1986).

While most correctional positions in the United States have specified requirements, there is little uniformity in either entry requirements or application procedures across different jurisdictions. Critics point out that limited requirements and poor screening procedures are key deficiencies in U.S. corrections (Champion 1990). When describing the limited background necessary to become a prison guard, Allen and Simonsen (1989, 563) comment that there "seem to be quite minimal requirements for a job that commands so much influence over the lives and rights of inmates." While some state prison systems have fairly extensive require- ments and screening procedures—involving standardized applicant testing, physical examination, psychological evaluation, background investigation, and a personal interview—other states require no more than an ability to read and write (*Correc- tions Compendium* 1984). In sharp contrast to Japan, employment as a prison guard in the United States is distinguished by a number of interrelated characteristics: low pay, minimal prestige, poor training, and high rates of burnout (Champion 1990; American Correctional Association 1988; Whitehead and Lindquist 1986).

Problems in the recruitment of prison guards in the United States are also exacerbated by skyrocketing prison populations and massive construction pro- grams, necessitating increasing numbers of new prison guards (Allen and Simonsen 1989). In contrast, the size of Japan's corrections system and its correctional population has remained fairly stable in recent decades. Johnson and Hasegawa (1987) point out, however, that Japan's corrections system has recruited new correctional personnel more heavily in recent years. This has been necessary in order to replace the large number of corrections officers who were hired after World War II, when Japan's correctional population was at least twice what it is today, and who are now at retirement age.

The recruitment of correctional personnel is probably most similar in Japan and the United States in the case of probation and parole officers. Both countries usually require a bachelor's degree and some form of competitive application (*Corrections Compendium* 1987; Parker 1986; Rehabilitation Bureau 1981). Additionally, com- petition for employment in probation and parole is keen in both Japan and the United States. However, the prestige attached to government work in Japan and the very limited number of probation and parole officers—792 throughout the entire nation—may make competition for such positions even greater in Japan than in the United States.

A final area of contrast in recruitment practices is the promotion and selection of supervisory and administrative personnel. In Japan, selection of senior level personnel and promotion to administrative positions are almost always based upon a competitive examination process and extensive advanced training (Corrections Bureau 1982; Rehabilitation Bureau 1981). In the United States, promotion is based largely on seniority, rather than competitive application and training (Allen and Simonsen 1989).

Training   Systematic and extensive employee training has been an integral part of Japanese corrections since the inception of a formal corrections system. In Japan's contemporary corrections system, training is provided to institutional employees by the Corrections Bureau's Training Institute for Correctional Personnel and to proba- tion officers by the Research and Training Institute of the Ministry of Justice (Clifford 1976). Both institutes provide extensive training programs that are struc- tured into courses and designed explicitly to provide academic and practical educa- tion for all levels of employment. Training for new correctional personnel is particularly intensive, while supervisory and administrative training is offered to individuals selected on the basis of competitive examination or merit. One unique training opportunity provided by the Training Institute for Correctional Personnel is the research fellowship course that allows individual "correctional officers to pursue research and study on subjects related to the theory, system or practice of correctional services" (Corrections Bureau 1982, 12; Rehabilitation Bureau 1981).

Training is not nearly such a characteristic feature of corrections in the United States. Because of the decentralized and fragmented structure of the corrections system, the responsibility for training correctional personnel is spread among the various branches and levels of government with some correctional jurisdiction, resulting in training programs of quite different structure and extent. The federal system is noted for fairly systematic and extensive training, but the training programs of state and local correctional systems are usually not as systematic or extensive, nor are they routinely coordinated through a central training center (Allen and Simonsen 1989; Allen et al. 1985).

It is abundantly clear, however, that no correctional jurisdiction in the United States comes even close to providing the extent of training found in the Japanese correctional system. In Japan, new prison guards are trained for a full six months and receive regular training after that. Although there is tremendous variation in the training of new prison guards in the United States, the average training period is four to six weeks, with many jurisdictions failing to provide training beyond the entry level (Corrections Bureau 1982; Parker 1986; American Correctional Association 1986). Furthermore, the training in a number of states is essentially on-the-job training with little class time (Allen and Simonsen 1989). Training programs for new prison guards in the United States fail to offer substantive materials that equip guards with the skills and insight necessary to respond to prison problems and issues in appropriate ways. Training in firearms, conducting searches, and prison rules and regulations is common, but training programs frequently fail to provide an essential background in criminal and civil rights law, crisis intervention, or human relations (Shannon 1987).

Training programs for probation and parole officers in Japan and the United States display similar patterns of differences. A National Manpower Survey (1978) found that approximately 80 percent of all probation and parole agencies in the United States provide some employee training. In 22 percent of the agencies, in-service training was the only form of training provided with no special courses for entry level officers. Although states vary widely, the average length of courses was about one week (38 hours) (Allen et al. 1985).

Japan's training program for probation and parole officers is far more extensive. All newly appointed probation officers must complete a 92-day (411 hours) "primary course" offered by the Research and Training Institute. This course offers an array of topics rarely found in probation officer training programs in the United States, ranging from laws and procedures to counseling and casework techniques to field work and visits to criminal justice agencies (Parker 1986; Rehabilitation Bureau 1981). Beyond this initial training, the Institute provides regularly scheduled in-service training courses for experienced officers, senior officers, and supervisors. The Institute's administration courses are offered to officers specially selected to take supervisory positions.

Such systematic selection and training of correctional administrators contrast sharply with the recruitment and training of correctional administrators in the United States. Personnel practices for correctional administrators in the United States have been criticized for their failure to identify and train those persons possessing the special skills necessary to be effective administrators (Champion 1990).

Management Styles   The hierarchical structure of corrections in both Japan and the United States tends to suggest a bureaucratic model of organization. However, one characteristic of bureaucracy that varies considerably in the correctional systems of Japan and those in the United States is the relations between supervisors and subordinates (Champion 1975, 1990).

We have already seen that Japan's correctional system is centralized with a clear hierarchy of authority. While this structure explicitly reflects the Japanese value of hierarchy, other core values influence how this hierarchical structure operates. The value of hierarchy in Japanese culture encompasses not only a vertical differentiation of authority and a respect for such authority but also a mutual appreciation for the status of supervisor and subordinate and the obligations that go along with these roles. This value of hierarchy, together with the values of harmony and group-relatedness, has led to a management style in corrections that Archambeault and Fenwick (1988, 16) describe as a "team perspective," where supervisory and line workers interact closely and are mutually dependent. We have pointed to this style of management in our discussion of management techniques used by the police in Japan. Although correctional managers perform different work, they solicit and respect the ideas of subordinates and allow them active participation in decision making. Supervisors deal with workers as individuals and demonstrate concern for their total well-being—social, family, and financial (Archambeault and Fenwick 1988). The supervisor–worker relationship approximates the traditional *oyabun-kobun* relationship in which the roles of superior and subordinate are characterized by mutual dependency and respect, loyalty, obligation, and service. Thus, the management style promoted in Japanese corrections is far from the impersonal relationships that exist in many bureaucratic organizations. Some have suggested that greater levels of employee participation in decision making, especially in decisions affecting their work, make for greater job satisfaction and greater loyalty to the organization (Champion 1990). This appears to be true in Japanese corrections.

The management style in U.S. correctional systems is far different and more varied. The different correctional systems in the United States are described most often as bureaucratic organizations (Archambeault and Fenwick 1988; Barak-Glantz 1986; Snarr and Wolford 1985). Management styles within these correctional bureaucracies appear to vary in different jurisdictions—federal, state, and local—and in different types of correctional operations—prisons, parole, probation, and other community-based programs.

A prison has been described as an "impersonal authoritarian bureaucracy using threat and intimidation to manage staff and inmates"; however, this is probably more true of prisons before World War II when autocratic wardens wielded almost absolute control (Archambeault and Fenwick 1988, 8; Bartollas 1981). In recent decades prison management that allows correctional officers to participate in decision making has become more popular (Champion 1990; Barak-Glantz 1986) though it is difficult to say how extensive this management style has become in U.S. prisons. Archambeault (1982a, 1982b) has suggested that the management style used in Japanese prisons is highly relevant to the current state of U.S. prisons.

The management of probation and parole officers in U.S. corrections is an entirely different issue. We saw earlier in this chapter that the organization of probation and parole in the United States is probably the most administratively varied form of corrections (Abadinsky 1987). Additionally, the practical reality of the probation and parole officer's dual role—investigation and supervision—requires that individual officers be delegated significant authority and independence (Clear and Cole 1990). As a result, even though probation and parole may be organized bureaucratically, the management of officers involves decentralized decision making and delegated authority.

The only conclusion that can be drawn about management styles in U.S. corrections is that they are extremely varied, and such diversity is exacerbated by the decentralized structure of U.S. corrections (Champion 1990).

SUMMARY

Throughout this chapter we have noted that Japan's national corrections system results in a consistency and standardization of correctional policy and practice not found in the United States. In Japan, just two bureaus within the Ministry of Justice operate all correctional programs. In contrast, the correctional enterprise in the United States is widely decentralized and fragmented among the various levels and branches of government. The net result of such variation in correctional structure is that Japan has a much greater clarity of purpose and more unified and coordinated system of corrections as compared to the United States. Then, too, Japan's correctional system includes widespread public involvement in which citizens provide advisory assistance and play a vital role in providing direct services, especially those efforts directed at resocializing offenders. To a great degree, the structure and practice of corrections reflect and reinforce each country's cultural values. This is evidenced, as we have seen, by variation in the use of rehabilitation, the rights granted to prison inmates, and personnel practices.

DRAWING CONCLUSIONS: LEARNING FROM COMPARATIVE CROSS-CULTURAL STUDY

One of the fundamental dilemmas confronting any democracy is how to guarantee a just society in which there is a proper balance between what appear to be two insistent but conflicting demands: the desire for individual freedom and autonomy and the need for collective order and control. Much of the history of America could be written in terms of the ongoing struggle to strike such a balance. The American Revolution, the Civil War, and the Civil Rights Movement can all be seen as tidal marks in this struggle.

Japan's history as a democratic society is much more recent than that of the United States, but Japanese history can also be read as the slow movement of a nation and people toward greater freedom and autonomy. Certainly from the period of the Meiji Restoration until today, the Japanese have confronted the problem of developing a system that allows adequate individual autonomy while maintaining appropriate collective control.

To be sure, when we look at these two societies today, we can see major differences in the ways each has achieved its own unique balance. Our examination of the cultural development in each society helps us understand why people in the United States have placed greater emphasis on freedom and individualism and why the Japanese have stressed responsibility, duty, and the group. Because each society has adopted a different set of values, each has achieved a different balance and produced a different system of social control.

The basic perspective of this book is influenced strongly by this understanding. In the preceding chapters our comparative analysis of crime and justice in these societies was informed by the *anthropological–historical* approach, recognizing that in every society, central, or core, cultural values develop from the interaction of land and people in the process of historic development.

As we pointed out, the very different combinations of these elements have produced two societies with quite distinct core values. Japan's history of autocratic government and its economic development, homogeneous population, and long tradition of hierarchy have resulted in a set of values that emphasize that the individual's interests are best served in the context of the group and its welfare. This

148

is a very different emphasis than that found in the United States, where the core values of freedom and individualism reflect the concerns of a diverse, immigrant population who came to these shores seeking autonomy and freedom. The resistance to centralized authority and the emphasis upon individual rights become reinforced by the ethnic, racial, and economic diversity that are such a central part of U.S. history.

The anthropological–historical approach also argues that a society's core values shape the behaviors of its members. It argues that while values are abstract concepts, they represent deep-seated beliefs that influence and mold the normative structures of a society and frame the relationships among its members. Put simply, different values produce different behaviors.

Our review of crime and justice in Japan and the United States indicates clearly that the differences in crime and social control in these two societies are a reflection of significant differences in their cultures. In Japan, the core values of group-relatedness, respect for tradition, harmony, and hierarchy have led to very strong forms of informal social control. The ethnically homogeneous Japanese stress conformity to group norms, and individuals prize the approval of the groups that monitor their behaviors and provide their identities. As a consequence, there is relatively little crime, and the structures of formal social control operate with effectiveness.

On the other hand, the American values of freedom, independence, individualism, and diversity have resulted in a society where informal controls are relatively weak. Because there is a great deal of ethnic, racial, and economic heterogeneity, there is no strong group consensus. Because there is much less emphasis placed upon either conformity or social approval and because there is far less economic equality in the society, there is a great deal more crime than in Japan. The net result of these cultural characteristics is a heavy reliance upon formal systems of social control. In the minds of many people in the United States and in contemporary criminal justice policy, conformity is more a matter of external compulsion than of internal compliance.

We also noted that the relationship between informal and formal social control mechanisms is highly interactive. When informal controls are strong, formal controls are more efficient and effective; and when informal controls are weak, formal controls become less efficient and require greater expenditures of time, energy, and resources.

Japan's low crime rate suggests either that Japanese culture effectively limits criminal behavior or that Japan's criminal justice system is uniquely able to suppress and control crime. In other words, either Japanese society has incredibly effective informal controls or its institutions of formal control are especially adept at controlling crime. However, as we have seen, both of these presuppositions may be correct. Japan has a remarkably low crime rate not simply because Japan has an effective criminal justice system but also because Japan has very strong informal social controls that successfully inhibit criminal behavior. We have argued that much of the efficiency and effectiveness of Japan's criminal justice system develops out of a cultural climate that strongly affects the way in which Japanese respond to law and order. Japan's pervasive system of informal control bolsters formal mechanisms of social control.

APPROPRIATING METHODS OF CRIME CONTROL

It is truly tempting to look at Japan's low crime rate with envy and ask, "What do they do that controls crime so well?" The implication, of course, is that perhaps our society can put in a quick fix by borrowing what works in Japan and incorporating it into our own criminal justice system.

It has been our basic argument, however, that a society's criminal justice system is shaped by the cultural environment—the prevailing values and norms—of that society. Consequently, any attempt to understand and apply another country's criminal justice practices must carefully consider the cultural context from which they emerged as well as that to which they will be applied.

To transplant Japan's system of control to U.S. soil in wholesale fashion is impossible. As Karel van Wolferen (1990, 17) argues,

> the "learn from Japan" approach has glossed over some crucial differences between Japan and the West. The adoption of parts of the System (*sic*) is not likely to work without most of the rest of the Japanese package, and the costs of that package cannot be paid by the West. An evolution of Western practices in Japanese directions would entail the reproduction of conditions inconceivable as long as social and intellectual freedom are valued.

American values grow out of an entirely different context of ethnic, racial, religious, and social diversity. If systems of formal control appear to be far less effective than their Japanese counterparts, the major reason is that the core values in American society do not provide strong informal social control. Japan has a remarkably low crime rate not simply because it has an effective criminal justice system but also because it has very strong informal social controls that successfully inhibit criminal behavior. While the Japanese are by no means bereft of individualism, the independence they exercise takes on far different forms than those in the United States. For Americans, freedom, equality, and independence lead to a situation in which weak informal controls do not lend strong support to formal control mechanisms.

It is also important to see that it is not simply the way Japan's criminal justice system is organized or structured that makes it so successful in controlling crime. In fact, although there are differences in structure between Japan and the United States—national as compared to state and federal courts, for example—the Japanese system is not all that different. Clifford (1976, 50) points out that "the Japanese system looks very much the same as those of the West because it has been borrowed wholesale from or intensively modeled on the laws and institutions of Germany, France, and the United States."

Even though the structures of criminal justice are quite similar in Japan and the United States, the way in which these structures operate in practice is significantly different. As Clifford (1976, 6) notes, Japan's system is dissimilar not so much because of its form or structure but because of the

> style and meaning . . . the structure gradually acquires in a Japanese context. It is the old story of how the Japanese have absorbed culture from the West without westernizing, the way in which they have been able to adopt modern methods and make them unmistakably Japanese in everything that matters.

It is, therefore, not simply the structures—the law, the police, or the courts—that produce the low crime rate in Japan. It is the total system in the context of its cultural setting. It is the set of values that people accept and that inform their behavior. Japanese commit less crime because they are a cohesive society in which group membership provides a constant control on behavior. Japanese commit less crime because to break the law disturbs the harmony so valued in a densely populated society where there is little privacy. Japanese commit less crime because there is essentially a single set of basic values that are shared among a tradition-oriented people. Japanese commit less crime because to do so is to bring shame not only upon oneself but also upon one's family and associates.

This becomes more evident when we ask the question, "Who commits crime?" Examination of the data in both Japan and the United States indicates clearly that the bulk of criminal activity is carried out by what might be termed "outsiders"—persons who do not have a place in the opportunity structure, or who really have no stake in the system, and who perceive that they have little chance of becoming a vested part of the larger society.

If we look at the kinds of crime and disorder that seem to disturb people in the United States the most—drug dealing, predatory street crime, disorder, gang-related random violence—and ask who it is that commits most of these kinds of crimes, we see that it is that part of society that has always been involved in this sort of activity: the disadvantaged, people who have nothing to gain by conformity and who have nothing to lose by deviating from society's norms. These are often people who are marginal in relation to the value systems of the larger society, people who are little influenced by the educational system, people for whom the ideas of delayed gratification or work ethic have little significance. These are people for whom the informal systems of social control of the larger society have little meaning or consequence. They are what many now call the "undercaste" of American society.

Robert Merton (1957, 146) helps us understand this. He argues that our society has become crimogenic because of the heavy emphasis on success and the failure to provide a major segment of the population with access to legitimate means of attaining success:

It is only when a system of cultural values extol, virtually above all else, certain *common* success-goals for the *population at large* while the social structure rigorously restricts or completely closes access to approved modes of reaching these goals *for a considerable part of the same population,* that deviant behavior ensues on a large scale. Otherwise said, our egalitarian ideology denies by implication the existence of non-competing individuals and groups in the pursuit of pecuniary success. Instead, the same body of success-symbols is held to apply for all. Goals are held to transcend class lines, not to be bound by them, yet the actual social organization is such that there exist class differentials in accessibility of the goals. In this setting, a cardinal American virtue, "ambition," promotes a cardinal American vice, "deviant behavior."

This is not to say that all crime is the product of the disadvantaged. While we have focused on crimes of violence in this study, we realize that some of the most significant criminal activity in the United States is white collar crime. As James Coleman (1989, 8) points out:

By virtually any criterion . . . white collar crime is our most serious crime problem. The economic cost of white collar crime is vastly greater than the economic cost of street crime. And although it may be impossible to determine exactly how many people are killed and injured each year as a result of white collar crime, the claim that such crimes are harmless, nonviolent offenses can hardly be taken seriously.

White collar crime is committed by *advantaged* people—most often by people in positions of trust and authority. These are usually people who have already attained a measure of success, for whom the criminal act is a means to increase or magnify the success that they so highly value. As damaging as white collar crime is, however, it seldom arouses the same level of fear nor does it reflect the sort of violence that we find in the kind of predatory crime that has been the focus of this study.

Who is it that commits this type of predatory crime in Japan? Once again, it is those who are untouched by the informal controls of the larger society. Reexamination of the figures on crime committed by Boryokudan members—or the Yakuza— indicates their extensive involvement in crime and violence. These are people who have been alienated from society and who have no sense of ownership or possession in the mainstream of Japanese life. Recruited into the gangs because they were outsiders or loners, their reference group is no longer the legitimate order. What controls the behavior of a Yakuza associate is the informal control mechanisms of the gang.

If Japan has less violent crime than the United States, certainly one major reason is that Japan is a homogeneous society with far greater cohesion and solidarity. To say it another way, there are a far smaller number of people in Japanese society who feel themselves to be cut off and separated from the mainstream of Japanese life. The result: far stronger informal controls and sharply reduced levels of crime.

WHAT CAN BE LEARNED

While we have just argued that cultural differences simply will not allow wholesale borrowing from the Japanese, at the same time there are features of the Japanese system that can be adapted for use in the United States. To expect rapid major cultural changes to accommodate changes in the justice system would be unrealistic. Culture—especially nonmaterial culture—develops slowly and resists change.

For that reason it would be unrealistic to anticipate any easy way for our society to develop cultural mechanisms or social structures that would provide for strong, uniformly accepted, informal social controls. At least two factors present almost insurmountable obstacles. First, the U.S. population is simply too diverse. Differences of race, ethnic heritage, economic status, religious belief, occupation, educational background, and the myriad other qualities that make up the diversity of U.S. society inhibit movement toward any universally acceptable consensus. Second, the love of freedom and independence would strongly resist any attempt to impose universal standards of behavior. For example, any attempt to teach moral or ethical behavior in the public schools would be strongly resisted.

However, culture is an adaptive system, and when change is required for the system's survival, culture can change (Currie 1989). For over 200 years the United States was a segregated society. Despite the Constitution and the Emancipation Proclamation, prejudice and discrimination were accepted patterns of behavior throughout the United States. Racism still exists, but the civil rights revolution of the 1960s and 1970s created major changes in American culture. There is still a long way to go, but Americans have taken major strides toward providing equality of opportunity.

Are Americans also willing to accept changes which would influence the character and quality of criminal justice in America? Have Americans reached the point where the costs of crime are no longer acceptable and where more radical solutions might be adopted, where the value of order might be seen to be worth restricting some personal freedom? Americans are an intensely pragmatic people. They tend to support what works and to withdraw support from programs that offer little promise of achieving goals. The attempts to win the "war on crime" have obviously produced few victories. It may well be that Americans may be more amenable to change than in previous decades. However, although there are some indications that this might be the case, we would argue that any attempts to change the justice system that do not understand and reflect basic American values are doomed to failure.

Decriminalization

What can we learn from Japan that might be adapted to the United States? One possible change is in the area of criminal law. Earlier we pointed out that a major difference between Japanese and U.S. criminal law is the extent to which morality is legislated. It is frequently observed that in the United States "sin" is defined as "crime." This obsession with controlling public morals is one that has led to serious problems for the U.S. justice system. As Walker (1989) points out, the Eighteenth Amendment, which prohibited the sale of alcohol, may have undermined respect for the law. Insistence on police control of so-called victimless crimes, such as prostitution and gambling, requires major expenditures of time and energy that divert resources from more critical areas of police work. Further, in the past, police attempts to control vice have been a major source of police corruption (Manning and Redlinger 1977).

Japan, operating out of a different moral and ethical system, approaches these problems in a very different way. As we have seen, the Japanese do not legislate morality. Japan's criminal law simply does not deal with many of these moral issues as crime (Hirano 1963). However, because there is strong consensus about moral issues, morality is regulated through informal controls. These controls are vested in the community rather than in the law, the courts, or the police.

Would it be possible for the United States to remove matters of morality from the realm of criminal law and use licensure or other regulatory devices to oversee them? What would happen if the United States decriminalized drugs such as marijuana and cocaine, if these drugs were treated as we currently treat alcohol? Some argue that this would result in even more widespread use of drugs, creating even greater social problems. Others argue that licensing drugs and making them available at much lower costs would both drastically reduce the amount of street crime associated with drug abuse and substantially decrease the huge profits that have fueled so much gang activity. The U.S. experience with alcoholic beverages suggests that licensure might indeed reduce criminal trafficking—bootlegging is not a major crime problem in today's society.

Although the outcome of decriminalization or deregulation is disputed (Walker 1989), many would argue that this kind of change might be accepted by the majority of people in the United States. Their willingness to accept state lotteries indicates a flexibility in the area of moral definitions. Further, a great many of them strongly believe that the government should not concern itself with what they perceive to be matters of personal freedom and choice. What becomes crucial in this sort of change is whether the community is willing to accept it as legitimate.

Pragmatically, what is important is that if issues of moral behavior were no longer defined as crime, police could direct their energies to other areas. Further, court systems might be freed for completing the adjudication process, and currently overburdened correctional institutions would have space to house offenders who pose a serious threat to society. Additionally, it is reasonable to assume that crime would be reduced if communities could regulate these matters in such a way that the large profits made from illicit activities would be eliminated.

Community Policing

Policing is an area where much has already been learned from Japan. This is an area where change has great potential for influencing crime rates. At the same time, law enforcement appears to be the major component of the criminal justice system with the fewest political obstacles to change. Our earlier examination of the history of policing in the United States indicated that, as the Reform Era evolved, the role of the police became increasingly narrowed to law enforcement and crime control. Police declared themselves to be professional experts on crime—the only ones qualified to fight the "war on crime." Citizens were expected to be the passive recipients of professional police service and protection. Civilian cooperation would be helpful, but law enforcement was a task for the professional, for the "thin blue line" that stood between society and the ravishing hordes of barbarians.

The net result was the development of a style of "professional" policing that relied on motorized patrol, the doctrine of rapid response to calls for emergency service, and an emphasis on the retroactive investigation of crime (Moore, Trojanowicz, and Kelling 1988). To supervise police activities, law enforcement managers came to rely upon a "command and control" style of management in which dense patterns of command and supervision were used to oversee rules that minutely prescribed police behavior. To increase efficiency and accountability, the centralized command structure of city police routinized policing, the role reduced by definition to a legalistic enforcement of the law. To remove ambiguity in the authority structure, the hierarchical, top-down paramilitary chain-of-command was adopted (Kelling, Wassermann, and Williams 1988).

However, despite these policies and practices, the police failed to win the "war on crime," and policing in the United States entered into a time of crisis. First, the rising tide of crime and disorder demonstrated that police strategies were not successful. Second, the accusation of police misconduct, especially during the early days of the civil rights struggle, coupled with the public's perception that the police were ineffective in combating crime, eroded a great deal of citizen confidence in the police. Finally, police management came under added stress when rank and file officers sought better working conditions through unionization (Walker 1983; Kelling 1988).

As a consequence of all this, progressive police leadership began to pay attention to the results of the research and experimentation of the 1970s. These findings present a strong argument that the basic strategies of "reform policing" are simply inadequate for contemporary society. Recognizing this fact,

> thinking police professionals have had to develop some new ideas. The key reformulation has been that police and the communities they are policing must try to become co-producers of crime prevention. Roughly speaking, this concept of co-production, of increased cooperation between police and the community, is what has taken hold as "Community Policing" (Skolnick and Bayley 1988a, 3).

Moore and Trojanowicz (1988, 9) give a basic description of community policing:

> In community policing, community institutions such as families, schools, neighborhood associations, and merchant groups are seen as key partners to the police in the creation of safe, secure communities. The success of the police depends not only on the development of their own skills and capabilities. Community policing acknowledges that police cannot succeed in achieving their basic goals without both the operational assistance and political support of the community. . . . Police agencies pursuing the strategy of community policing must become more open to community definitions and priorities of problems to be solved. . . . In community policing the community's views . . . about what constitutes a serious problem count. So do their views about what would be an appropriate police response.

In their transnational study of community policing, Skolnick and Bayley (1988b, 3) found that community policing programs are operating all around the globe. They also point to the fact that

> the oldest and best established community policing system in the world is the Japanese . . . who forged their system immediately after World War II out of a combination of traditional culture and American democratic ideals. Japanese policing has all the elements of community policing.

There have been a variety of programs bearing the label "community policing," but four elements appear to be at the core of this policing strategy: (1) community-based crime prevention, (2) reorientation of patrol activities to emphasize nonemergency servicing, (3) increased accountability to the public, and (4) decentralization of command (Skolnick and Bayley 1988a).

If community policing begins with community-based crime prevention, the

Japanese experience offers several valuable insights. First, one of the basic reasons Japanese policing works as well as it does is because of the close relationships Japanese police have developed with the community. Because they deal daily in face-to-face fashion with the citizens they serve, they become known and re-spected—a part of the community rather than an alien intrusive force separated from the people by a screen of glass and steel. While the structure of most U.S. cities would prohibit the use of the Japanese *koban* (police box), communities such as Detroit and Santa Ana, California, have introduced minipolice stations with success (Skolnick and Bayley 1988b). Foot or bicycle patrol could be used in many neighborhoods. The foot patrol experiments in Newark, New Jersey, and Flint, Michigan, have shown that communities in the U.S. would welcome this sort of police presence (Kelling 1981; Trojanowicz 1980).

Second, the Japanese neighborhood crime prevention associations provide a model for U.S. neighborhoods. Granted that while the Japanese tradition of the *gonin-gumi* has given Japanese culture a somewhat different idea of public participation, it may be possible for U.S. communities to organize neighborhood groups to work with local police in developing crime prevention programs. Pro-grams such as Neighborhood Watch (Rosenbaum, Lewis, and Grant 1985; Rosen-baum 1986, 1988) are a step in that direction.

However, we would argue that attempts to organize neighborhood groups to work with police will succeed only if and when police are willing to share power with the local community. If community policing gives the community only an affirming role, if it does not allow the community significant participation in establishing policing priorities and programs, it will not succeed. The key to community policing is that police and community become "co-producers" of a secure community (Kelling, Wasserman, and Williams 1988; Moore and Trojano-wicz 1988b).

Third, if community-based crime prevention is to occur, police will have to expand their perception of the police role to make the prevention of crime equal in importance to the law enforcement component. While much of what police do is directed to prevention—indeed the patrol strategy was directed to prevention—police in the U.S. have been better known for their reaction to crime than for an explicit emphasis upon crime prevention. Most departments have made efforts to speak to various groups about crime prevention strategies, but few police de-partments have attempted to develop systematic programs aimed at preventing crime. Rosenbaum (1988, 371) reports that

> most law enforcement administrators continue to view these police activities as auxiliary and tangential to "real" police work; for this reason police crime prevention programs never have received the status or the resources needed to function adequately.

In fact, in some communities crime prevention programs seem to have been abandoned to private security agencies.

People in the United States can learn a great deal from Japan's complex program of crime prevention that relies upon the cooperation and support of the community. Japan's program may be successful because the lower crime rates in Japan allow its police to expend more time and energy on developing prevention programs. Further, we would acknowledge that the basic problems of crime in the United States will not be solved with locks and antiburglar devices. Nor are we so naive as to expect prevention programs to have immediate major effects upon crime. However, these programs provide a basic beginning to an effort that brings police and citizens together and could produce an understanding within the community that peace and order are the responsibility of all (Moore, Trojanowicz, and Kelling 1988).

The second major element in community policing is the reorientation of patrol activities to emphasize nonemergency servicing. While American police can learn a great deal from the Japanese police about this aspect of the police role, it must be remembered that over the years the Japanese police have developed a very different relationship to the community. Bayley (1976a) and Clifford (1976) both argue that Japanese citizen attitudes toward the police—illustrated by their willingness to participate in the crime prevention associations—are those of partners in the effort to maintain an orderly society. People in Japan do not have the same "we versus they" perceptions about the police that people in the United States have.

The consequence of this is that the Japanese appear to be far more willing than Americans to accept a police presence not as a threat to individual rights but as a legitimate force for order. This, of course, enables the police not only to penetrate the community but to promote relationships that allow them to offer a broad range of services.

Thus, Japanese police are much more than law enforcers. As we have seen, Japanese police place heavy emphasis upon order maintenance and crime prevention. This is not simply crime prevention in terms of locks and burglar bars. Rather, police activity reaches into many areas of life in an attempt to aid the community to resolve problems that could lead to disorder. Especially important in this regard are the counseling services that have become a part of every Japanese police station. Bayley (1976a, 87) reports that "all police stations assign an experienced older officer, usually a sergeant, to general counseling." Police counseling is sought for a broad range of problems—from family disputes to questions about contracts and indebtedness. Trained in dispute resolution, the police are able to provide a helpful, informal conciliation. Japanese police recognize that since they are

> the most pervasive government agency in society, advice from them can save people agonizing steps. In most cases police counselors simply refer people to appropriate non-police offices (Bayley 1976a, 87).

It is important to recognize that this broader concept of the police role can be filled because, first, the public does not see the police as an oppressive alien force and, second, the police in Japan see this service as an integral part of their role, in keeping with the Japanese tradition of conciliation. This is very different from the situation in the United States.

Because police management in the United States has emphasized rapid response to emergency calls as a basic tactic, it has encouraged patrol officers to keep free of anything that would delay that response. What this has meant is that police and community have been separate elements. Policing is perceived to be the business of the law enforcement professionals who dispense this service to a dependent public. Because police deal with citizens only in terms of complaints, they tend to develop a somewhat distorted view of the community. In turn, because citizens seldom, if ever, speak to police except in emergency situations or when they have been stopped for a traffic violation, citizens develop a distorted view of the police. When police come into a community, they do so as strangers who are suspect and feared (Bittner 1980).

Further, because the role of the police has been defined as law enforcement and the strategies used have been designed "to catch crooks," many policeofficers look on other forms of service as social work and not "real police work" (Kelling and Moore 1988). Obviously, police already spend a great deal of time in performing this kind of service, but many do so unwillingly or assign it a low priority. Before community policing can begin to become a reality in the United States, basic attitudes within both the police and the community need to change, and specific strategies to accomplish this will have to be developed (Sparrow 1988).

One such strategy is police education and training. VanMaanen's (1985b) study of police training noted that the American system, which stresses the technical aspects of law enforcement, encourages the perpetuation of the police subculture and its values through the use of untrained field training officers. The longer and more intensive training of the Japanese police, most importantly their use of a specially trained mentor as field training officer, provides a model that U.S. police departments could well emulate. Admittedly, any intensification of police training would be expensive. However, if community policing is to become a reality in U.S. society, police need to receive added training in the nontechnical aspects of the police role. These aspects might include training in race relations, various intervention techniques, ways of utilizing available community services, and methods of dispute resolution.

One step that could be taken with a minimum of expense would be the upgrading of the field training experience. Programs like the one adopted by the San Jose, California, Police Department are based on systematic training and evaluation techniques used by carefully recruited and trained field training officers. Each new recruit is provided with opportunities to experience the full range of police activities and is evaluated by a number of FTOs before he or she is promoted out of the probationary status (McCampbell 1986). The tactic of upgrading personnel by recruiting officers with collegiate education has also become widespread in recent years.

The third major element in community policing is increased accountability to the public. During the Reform Era of policing in the United States, efforts to remove police from the influence of local ward politicians led to the centralization of police authority. Power became vested in local police administrators who served at the pleasure of the mayor, insulated from the direct influence of ward bosses. Although this reduced police corruption, it created a situation in which police became effectively insulated from the influence or control of the people they served.

As we argued above, if police and community are to become co-producers of an orderly society, police must begin to share power with the community they service. They can begin to do this by developing relationships with community groups, clubs, churches, and civic organizations that could provide them with information, give insight to particular problems, help define priorities, and aid in planning effective strategies (Kelling, Wassermann, and Williams 1988).

However, if that is to be done, the fourth major element in community policing must be developed: decentralization of command. Kelling and Moore (1988) make a convincing case for having operational and tactical decisions made at lower levels. By creating neighborhood police centers or beat offices and by giving officers at that level greater discretion to develop responses to community problems, the community can be more effectively enlisted in the task of maintaining order. If citizens see an immediate and specific police response to their problems or complaints, they are more likely to cooperate with the police.

This has been one of the strengths of the Japanese police system. As Clifford (1976, 79) has observed, while the Japanese police are "a very powerful and well-integrated national body," there is a "decentralization of the police with some local lay control of local policing." The National Police Agency allows tactical decisions to be made at the local level.

One of the important features of this decentralized control is increased participation by the rank and file in the decision-making process. As Kelling and Moore (1988, 11) note about participative management in policing:

> Chiefs have discovered that programs are easier to conceive and implement if officers themselves are involved in their development through task forces . . . and other organizational innovations that tap the wisdom and experience of sergeants and patrol officers.

In a previous chapter we noted that patrol officers in Japan are under even closer supervision than are rank and file in the United States. Yet the *kobun–oyabun* relationship between the Japanese patrolman and his superior allows the patrolman a good deal of input into decisions about local problems. The Japanese style of management, which emphasizes consensus, provides opportunity for subordinates to participate in the managerial process. American industrialists have borrowed management techniques, such as the "quality circle," in production organizations. The U.S. police might well review these techniques as ways to tap the hard-earned expertise and "street-smarts" of lower echelon officers. Additionally, there is reason to believe that reforms imposed from without are frequently circumvented by criminal justice professionals. Walker (1989, 44) documents the courtroom work group's ability to "evade, absorb, or blunt reform." The same resistance may be experienced in police reform that does not involve the line officer in its formulation.

To make these kinds of changes in policing involves much more than simply adopting a change in tactics or organizational structure. It requires the adoption of an entire strategy on the part of both the police and the community. The question, of course, is whether the police and the public are willing to commit themselves to such changes, given the core values of U.S. society. Skolnick and Bayley's (1988a) survey of community policing in sixteen nations around the world provides us with some degree of hope. Their report indicates that community policing is more than a buzzword. In places like Australia, Canada, Great Britain, and Singapore, elements of community policing have been adopted effectively.

It should also be recognized that the sort of change we are talking about here "is a change in the practices but not in the objectives of policing" (Skolnick and Bayley 1988a, 90). Police from the earliest days of institutionalized policing have been concerned with helping the community achieve and maintain a safe and orderly environment. We in no way mean to slight or deprecate their efforts. Community policing represents a theoretical and philosophical perspective which argues that, for police to be effective in contemporary society, they need to enlist the support and counsel of the communities they are sworn to protect. Japanese policing, the exemplar of community policing, provides us with evidence of its effectiveness.

Alternative Dispute Resolution

A third area in which the United States might learn from Japan is the use of alternative procedures in the adjudication process. There are a number of things that could be examined in this area, but we wish to focus on those that fit the general description of alternative dispute resolution (ADR).

Review of the materials on adjudication practices suggests that the justice system in the United States has been strongly influenced by the recent rise in the rates of drug-related crime and the subsequent volume of work that has fallen upon the courts. Any comparison between the Japanese and American adjudication systems must begin with the realization that the American court system is swamped with both civil and criminal litigation. This is one of the most serious problems confronting the justice system in the U.S. today. There is some debate about the impact of the increasing number of cases that are being filed in both the civil and criminal courts (Daniels 1984, 1985; Sarat 1985; Galanter 1983), but the fact is that cases pending trial in courts at federal, state, and local levels have increased steadily in recent years (Marvell 1985, 1987; Neubauer 1986; Flango and Ito 1984). Comprehensive data on adjudication at the level of the state courts are difficult to obtain. By far the most accurate court data we have come from the federal court system. However, the U.S. district court data on criminal cases deal only with violations of federal criminal law, which are, of course, only a fraction of the crimes committed in the United States, but these data do give us some idea of the court overcrowding problem.

Although the number of authorized judgeships in U.S. district courts increased 11.4 percent (from 516 to 575) between 1981 and 1987, the number of criminal cases filed increased from 30,681 to 43,261, or 41 percent. However, despite the addition of nearly sixty judges, the number of cases pending before the courts increased from 15,866 to 24,458, for an increase of 54 percent over the 1981 level (Flanagan and Jamieson 1989, 531–532). The rate of overcrowding at the state level may be assumed to be as great or greater. Wise (1989) reports that during 1988 the New York state courts' list of criminal cases awaiting trial increased by 33 percent.

There are at least two major reasons for this overcrowding in the courts. First, concern over drug-related and predatory street crime has resulted in a "get tough" approach on the part of law enforcement that has produced a sharp increase in the number of arrests. For example, the New York City Office of Criminal Justice Coordination has recently predicted that the city's "Buy and Bust" drug control operation would "increase criminal case loads by 21,000 a year" (*New York Law Journal* 1988, 1). This appears to be duplicated in the federal court system. Between 1980 and 1987, the U.S. district courts experienced a 153.2 percent increase in the number of prosecutions for drug offenses. The 17,729 prosecutions for drug offenses in 1987 accounted for 30.6 percent of all criminal cases tried in U.S. district courts during that year (Hester and Kaplan 1989).

The second major reason for overcrowding in the courts is the steady increase in the number of civil suits being filed. As Marvell (1987) points out, steady growth in civil caseloads has led to nearly a 45 percent increase between 1976 and 1986. This increase in civil litigation impacts on the criminal courts in that the increasing demand of the civil caseload impinges on the number of courts and judges that can be used for criminal trials.

Overcrowded courts impact negatively on the justice process in a number of ways. If it is true that "justice delayed is justice denied," then the increasingly long delays between arrest or arraignment and trial creates a system of injustice. This is especially true for indigent arrestees who are unable to arrange bail and who may spend months, if not years, awaiting trial (*Los Angeles Daily News* 1988). This situation also leads to the severe overcrowding of the county jails that house prisoners awaiting trial (Kline 1988). Because both state and federal courts have ruled that excessive overcrowding constitutes a violation of civil rights, many jurisdictions are forced to release pretrial detainees. A similar situation exists in some state prison systems. Walker (1989, 80) reports that "seventeen states have emergency release laws that place a cap on prison populations and mandate release of some current inmates before new ones can be admitted."

As a result, many offenders appear to spend little or no time in jail, and this failure to provide the sanctions demanded by the law brings the law and the system of justice into disrespect. The classical theorist Beccaria (1963 [1764]) argued that punishment would deter crime if it was swift, certain, and appropriate. Today's overcrowded courts and penal system fail to provide criminal sanctions that will deter crime.

There are a number of ways in which this problem might be resolved. The nation could increase the total number of courts and judges and thus be able to process larger numbers of criminal defendants. This solution would not, of course, resolve all of the issues of overcrowding in the jails and prisons, and it would be an exceedingly costly procedure. The process could also be speeded up if court administration practices could be modified to become a more assembly-line process—perhaps by sharply restricting continuances and discovery procedures. This might, however, impinge on civil rights. Another response might be to simply stop arresting so many offenders. We have already discussed the implications of decriminalization. A fourth option to resolve the problem of overcrowding in the courts might be through the use of alternative dispute resolution (ADR).

The use of ADR could help to reduce court overcrowding in two ways. First, if the ADR mechanisms were used in a significant number of civil cases, courtrooms and judges now dedicated to civil litigation could be freed to work on the backlog of criminal cases. Second, the use of ADR for most of the minor, less serious criminal cases would prevent them from ever coming before the court.

Japan's courts are not immune to overcrowding (Haley 1978). Japanese courts have incredibly high caseloads because Japan has chosen to place statutory limitations on the number of prosecutors and judges in its system. However, even if Japan's courts are overcrowded, the system is able to operate successfully because the Japanese have a long history of avoiding litigation through the use of informal conciliation and the mediated settlement of disputes. As we pointed out in our discussion of adjudication in Japan, the time-honored tradition of *jidan,* as well as the more recent innovations of *Chotei* and *wakai,* have allowed the Japanese to develop a range of organized yet informal alternatives to litigation. Important in this is that the cultural values of harmony, hierarchy, and social order have encouraged these people to seek out and use nonjudicial and informal ways to settle differences. Because they see judicial litigation as disruptive of social harmony and threatening to the group, the Japanese have come to prefer nonjudicial means of resolving disputes. Further, their acceptance of subjective approaches to the law enables them to seek justice without the use of the adversarial approach that people in the United States seem to think is essential to the process.

To be sure, conciliation and mediation in informal settings have always been present in American society. Ministers, doctors, police, and community leaders have helped settle countless numbers of disputes and disagreements. However, these unorganized and informal efforts simply do not begin to deal adequately with either the rapid growth of civil litigation in the United States or the number of criminal cases that have flooded the courts. Even the extensive use of plea bargaining, which can be conceived of as a form of dispute resolution, has not eliminated the problem of overcrowding in the criminal courts.

Perhaps one of the major reasons for this is that Americans are simply not socialized to seek out alternative means of resolving disputes. For Americans, justice is somehow equated with legal procedure. Because of our objective approach to law, Americans seem to believe that justice is done only when the courts and legal channels are called into play. The ideal of the adversarial approach leads us to believe that somehow justice cannot be accomplished apart from trial and open confrontation. Our belief in civil rights and our experience in using the courts to secure those rights reinforces the belief that the only way to secure justice is to use judicial litigation (Jacob 1984).

In recent years, however, fueled by the rise in both civil and criminal litigation, the inability of the courts to provide speedy response, and the increasing expense involved, there has been an increasing interest in the development of ADR as a necessary option for the American court system. For example, McGillis (1986) reports that between 1975 and 1985 community dispute resolution centers were established in over 180 U.S. cities. These programs, which take a variety of different forms and formats, provide an alternative to normal court procedures. Most deal with minor civil or criminal matters by using techniques such as conciliation, arbitration, and mediation without the use of a judge. To train attorneys in these techniques, "at least 130 law schools now have course work in non-litigation dispute resolution processes such as negotiation, mediation, and arbitration" (Lowry 1987, 771).

The ADR programs appear to reach toward four basic goals: (1) to relieve congestion in the courts, as well as to reduce costs and delays, (2) to increase the community's involvement in the dispute resolution process, (3) to make justice more immediate and accessible, and (4) to provide more effective dispute resolution (Sander 1982). Developed and sponsored by both private and public agencies, ADR programs appear to be motivated by the desire to provide more humanitarian approaches, as well as to increase the efficiency of the system (McGillis 1986).

While there are many who place a great deal of confidence in ADR (Lambros 1987; Kahn 1987; Christian 1986), there are others who do not see these programs as a great legal panacea. Edwards (1986, 677) raises the fear that "ADR will replace the rule of law with non-legal value" and end up providing second-class justice. Murray (1987, 782) points out that the success of ADR will depend on whether or not lawyers will accept and make use of these programs in their practices:

> Lawyers are America's professional dispute resolvers. Our culture sends people directly to lawyers first for help in resolving what these people regard as serious disputes or problems. . . . The processes that lawyers accept and use are the ones that are legitimate. Therefore lawyers' standards for acceptance and use become a limit to the success of the ADR movement.

Other critics point out that while the programs have been successful in some areas, there is no strong evidence that ADR programs have freed up court dockets or sharply reduced costs. However, as McGillis (1986, 14) points out:

> The American people are not eagerly beating a path to the program's doors, although this may be more due to Americans' focus on court dispute settlement (as idealized on Perry Mason) than due to anything fundamentally wrong with dispute resolution programs.

The failure to significantly affect caseloads and costs may well be due to the fact that few Americans outside the legal community know about these programs and are unaware of the benefits they offer. We would argue that as long as the ADR movement in the United States remains largely unorganized, with no central agency to provide for promotion and support, ADR will continue to be a relatively ineffective alternative to litigation. One reason for this is that without some central organizing force to educate people about the informal dispute resolution process, people will simply remain unaware of its potential or its availability. Second, without some organizational foundation to provide legitimation, informal means of settling disputes will not be accepted or trusted by the U.S. public. It is not so much the informality of the process that the public distrusts, it is the lack of some legitimating organizational relationship between ADR programs and the justice system. If federal- and state-level authorities, working within the local communities, could provide the resources for community dispute resolution centers and encourage their use with financial incentives, the ADR movement might well become an accepted part of the justice system.

One of the major keys to the ADR approach is the enlistment and utilization of the local community. For example, in an ADR program entitled "Victim Offender Reconciliation Program" (VORP), trained volunteers from the local community serve as mediators between victims and offenders. This program tries to provide an opportunity for victims to confront those who have victimized them and to bring about both restitution and reconciliation. While these programs have been used primarily in cases of less serious crime, they offer promise of extrajudicial ways of allowing the victims of crime to see justice done and at the same time serve as means of pretrial diversion to keep many offenders from incarceration (Umbreit 1985a). The use of trained community volunteers in an organized and court-related format provides needed legitimation that makes this sort of program acceptable.

This same purpose is served in Japan with the use of the summary trial. Although Japan has not used plea bargaining in its adjudication process, it has made extensive use of the summary trial to bring speedy resolution to minor criminal cases. In these summary procedures, persons who have pled guilty to minor offenses or to offenses involving limited damages or punishment agree to have their case heard by a judge *in camera* in the absence of a prosecutor, defense attorney, or complainant. Evidence is submitted to the court, and the judge rules on guilt or innocence. In most cases punishment consists of restitution in the form of some payment made to the victim, a fine, or some form of community service (Araki 1985).

We would argue that similar programs could be developed in American courts. Indeed, in some jurisdictions summary jury trials have been used with good effect (Riskin 1985; Wilkinson 1987). In many communities where judges have been willing to explore the potential of these new approaches to the problem of justice, citizens have given strong approval (Umbreit 1985b). The core value of pragmatism, so strong in the development of the United States, supports programs of this sort when they are shown to provide justice that is both swift and inexpensive and that protects the civil rights of the participants. As we have suggested, however, the effective implementation of ADR in the United States will probably require that these programs be institutionalized into the justice system, even though the processes involved would ideally operate in an informal fashion.

Sentencing and Corrections

One decisive difference in sentencing and corrections in Japan and the United States is the incredible difference in the scale of the crime problem in the two societies. This difference is accentuated in the case of violent crime—the type of crime that most taxes sentencing and correctional strategies and resources. Violent crime in the United States is almost thirty times greater than in Japan. Consequently, the size of the correctional enterprise in the United States is substantially larger than in Japan. Current figures indicate that there are close to one million persons incarcerated in U.S. jails and prisons, whereas Japan's incarceration facilities house fewer than 60,000 inmates (Greenfeld 1989; Hester 1988; Ministry of Justice 1988). Because of this great difference in scale, it is difficult to compare the two systems and even more difficult to suggest which policies and programs might be adopted from one system to the other. As mentioned earlier in this chapter, the consideration of which policies and programs might be appropriated is made even more complex when differences in cultural values become part of the consideration. Some of the sentencing and correctional practices of Japanese authorities simply could not be used in the United States. The very size and complexity of the offender population, together with incompatible cultural values, would preclude their use. For example, the practice of providing an extensive vocational training and employment program in Japanese prisons would probably prove far too costly in the American context. Furthermore, because Japan's prisoner population is so small, business and industry do not seem to fear the competition of prison industries as do their counterparts in the U.S., nor does prison industry seem to violate the goal of a free marketplace that is so emphasized in the United States.

Another major hindrance to the adoption of Japanese sentencing and correctional methods is the decentralized and fragmented structure of criminal justice in the United States. The centralized structure of Japanese criminal justice has led to great clarity of purpose and consistency of practice in sentencing and corrections. This is clearly evident in Japan's system or recruiting and training judges and correctional personnel. Not only is the caliber of court and correctional employees high, but extensive training programs, operated by national agencies, generate clear and consistent goals and practices in both sentencing and corrections.

In contrast, the goals and practices of sentencing and corrections in the United States are diverse, ever-changing, and rarely applied consistently or completely. While the crime control model has come to dominate the U.S. justice system in recent years, the implementation of this model in sentencing and correctional practice has never met the tenets of classical thought upon which it is based. Beccaria (1963 [1764]) argued that penal sanctions will deter crime when they are swift, certain, and severe in their execution. Sanctions in the U.S. context are seldom either certain or swift, and all too often they vary from not at all severe to far too severe.

Part of the problem derives from the great variance in sentencing practices brought about by the diversity of the courts in the state and federal system and the way in which the system selects and employs judges. Because judges have no common training in judicial practice and because the United States has no firm national policy on criminal sanctioning, sentencing has often varied widely from one jurisdiction to the next (Inciardi 1990; Forst 1982).

The problem of certainty in criminal sanctions in the United States is confounded by adjudication practices in which very few cases actually go to trial. Extensive prosecutorial discretion and the widespread use of plea bargaining produce a system of justice which is heavily negotiated (Walker 1989). While Japan's justice system also makes limited use of criminal trials, plea bargaining is illegal and as a result, prosecutorial discretion rarely involves "striking a deal." Such a negotiated process of justice in American courts undermines a sense of certainty.

Penal sanctions in American courts are also seldom swift in their execution. Once again, overcrowded courts, along with the emphasis placed upon the civil rights of the accused, lead to lengthy delays between arrest and resolution of the criminal charges (Mahoney, Sipes, and Ito 1985; Church et al. 1978).*

Finally, penal sanctions in the United States appear to be based increasingly

---

*Delays in courts are often attributed to overworked judges and understaffed courts. Yet as Cole (1989, 427) notes, the informal legal culture is especially important: "The participants [of the courts] become adapted to a certain pace of litigation, and these expectations are translated into others in regard to the way cases should proceed. What is viewed as the normal speed for the disposition of criminal cases in one system may be viewed as undue haste in another."

upon incarceration. While American courts make frequent use of fines for minor offenses (Hillsman, Sichel, and Mahoney 1984; Hillsman et al. 1987), both the tendency to use incarceration for serious offenses and the length of sentence imposed have increased in recent years (Greenfeld 1989, 6; Jamieson and Flanagan 1989, 550). Part of this change in sentencing practice may be due to the influence of public opinion upon the courts, when public outcries caused by the fear of predatory crime have led to more punitive sentencing practices (Jamieson and Flanagan 1989). The outcome of this change has been serious overcrowding in U.S. prisons, where offenders are being released early and a majority of states operate prisons under conditions which appellate courts have ruled to be "cruel and unusual punishment" (Zawitz 1988; Schlesinger 1987).

Sentencing and corrections in Japan appear to be guided by a philosophy that reflects an appreciation for the classical approach, yet one that is tempered by Japanese cultural values. The practice of sentencing and corrections in Japan is based upon the dual purposes of retribution and rehabilitation. Our study of sentencing and corrections in Japan indicates that the Japanese focus on both certainty and selective severity in a cultural context that produces justice more certainly than does the American system. The element of certainty in the Japanese system begins with the fact that Japanese police have a much higher rate of clearing crimes than do their U.S. counterparts. For example, while U.S. police cleared 17.5 percent of all larceny cases in 1986, Japanese police cleared 58.7 percent (Jamieson and Flanagan 1989; Ministry of Justice 1988). Comparison of the Uniform Crime Report and the National Crime Survey in the United States suggests that only about one-third of all the crimes committed are reported to the police (Zawitz 1988, 34). Although we have no comparable figure for the Japanese, a 1974 study conducted by the National Police Agency indicates that the amount of unreported crime in Japan is much smaller than in the United States (Ames 1981). In Japan, criminal offenses are more likely to be reported, and offenders are more likely to be apprehended.

Once arrested, police, prosecutors, and judges in Japan exercise an unparalleled amount of discretion: *Bizai-shobun* (police discretion in referring cases to the prosecutor), nonprosecution, suspension of prosecution, summary court procedures, modified public trials, and intensive use of suspended sentences (Araki 1985). Previous chapters have depicted such discretion as being clearly based in the goal of rehabilitation yet rehabilitation that is decisively Japanese. This goal of rehabilitation is readily mobilized for offenders who admit guilt, express remorse, and are willing to make restitution. In this way the goal of retribution yields to values of group-relatedness and benevolent authority. Thus, rehabilitation, as it is practiced in Japan, focuses on restoring the offender to the community through a process of resocialization. In the Japanese cultural context, discretion fosters a system of individualized and subjective justice, yet one that produces a high level of certainty that offenders will be dealt with in an appropriate fashion.

The Japanese system appears to be more lenient in its sentencing policy, yet review of the data indicates it is actually severe in its treatment of violent offenders, especially repeat offenders. Recidivists are given longer sentences and serve longer periods of time than nonviolent nonrecidivists. The classical notion of severity appears to be selectively applied (Ministry of Justice 1989).

Despite these differences in philosophy, there are some elements of the Japanese system of sentencing and corrections that might translate well to the American situation. Certainly one of those elements is Japan's more limited use of prisons as a sanctioning device. As we noted in the chapters on adjudication and corrections, Japanese judges tend to send a far smaller proportion of its criminal population to prison. A large number of criminal cases are suspended without prosecution, and many convicted offenders are given suspended sentences. As a result, the largest segment of the Japanese prison population appears to be offenders with records of serious crime (Ministry of Justice 1988).

Perhaps judicial and correctional authorities in the United States might seriously consider how the Japanese use incarceration. Norval Morris and Michael Tonry (1990a, 1990b) have cogently argued that current sentencing policy in the United States operates at the extreme ends of a continuum of penal sanctions: At one end many offenders are released with little or no sanctions being employed; at the other end many are needlessly incarcerated for long periods of time:

> At present, too many criminals are in prison and too few are the subject of enforced controls in the community. We are both too lenient and too severe; too lenient with many on probation who should be subject to tighter controls in the community, and too severe with many in prison and jail who present no serious threat to community safety if they were under control in the community (Morris and Tonry 1990b, 3).

They go on to argue for the development of a rational sentencing system that makes more extensive use of " 'intermediate punishments'—intensive probation, substantial fines, community service orders, residential controls, treatment orders" (Morris and Tonry 1990b, 4).

To be sure, these programs are being used in many communities at the present time, but the amount of consideration and resources devoted to developing and implementing nonincarcerative forms of punishment is minimal (Morris 1987). For example, Morris (1987) argues that U.S. courts have not extended the use of fines to a broad range of offense applications as have a number of other countries. While they are not a panacea, sentences of nonincarceration provide alternative forms of sanctioning and offer a means of keeping the offender in the community. One of the major themes we have seen in the corrections philosophy of Japan is that of helping the offender become reintegrated into the community. Since the inception of the penitentiary in the United States, a recurrent concern has been the great difficulty incarcerated offenders have in returning to the community. Programs that focus on the middle range of criminal sanctions offer promise of making that return to the community unnecessary.

Two factors are important in making more extensive use of midrange sentencing and correctional options. First, we recognize that some offenders—even first offenders—need to be incarcerated for the well-being of society. We also recognize that it is extremely difficult to predict future criminal behavior (Walker 1989). Nevertheless, perhaps the American justice system could emulate the Japanese system in directing the use of incarceration for violent, repeat offenders. While Peter Greenwood (1982) and others have already advocated far more extensive use of "selective incapacitation," the Japanese practice of incarceration points clearly to the need for a focused incarceration policy in the United States. Granted, the fragmented nature of corrections in the U.S. would make this difficult, but the prevalence of overcrowding in U.S. jail and prison facilities requires a more logical and consistent use of incarceration resources (Zedlewski 1987). At the same time, such focused use of incarceration would allow less serious offenders to receive their just deserts in the local community.

This last comment leads directly to a second factor. If corrections are to become community-based, then our system needs to get community members involved. While the use of volunteers in corrections is certainly not new in the United States, the extensive use of volunteers—to the degree that correctional volunteers are incorporated into Japan's correctional programs—has not been adequately considered. Nevertheless, Japan's heavy use of volunteers as probation officers and in various community-based rehabilitation hostels provides us with working models of how individuals and groups can become involved in corrections.

One other lesson we can learn from Japan lies in the area of correctional administration and personnel. In Japan, correctional employees are carefully recruited and extensively trained. Because correctional personnel are employees of the national government, they are people with some status in the community, and their salaries and benefits reflect that status.

By contrast, corrections personnel in the U.S. are often perceived as having very low-status jobs. There is little prestige in being a guard at a state prison, and there is even less in being an officer at a county jail. Few of our correctional systems offer extensive training, and salaries and benefits—especially at the entry level—tend to discourage better-educated and more-talented applicants.

We recognize that any attempt to introduce changes in these areas will be incredibly difficult. The size of America's correctional systems has reached such proportions that even minor changes face major obstacles. Certainly recent legislation in the "war on drugs," with its premise that the United States must build yet more prisons, only exacerbates the problem.

The primary lessons that Japan holds out for corrections in the U.S. are its emphasis upon the community and its strong belief that its primary purpose is to resocialize offenders so they return to the community, family, and work groups.

CONCLUSION

We have argued consistently throughout this book that Japan and the United States represent two fundamentally different cultural systems and that, in terms of criminal justice practice, what works in one system will not necessarily work in the other. We have argued that the history, tradition, and population of each society have produced core cultural values that strongly influence both criminal behavior and the nation's response to crime. If we wish to adopt strategies and techniques from the Japanese, these adoptions must reflect American values or be adaptable to them.

In our review of what we might adopt from Japan, a common theme appears to emerge: community participation and responsibility. Our review has suggested that one of the most salient things we can learn from the Japanese experience is the need to allow the community to help define and respond to the problems of crime and order. In this vein we have argued that the community should be encouraged to take on a larger responsibility in establishing informal controls and social order. Not all communities and neighborhoods are alike. Given some basic guidelines, each community, working with representative groups, could define, within the parameters of the law, its own definition of orderly behavior.

Our review of policing points clearly to the need for developing a coalition between the police and the community so that they become co-producers of an orderly society. By developing cooperative relationships between police and the neighborhoods they serve, the quality of police service could be greatly enhanced. But this can occur only when the police are willing to enlist neighborhood participation both in the establishment of policing priorities and in the order-maintenance function.

Our examination of the adjudication process in the United States points to a legal system in which the process of attaining justice has been delegated to the courts and the legal professionals. Once again, we would argue that the community can and should develop organized but informal structures that allow for individual participation. The development of community dispute resolution centers that provide a variety of ADR mechanisms is not an impossible dream, nor is it a response that contradicts the values of individual freedom and human rights.

Our overburdened system of corrections would also benefit from community participation. While the United States does not have the same record of volunteer participation in corrections as Japan, public involvement in a wide range of programs is certainly consistent with our concept of participatory democracy. By increasing the use of volunteers in the probation process, establishing community service restitution programs, and developing preincarceration halfway centers within the local community, we might be able to reduce our prison population. If nothing else, we would be able to restore a great many persons to the community and perhaps lower recidivism rates.

We would argue that this kind of community focus in criminal justice is in harmony with the core values of American culture. The United States boasts that it is a bastion of participatory democracy—that we are a people whose freedom and rights are best preserved when they are exercised in the democratic process. That process is certainly enhanced when members of the community begin to work with one another to achieve the basic goals of a free and orderly society.

Will all of this stop crime in U.S. society? It is our firm belief that as long as economic inequality and social and racial injustice exist, crime will continue to be a major problem. But while crime will never be eradicated, it can be significantly reduced.

Perhaps even more important, programs and processes that we have discussed would help build a community of shared values and beliefs that would create a climate in which informal means of social control might make formal controls more effective.

Japan and the United States are in many ways remarkably alike. They are modern, industrial, literate, technologically oriented societies. Yet, as we've seen, they are very different nations and peoples, with very different histories and cultures. These differences have produced great dissimilarity in crime and justice in the two societies.

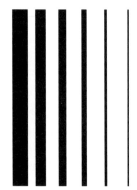

BIBLIOGRAPHY

Abadinsky, Howard. *Probation and Parole: Theory and Practice.* 3rd ed. Englewood Cliffs, NJ: Prentice-Hall, 1987.

———. *Law and Justice: An Introduction.* Chicago: Nelson-Hall, 1988.

Abe, H. "Criminal Justice in Japan: Its Historical Background and Modern Problems." *American Bar Association Journal* 47 (1961): 555–559.

———. "Education of the Legal Profession in Japan." In *The Japanese Legal System,* edited by Hideo Tanaka, pp. 566–581. Tokyo: The University of Tokyo Press, 1976.

Abel, Richard L., ed. *The Politics of Informal Justice: Vol. 1, The American Experience.* New York: Academic Press, 1982.

Abraham, Henry J. *The Judicial Process: An Introductory Analysis of the Courts of the United States, England, and France.* 5th ed. New York: Oxford Press, 1986.

Adler, Freda. *Nations Not Obsessed with Crime.* Littleton, CO: Fred B. Rothman, 1983.

Alderson, John C. "Hong Kong, Tokyo, Peking: Three Police Systems Observed." *Police Studies* 3 (1981): 3–13.

Allen, Francis A. "Legal Values and the Rehabilitative Ideal." *Journal of Criminal Law, Criminology, and Police Science* 50 (1959): 226–232.

———. *The Borderland of Criminal Justice.* Chicago: University of Chicago Press, 1964.

Allen, Harry E., Eskridge, Chris W., Latessa, Edward J., and Vito, Gennaro F. *Probation and Parole in America.* New York: The Free Press, 1985.

Allen, Harry E., and Simonsen, Clifford E. *Corrections in America: An Introduction.* 5th ed. New York: Macmillan, 1989.

Allen, Joan V. "The Japanese Judicial System." *San Fernando Valley Law Review* 12 (1984): 1–10.

Allen-Bond, Marc. "Policing Japan." *Law and Order* 32 (1984): 46–52.

Almond, Brenda, and Wilson, Bryan, eds. *Values: A Symposium.* Atlantic Highlands, NJ: Humanities Press, 1988.

Alpert, Geoffrey P., and Dunham, Roger P. *Policing Urban America.* Prospect Heights, IL: Waveland Press, 1988.

American Correctional Association. *Vital Statistics in Corrections.* College Park, MD: American Correctional Association, 1986.

———. *Directory.* College Park, MD: American Correctional Association, 1988.

American Friends Service Committee. *Struggle for Justice.* New York: Hill and Wang, 1971.

Ames, Walter L. "Police and Community in Japan." Ph.D. diss., University of Michigan, 1976.

———. "The Japanese Police: A General Survey." *Police Studies* 2 (1979a): 6–10.

———. "The Japanese Police: On the Beat." In *Current Studies in Japanese Law,* edited by Gary Whitmore, pp. 43–63. Ann Arbor: University of Michigan Press, 1979b.

———. *Police and Community in Japan.* Berkeley: University of California Press, 1981.

Anesaki, Masaharu. *History of Japanese Religion.* Rutland, VT: Charles E. Tuttle, 1963.

Angell, John E. "Toward an Alternative to the Classic Police Organizational Arrangements." In *Managing the Police Organization,* edited by Larry K. Gaines and Truett A. Rick, pp. 103–119. St. Paul, MN: West, 1977.

Araki, Nobuyoshi. "The Flow of Cases in the Japanese Criminal Justice System." *Crime and Delinquency* 31 (1985): 601–629.

———. "The Role of Police in Japanese Society." *Law and Society Review* 22 (1988): 1033–1036.

Archambeault, William G. "Management Theory Z: Implications for Correctional Survival Management." *Federal Probation* 46 (1982a): 7–11.

———. "Management Theory Z: Implication for Managing the Labor Intensive Nature of Work in Prison." *The Prison Journal* 62 (1982b): 58–67.

Archambeault, William G., and Fenwick, Charles R. "A Comparative Analysis of Japanese and American Police Organizational Management Models: The Evolution of a Military Bureaucracy to a Theory Z Organization." *Police Studies* 6 (1983): 3–12.

———. "Differential Effects of Police Organizational Management in Cultural Context: Comparative Analysis of South Korean, Japanese, and American Law Enforcement." *Police Studies* 8 (1985): 1–12.

———. "A Comparative Analysis of Culture, Safety, and Organizational Management Factors in Japanese Prisons." *The Prison Journal* 68 (1988): 3–23.

Archer, Dane, and Gartner, Rosemary. "Violent Acts and Violent Times: A Comparative Approach to Postwar Homicide Rates." *American Sociological Review* 41 (1976): 937–963.

———. "Homicide in 110 Nations: The Development of the Comparative Crime Data File." In *Readings in Comparative Criminology,* edited by Louise I. Shelley, pp. 78–99. Carbondale: Southern Illinois University Press, 1981.

———. *Violence and Crime in Cross-National Perspective.* New Haven, CT: Yale University Press, 1984.

Asakura, Kyoichi, Tenbashi, Hideo, and Okabe, Shunroku. "A Study on Rehabilitation Activities in Prison Facilities—Japan." In *International*

Summaries, Vol. 2, translated by Michael McCaskey, pp. 59–64. National Criminal Justice Reference Service. Washington, DC: USGPO, 1978.

Avison, William R., and Loring, Pamela L. "Population Diversity and Cross-National Homicide." *Criminology* 24 (1986): 733–749.

Balch, Robert W. "The Police Personality: Fact or Fiction? *The Journal of Criminal Law, Criminology, and Police Science* 63 (1972): 106–119.

Banton, Michael. "The Social Definition of the Police Officer's Role." In *The Sociology of Punishment and Correction,* edited by Norman Johnston, Leonard Savitz, and Marvin E. Wolfgang, pp. 17–25. New York: Wiley, 1970.

Barak-Glantz, Israel L. "Toward a Conceptual Schema of Prison Management Styles." *Prison Journal* 60 (1986): 42–60.

Bartollas, Clemens. *Introduction to Corrections.* New York: Harper & Row, 1981.

———. *Correctional Treatment: Theory and Practice.* Englewood Cliffs, NJ: Prentice-Hall, 1985.

Bayley, David H. *Forces of Order: Police Behavior in Japan and the United States.* Berkeley: University of California Press, 1976a.

———. "Learning About Crime: The Japanese Experience." *Public Interest* 44 (1976b): 55–68.

———. "Modes and Mores of Policing the Community in Japan." In *Law and Society: Culture Learning Through Law,* edited by Richard Vuylsteke. Honolulu, HA: East West Center, 1976c.

———. "Community Policing in Japan and Singapore." In *Community Policing: Proceedings 2–3,* edited by James Morgan, pp. 19–35. Canberra, Australia: Australian Institute of Criminology, 1984.

———. *Patterns of Policing: A Comparative International Analysis.* New Brunswick, NJ: Rutgers University Press, 1985.

Bayley, David H., and Mendelsohn, Harold. *Minorities and the Police.* New York: The Free Press, 1969.

Beasley, W. G. *The Modern History of Japan.* New York: Praeger, 1963.

Beccaria, Cesare. *On Crimes and Punishments.* 5th ed. Translated by Henry Paolucci. Indianapolis, IN: Bobbs-Merrill, 1764 (1963).

Beer, Lawrence Ward. *Freedom of Expression in Japan: A Study in Comparative Law, Politics, and Society.* Tokyo: Kodansha, 1984.

Befu, Harumi. *Japan: An Anthropological Introduction.* San Francisco: Chandler, 1971.

Bell, Daniel. "Crime as an American Way of Life." In *The End of Ideology,* edited by Daniel Bell, pp. 115–158. Glencoe, IL: The Free Press, 1960.

Bellah, Robert N. *Tokugawa Religion.* New York: The Free Press, 1957.

———. "Japan's Cultural Identity." *Journal of Asian Studies* 4 (1965): 573–578.

———. *Beyond Belief: Essays on Religion in a Post-Traditional World.* New York: Harper & Row, 1970.

———. "Continuity and Change in Japanese Society." In *Stability and Social Change,* edited by Bernard Barber and Alex Inkeles, pp. 377–404. Boston: Little, Brown, 1971.

———. *The Broken Covenant: American Civil Religion in Time of Trial.* New York: Seabury Press, 1975.

Bellah, Robert N., Madsen, Richard, Sullivan, William M., Swindler, Ann, and Tipton, Steven M. *Habits of the Heart.* Berkeley: University of California Press, 1985.

Bendansan, Isaiah. *The Japanese and the Jews,* translated by Richard L. Gage. Tokyo: Weatherhill, 1972.

Benedict, Ruth. *The Chrysanthemum and the Sword.* New York: Meridian, 1946.

Benjamin, R. W. "Images of Conflict Resolution and Social Control: American and Japanese Attitudes Toward the Adversary System." *Journal of Conflict Resolution* 19 (1975): 123–137.

Bennett, J. W., and Nagai, Michio. "Echoes: Reactions to American Anthropology—Japanese Critique of Benedict's 'Chrysanthemum and the Sword'." *American Anthropologist* 55 (1954): 404–411.

Bennett, Richard R., and Lynch, James P. "Does a Difference Make a Difference? Comparing Cross-National Crime Indicators." *Criminology* 28 (1990): 153–181.

Berezin, Eric Paul. "A Comparative Analysis of the U.S. and Japanese Juvenile Justice Systems." *Juvenile and Family Courts Journal* 33 (1982): 55–62.

Berger, Peter. *The Sacred Canopy.* Garden City, NY: Doubleday, 1967.

Berger, Peter, and Luckman, Thomas. *The Social Construction of Reality.* New York: Doubleday, 1967.

Birbeck, Christopher H. "Understanding Crime and Social Control Elsewhere: A Geographic Perspective on Theory in Criminology." *Research in Law, Deviance and Social Control* 7 (1985): 215–246.

Bittner, Egon. *The Functions of Police in Modern Society.* Cambridge, MA: Oleschlager, Gunn, and Hain, 1980.

———. "The Quasi-Military Organization of the Police." In *Managing the Police Organization,* edited by Larry K. Gaines and Truett A. Ricks, pp. 200–210. St. Paul, MN: West, 1977.

Black, Donald. *The Behavior of Law.* New York: Academic Press, 1976.

———. *The Manners and Customs of the Police.* New York: Academic Press, 1980.

———. "Crime as Social Control." *American Sociological Review* 48 (1983): 34–45.

Block, Richard, ed. *Victimization and Fear of Crime: World Perspectives.* U.S. Department of Justice, Bureau of Justice Statistics. Washington, DC: USGPO, 1984.

Blodgett, Nancy. "A Look at Today's Lawyer." *ABA Journal* 1 (1986): 47–52.

Blumberg, Abraham S., and Niederhoffer, Elaine, eds. *The Ambivalent Force.* 3rd ed. New York: Holt, Rinehart & Winston, 1985.

Bok, Derek. *Annual Report to the Board of Overseers.* Boston: Harvard University, 1983.

Boland, Barbara, Conly, Catherine H., Warner, Lynn, Sones, Ronald, and Martin, William. *The Prosecution of Felony Arrests, 1986.* U.S. Department of Justice, Bureau of Justice Statistics. Washington, DC: USGPO, 1989.

Boland, Barbara, and Forst, Brian. *The Prevalence of Guilty Pleas.* U.S.

Department of Justice, Bureau of Justice Statistics. Washington, DC: USGPO, 1984.

Boland, Barbara, Logan, Wayne, Sones, Ronald, and Martin, William. *The Prosecution of Felony Arrests, 1982*. U.S. Department of Justice, Bureau of Justice Statistics. Washington, DC: USGPO, 1988.

Boland, Barbara, and Sones, Ronald. *The Prosecution of Felony Arrests, 1981*. U.S. Department of Justice, Bureau of Justice Statistics. Washington, DC: USGPO, 1986.

Bolz, Herbert F. "Judicial Review in Japan: The Strategy of Restraint." *Hastings International and Comparative Law Review* 4 (1980): 87–142.

Bordua, David J. "Recent Trends: Deviant Behavior and Social Control." *Annals of the American Academy of Political and Social Science* 369 (1969): 149–163.

Bordua, David J., and Reiss, Albert J. "Command, Control, and Charisma: Reflections on Police Bureaucracy." In *Managing the Police Organization,* edited by Larry K. Gaines and Truett A. Ricks, pp. 211–222. St. Paul, MN: West, 1977.

Brosi, Kathleen B. *A Cross-City Comparison of Felony Case Processing*. U.S. Department of Justice, Bureau of Justice Statistics. Washington, DC: USGPO, 1979.

Brown, Michael K. *Working the Street: Police Discretion and the Dilemmas of Reform*. New York: Russell Sage Foundation, 1981.

———. "A Typology of Operational Styles." In *The Ambivalent Force,* edited by A. S. Blumberg and E. Niederhoffer, pp. 195–207. New York: Holt, Rinehart & Winston, 1985.

Brusten, M., Graham, N., Herriger, P., and Malinowski, P., eds. *Youth Crime, Social Control and Prevention: Theoretical Perspectives and Policy Implications*. Wuppertal, DRG: Bergische Universitat—Gesamthochschule FB Gesellschaftswissenschaften, 1984.

Brzezinski, Zbigniew. *The Fragile Blossom: Crisis and Change in Japan*. New York: Harper & Row, 1972.

Bunge, Frederica M. *Japan: A Country Study*. Washington, DC: USGPO, 1981.

Burden, Ordway. "Japan's Traditional Attitudes Affect the Police Role There." *Law Enforcement News* 5 (1979): 8.

Burks, Ardath. *Japan: Profile of a Post Industrial Power*. Boulder, CO: Westview Press, 1984.

Buruma, I. "Tattoos in Pinstripes." *Far Eastern Economic Review* 126 (1987): 47.

Cafferty, Pastora S. J., Chiswick, Barry S., Greeley, Andrew M., and Sullivan, Teresa A. *The Dilemma of American Migration: Beyond the Golden Door*. New Brunswick, NJ: Transaction Books, 1983.

Calista, D. J. "Postmaterialism and Value Convergence: Priorities of Japanese Compared with Their Perceptions of American Values." *Comparative Political Studies* 16 (1984): 529–555.

Campbell, Colin, and Wiles, Paul, eds. *Law and Society: Readings in the Sociology of Law*. New York: Barnes & Noble, 1979.

Cavan, Ruth S., and Cavan, Jordan T. *Delinquency and Crime: Cross Cultural Perspectives*. New York: Lippincott, 1968.

Chaiken, Jan M. "What Is Known about Deterrent Effects of Police Activities?" In *Thinking about Crime,* edited by James Q. Wilson, Ch. 5. New York: Basic Books, 1975.

Chaiken, Jan M., and Chaiken, Marcia R. "Crime Rates and the Active Criminal." In *Crime and Public Policy,* edited by J. Q. Wilson, pp. 11–29. San Francisco: ICS Press, 1983.

Chalfant, H. Paul, Beckley, Robert E., and Palmer, C. Eddie. *Religion in Contemporary Society*. 2nd ed. Palo Alto, CA: Mayfield, 1987.

Chambliss, Willian J., and Nagasawa, R. H. "On the Validity of Official Statistics: A Comparative Study of White, Black, and Japanese High-School Boys." *Journal of Research in Crime and Delinquency* 6 (1969): 71–77.

Chambliss, William J., and Seidmen, Robert B. *Law, Order, and Power*. Reading, MA: Addison-Wesley, 1971.

Champion, Dean J. *Sociology of Organizations*. New York: Harper & Row, 1975.

———. *Corrections in the United States: A Contemporary Perspective*. Englewood Cliffs, NJ: Prentice-Hall, 1990.

Chang, Dae H., ed. *Criminology: A Cross-Cultural Perspective,* Vols. I and II. Durham, NC.: Carolina Academic Press, 1976.

Chang, Dae H., and Blazicek, Donald L. *An Introduction to Comparative and International Criminology*. Durham, N.C.: The Acorn Press, 1986.

Christian, Thomas. "Community Dispute Resolution: First Class Process or Second Class Justice?" *New York University Review of Law and Social Change* 14 (1986): 771–783.

Christiansen, Karl O. "Industrialization, Urbanization, and Crime." *Resource Material Series* 8 (1974): 6–7.

Church, Thomas, Jr., Carlson, Alan, Lee, Jo-Lynn, and Tan, Teresa. *Justice Delayed,* 1978.

Civiletti, Benjamin. "Zeroing in on the Real Litigation Crisis: Irrational Justice, Needless Delays, Excessive Costs." *Maryland Law Review* 46 (1986): 40–48.

Clear, Todd R. "Three Dilemmas in Community Supervision." *The Prison Journal* 59 (1979): 2–16.

Clear, Todd R., and Cole, George F. *American Corrections*. Pacific Grove, CA: Brooks/Cole, 1990.

Clifford, William. *Crime Control in Japan*. Lexington, MA: Lexington Books, 1976.

Clinard, Marshall B. *Cities with Little Crime: The Case of Switzerland*. Cambridge, MA: Cambridge University Press, 1978.

Clinard, Marshall B., and Abbott, Daniel J. *Crime in Developing Countries: A Comparative Perspective*. New York: Wiley, 1973.

Clinard, Marshall B., and Meier, Robert F. *Sociology of Deviant Behavior*. 7th ed. New York: Holt, Rinehart & Winston, 1989.

Cohen, Bernard, and Chaiken, Jan M. *Police Background Characteristics and*

Performance. Washington, DC: Law Enforcement Assistance Administration, 1972.

Cohen, Neil P., and Rivkin, Dean Hill. "Civil Disabilities: The Forgotten Punishment." *Federal Probation* 35 (1971): 19–25.

Cohen, Stanley. "Western Crime Control Models in the Third World: Benign or Malignant?" In *Research in Law, Deviance, and Social Control*, Vol. 4, edited by S. Spitzer and R. Simon, pp. 85–119. Greenwich, CT: J.A.I. Press, 1982.

Cole, George F. *The American System of Criminal Justice*. 5th ed. Pacific Grove, CA: Brooks/Cole, 1989.

Cole, George F., Frankowski, S. J., and Gertz, M. G., eds. *Major Criminal Justice Systems*. Newbury Park, CA: Sage, 1981.

Coleman, James W. *The Criminal Elite: The Sociology of White Collar Crime*. 2nd ed. New York: St. Martin's Press, 1989.

Coleman, Lee. "What Is American? A Study of Alleged American Traits." *Social Forces* 19 (1941): 492–499.

Coleman, Rex, and Haley, John Owen. *An Index to Japanese Law: A Bibliography of Western Language Materials 1867–1973*. Tokyo: University of Tokyo Press, 1975.

Conklin, J. E. *Criminology*. 2nd ed. New York: Macmillan, 1981.

Corrections Bureau. *Corrections Institutions in Japan*. Tokyo: Ministry of Justice, 1982.

Corrections Compendium. "Correctional Officers." *Corrections Compendium* 8 (1984): 1–4.

———. "Survey: Parole Officers." *Corrections Compendium* 12 (1987): 10–14.

Coser, Lewis A. "The Notion of Social Control in Sociological Theory." In *Social Control: Views from the Social Sciences*, edited by Jack P. Gibbs, pp. 13–32. Newbury Park, CA: Sage, 1982.

Coulborn, Rushton, ed. *Feudalism in History*. Princeton, NJ: Princeton University Press, 1956.

Coulson, Robert. "The Immediate Future of Alternative Dispute Resolution." *Pepperdine Law Review* 14 (1987): 773–775.

Crane, Diana. "Cultural Differentiation, Cultural Integration." In *Social Control: Views from the Social Sciences*, edited by Jack P. Gibbs, pp. 229–244. Newbury Park, CA: Sage, 1982.

Cressey, D. R. *Criminal Organization*. New York: Harper & Row, 1972.

Cromwell, Paul F., Killinger, George G., Kerper, Hazel B., and Walker, Charles. *Probation and Parole in the Criminal Justice System*. 2nd ed. St. Paul, MN: West, 1985.

Crutchfield, Robert, Geerken, Michael, and Gove, Walter R. "Crime Rates and Social Integration." *Criminology* 20 (1982): 467–478.

Culbertson, Robert G., ed. *Order Under Law: Readings in Criminal Justice*. Prospect Heights, IL: Waveland Press, 1984.

Cullen, Francis T., and Gilbert, Karen E. *Reaffirming Rehabilitation*. Cincinnati, OH: Anderson, 1982.

Cunniff, Mark A. *Felony Sentencing in 18 Local Jurisdictions*. U.S. Department of Justice, Bureau of Justice Statistics. Washington, DC: USGPO, 1985.

———. *Sentencing Outcomes in 28 Felony Courts, 1985*. U.S. Department of Justice, Bureau of Justice Statistics. Washington, DC: USGPO, 1987.

Curran, Barbara A. "American Lawyers in the 1980's: A Profession in Transition." *Hastings International and Comparative Law Review* 4 (1986): 88–142.

Curran, James T., Fowler, Austin, and Ward, Richard H. *Police and Law Enforcement, 1972*. New York: AMS Press, 1973.

Currie, Elliott. "Confronting Crime: Looking Toward the Twenty-First Century." *Justice Quarterly* 6 (1989): 5–25.

Dando, Shigemitsu. *Japanese Criminal Procedure*. Translated by B. J. George, Jr. South Hackensack, NJ: Fred B. Rothman, 1965.

———. "System of Discretionary Procedure in Japan." *The American Journal of Comparative Law* 18 (1970): 518–531.

———. "Elements of Penal Law: General Parts." In *The Japanese Legal System*, edited by Hideo Tanaka, pp. 316–320. Tokyo: The University of Tokyo Press, 1976.

Daniels, Stephan. "Ladders and Bushes: The Problem of Caseload and Studying Court Activities Over Time." *American Bar Foundation Research Journal* 1984: 751–795.

———. "We Are Not a Litigious Society." *The Judges Journal* 24 (2) (1985): 18–21, 47–50.

deCrevecouer, J. Hector St. John. *Letters from an American Farmer*. New York: Penguin Books, 1981.

deToqueville, Alexis. *Democracy in America*. Translated by George Lawrence; edited by J. P. Mauyer. New York: Doubleday, 1969.

DeVos, George A. "The Relation of Guilt Toward Parents to Achievement and Arranged Marriage Among the Japanese." *Psychiatry: Journal for the Study of Interpersonal Processes* 23 (1960): 3.

———. *Socialization for Achievement: Essays on the Cultural Psychology of the Japanese*. Berkeley: University of California Press, 1973.

Doi, Takeo. "Understanding Japanese Personality Structure." In *Japanese Culture: Its Development and Characteristics*, edited by Robert J. Smith and Richard K. Beardsley, pp. 132–139. Chicago: Aldine, 1962.

———. *The Anatomy of Dependence*. Translated by John Bester. Tokyo: Kodansha International, 1973.

Dower, John W. *Empire and Aftermath: Yoshida Shigeru and the Japanese Experience, 1878–1954*. Cambridge, MA: Harvard University Press, 1979.

Durkheim, Emile. *The Division of Labor in Society*. Translated by W. D. Halls. New York: The Free Press, 1893 (1984).

———. *Rules of the Sociological Method*. Translated by George E. G. Catlin. New York: The Free Press, 1895 (1938).

———. *Suicide*. Translated by John A. Spaulding and George Simpson. New York: The Free Press, 1897 (1951).

Eck, J. E. *Solving Crimes: The Investigation of Burglary and Robbery*. Washington, DC: Police Executive Research Forum, 1982.

Eck, J. E., and Spelman, W. *Problem Solving: Problem Oriented Police in Newport News*. Washington, DC: Police Executive Research Forum, 1987.

Edgerton, Robert. *Deviance: A Cross-Cultural Perspective*. Menlo Park, CA: Cummings, 1976.

Edwards, Harry T. "Alternative Dispute Resolution: Panacea or Anathema?" *Harvard Law Review* 99 (1986): 668–684.

Embree, John F. *Suye Mura: A Japanese Village*. Chicago: University of Chicago Press, 1964.

Evan, W. M. *Law and Society: Exploratory Essays*. New York: The Free Press, 1962.

Evans, S. S., and Scott, J. E. "The Seriousness of Crime Cross-Culturally: The Impact of Religiosity." *Criminology* 22 (1984): 39–59.

Farnsworth, E. Allan. *An Introduction to the Legal System of the United States*. New York: Oceana Publications, 1963.

Federal Bureau of Investigation. *Uniform Crime Reporting Handbook*. Washington, DC, 1980.

Feeley, Malcolm. *Foreword* in Nobuyoshi Araki's "The Flow of Criminal Cases in the Japanese Criminal Justice System." *Crime and Delinquency* 31 (1985): 601–604.

Feeney, Floyd. "Comment: Japanese Criminal Justice—Some Brief Comparisons." In Nobuyoshi Araki's "The Flow of Criminal Cases in the Japanese Criminal Justice System." *Crime and Delinquency* 31 (1985): 627–629.

Fenwick, C. R. "Crime Control in Japan: Implications for the United States." *International Journal of Comparative and Applied Criminal Justice* 6 (1982): 62–71.

———. "Juvenile Delinquency in Japan: Application of a Role Relationship Model." *International Journal of Comparative and Applied Criminal Justice* 7 (1983a): 120–127.

———. "Law Enforcement, Public Participation and Crime Control in Japan: Implications for American Policing." *American Journal of Police* 3 (1983b): 83–109.

———. "Culture, Philosophy and Crime: The Japanese Experience." *International Journal of Comparative and Applied Criminal Justice* 9 (1985): 10–30.

Ferdinand, T. "The Criminal Patterns of Boston since 1849." *American Journal of Sociology* 73 (1967): 84–99.

Fiala, Robert, and LaFree, Gary. "Cross-Cultural Determinants of Child Homicide." *American Sociological Review* 53 (1988): 432–445.

Fishman, Gideon, and Dinitz, Simon. "Japan: A Country with Safe Streets." In *Advances in Criminological Theory*, Vol. I, edited by William S. Laufer and Freda Adler, pp. 111–126. New Brunswick, NJ: Transaction Publishers, 1989.

Flanagan, Timothy J., and Jamieson, Katherine M., eds. *Sourcebook of Criminal Justice Statistics—1987*. U.S. Department of Justice, Bureau of Justice Statistics. Washington, DC: USGPO, 1988.

Flango, Victor, and Ito, Jeanne. "Advanced Caseload Report, 1983." *The State Court Journal* 8 (1984): 8–15.

Fodella, Gianni, ed. *Social Structures and Economic Dynamics in Japan Up to 1980.* Milan, Italy: Institute of Economic and Social Studies for East Asia, Luigi Bocconi University, 1975.

Fogelson, Robert M. *Big-City Police.* Cambridge, MA: Harvard University Press, 1977.

Forbis, William H. *Japan Today: People, Places.* New York: Harper & Row, 1975.

Forst, Martin L. "Sentencing Disparity: An Overview of Research and Issues." In *Sentencing Reform: Experiments in Reducing Disparity,* edited by Martin L. Forst, pp. 9–34. Newbury Park, CA: Sage, 1982.

Friday, Paul C. "Problems in Comparative Criminology: Comments on the Feasibility and Implications of Research." *International Journal of Criminology and Penology* 1 (1973): 151–160.

Friedman, Lawrence M. *American Law: An Introduction.* New York: Norton, 1984.

Fujimoto, T. "Social Class and Crime: Case of Japanese Americans." *Issues in Criminology* 10 (1975): 73–93.

———. *Crime and Delinquency Among the Japanese Americans.* Tokyo: Institute of Comparative Law in Japan, 1978.

Fukutake, Tadashi. *Japanese Society Today.* Tokyo: University of Tokyo Press, 1974.

———. *The Japanese Social Structure: Its Evolution in the Modern Century.* Tokyo: University of Tokyo Press, 1982.

Gaines, Larry K., and Ricks, Truett A., eds. *Managing the Police Organization.* St. Paul, MN: West, 1977.

Galanter, Mark. "Reading the Landscape of Disputes." *UCLA Law Review* 31, no. 4 (1983): 36–51.

———. "The Day After the Litigation Explosion." *Maryland Law Review* 46 (1986): 3–39.

Gartner, Rosemary. "The Victims of Homicide: A Temporal and Cross-National Comparison." *American Sociological Review* 55 (1990): 92–106.

George, B. J., Jr. "The Impact of the Past Upon the Rights of the Accused in Japan." *American Journal of Comparative Law* 14 (1965): 672–685.

Gibbons, Don C. *The Criminological Enterprise: Theories and Perspectives.* Englewood Cliffs, NJ: Prentice-Hall, 1979.

———. *Society, Crime, and Criminal Behavior.* 5th ed. Englewood Cliffs, NJ: Prentice-Hall, 1987.

Gibbons, Don C., and Jones, Joseph F. *The Study of Deviance.* Englewood Cliffs, NJ: Prentice-Hall, 1975.

Gibbs, Jack P. "Norms: The Problem of Definition and Classification." *American Journal of Sociology* 70 (1965): 586–594.

———. *Crime, Punishment and Deterrence.* New York: Elsevier, 1975.

———. "Social Control, Deterrence, and Perspectives on Social Order." *Social Forces* 56 (1977): 408–423.

———, **ed.** *Social Control: Views from the Social Sciences.* Newbury Park, CA: Sage, 1982a.

————. "Law as a Means of Social Control." In *Social Control: Views from the Social Sciences,* edited by Jack P. Gibbs, pp. 83–114. Newbury Park, CA: Sage, 1982b.

Gibbs, Jack P., and Erickson, Maynard. "Conceptions of Criminal and Delinquent Acts." *Deviant Behavior* 1 (1979): 71–100.

Gibney, Frank. *Japan: The Fragile Superpower.* New York: Norton, 1975.

Golden, Hilda H. *Urbanization and Cities.* Lexington, MA: Heath, 1981.

Goldstein, Herman. "Police Policy Formulation: A Proposal for Improving Police Performance." In *Managing the Police Organization,* edited by Larry K. Gaines and Truett A. Ricks, pp. 282–304. St. Paul, MN: West, 1977a.

————. *Policing a Free Society.* Cambridge, MA: Bellringer Publications, 1977b.

————. "Improving Policing: A Problem-Oriented Approach." *Crime and Delinquency* April (1979): 236–258.

Goodman, Marcia E. "The Exercise and Control of Prosecutorial Discretion in Japan." *Pacific Basin Law Journal* 5 (1986): 16–95.

Gourman, Jack. *The Gourman Report: A Rating of Graduate and Professional Schools.* Los Angeles: National Education Standards, 1985.

Greenberg, David. "On One-Dimensional Criminology." *Theory and Society* 3 (1976): 610–621.

Greenberg, Douglas. *Crime and Law Enforcement in the Colony of New York, 1691–1776.* Ithaca, NY: Cornell University Press, 1976.

Greenfeld, Lawrence A. *Prisoners in 1987.* U.S. Department of Justice, Bureau of Justice Statistics. Washington, DC: USGPO, 1988.

————. *Prisoners in 1988.* U.S. Department of Justice, Bureau of Justice Statistics. Washington, DC: USGPO, 1989.

Greenwood, Peter. *Selective Incapacitation.* Santa Monica, CA: Rand Corporation, 1982.

Gurr, Ted. "Crime Trends in Modern Democracies Since 1945." *International Annals of Criminology* 16 (1977): 41–86.

Gurr, T. R., Grabowski, P. N., and Hula, R. C. *The Politics of Crime and Conflict: A Comparative History of Four Cities.* Newbury Park, CA: Sage, 1977.

Gusfield, Joseph R. *Symbolic Crusade.* Urbana: University of Illinois Press, 1963.

Hahn, Elliott. "An Overview of the Japanese Legal System." *Northwestern Journal of International Law and Business* 5 (1983): 517–539.

Haley, John O. "The Myth of the Reluctant Litigant." *Journal of Japanese Studies* 4 (1978): 359–390.

————. "Sheathing the Sword of Justice in Japan: An Essay on Law Without Sanctions." *Journal of Japanese Studies* 8 (1982): 265–281.

Hall, John W. "Feudalism in Japan—A Reassessment." *Comparative Studies in Society and History* 5 (1962): 15–51.

Hall, John W., and Beardsley, Richard K., eds. *Twelve Doors to Japan.* New York: McGraw-Hill, 1965.

Halleck, Seymour L., and Witte, Ann D. *American Prison Systems: Punishment and Justice.* Englewood Cliffs, NJ: Prentice-Hall, 1977a.

————. "Is Rehabilitation Dead?" *Crime and Delinquency* 23 (1977b): 379–382.

Hamilton, V. Lee, and Sanders, Joseph. (with Yoko Hosoi, Zensuke Ishimura, Nozomu Matsubara, Harua Nishimura, Nobuho Tomita, and Kenzuhiko Tokoro). "Universals in Judging Wrongdoing: Japanese and Americans Compared." *American Sociological Review* 48 (1983): 199–211.

Handler, Joel F. *Social Movements and the Legal System.* New York: Academic Press, 1978.

Hane, Mikiso. *Peasants, Rebels and Outcasts: The Underside of Modern Japan.* New York: Pantheon Books, 1982.

Hansmann, Henry B., and Quigley, John M. "Population Heterogeneity and the Sociogenesis of Homicide." *Social Forces* 61 (1982): 206–223.

Hartmann, Francis X., ed. "Debating the Evolution of American Policing." *Perspectives on Policing* 5 (1988): 1–10. Department of Justice. Washington, DC: USGPO.

Hasegawa, Nyozekan. *The Japanese Character: A Cultural Profile.* Tokyo: Kodansha International, 1965.

Hashimoto, Kiminobu. "The Rule of Law: Some Aspects of Judicial Review of Administrative Action." In *Law in Japan: The Legal Order in a Changing Society,* edited by Arthur T. vonMehren, pp. 239–273. Cambridge, MA: Harvard University Press, 1963.

Hattori, Takaaki. "The Legal Profession in Japan: Its Historical Development and Present State." In *Law in Japan: The Legal Order in a Changing Society,* edited by Arthur T. vonMehren, pp. 111–152. Cambridge, MA: Harvard University Press, 1963.

Hawkins, Richard, and Alpert, Geoffrey P. *American Prison Systems: Punishment and Justice.* Englewood Cliffs, NJ: Prentice-Hall, 1989.

Hazard, Geoffrey C., Jr., ed. *Law in a Changing America.* Englewood Cliffs, NJ: Prentice-Hall, 1968.

Heald, Gordon. "A Comparison Between American, European, and Japanese Values." In *Values: A Symposium,* edited by Brenda Almond and Bryan Wilson, pp. 75–90. Atlantic Highlands, NJ: Humanities Press, 1988.

Henderson, Dan F. "Some Aspects of Tokugawa Law." *Washington Law Review* 27 (1952): 85–109.

————. *Conciliation and Japanese Law, Tokugawa and Modern,* Vols. I & II. Seattle: University of Washington Press, 1965.

————. *The Constitution of Japan: Its First Twenty Years, 1947–67.* Seattle: University of Washington Press, 1968a.

————. "The Evolution of Tokugawa Law." In *Studies in the Institutional History of Early Modern Japan,* edited by John W. Hall and Marius B. Jansen, pp. 203–229. Princeton, NJ: Princeton University Press, 1968b.

Hester, Thomas. *Probation and Parole, 1987.* U.S. Department of Justice, Bureau of Justice Statistics. Washington, DC: USGPO, 1988.

————. *Correctional Populations in the United States, 1986.* U.S. Department of Justice, Bureau of Justice Statistics. Washington, DC: USGPO, 1989.

Hester, Thomas, and Kaplan, Carol G. *Federal Criminal Cases, 1980–87.*

U.S. Department of Justice, Bureau of Justice Statistics, Special Report. Washington, DC: USGPO, 1989.

Heusken, Henry C. J. *Japan Journal 1855–1861.* New Brunswick, NJ: Rutgers University Press, 1964.

Hicks, Randolph D. "Some Observations on Japanese and American Policing." *Journal of Police and Criminal Psychology* 1 (1985): 68–78.

Hillsman, Sally T., Mahoney, Barry, Cole, George F., and Auchter, Bernard. "Fines as Criminal Sanctions." *Research in Brief,* National Institute of Justice. Washington, DC: USGPO, 1987.

Hillsman, Sally T., Sichel, Joyce L., and Mahoney, Barry. *Fines in Sentencing: A Study in the Use of the Fine as a Criminal Sanction.* The Vera Institute of Justice, the Institute of Court Management, and the U.S. Department of Justice, Bureau of Justice Statistics. Washington, DC: USGPO, 1984.

Hirano, Ryuichi. "The Accused and Society: Some Aspects of Japanese Criminal Law." In *Law in Japan: The Legal Order in a Changing Society,* edited by Arthur T. vonMehren, pp. 274–296. Cambridge, MA: Harvard University Press, 1963.

Hirschi, Travis. *Causes of Delinquency.* Berkeley: University of California Press, 1969.

Hoebel, E. Adamson. *The Law of Primitive Man.* Cambridge, MA: Harvard University Press, 1964.

Hoffman, Vincent J. "The Development of Modern Police Agencies in the Republic of Korea and Japan: A Paradox." *Police Studies* 5 (1982): 13–16.

Hoge, Dean R., and Roozen, D. A. *Understanding Church Growth and Decline.* New York: Pilgrim Press, 1979.

Holmberg–Okuba, Susan, Carol. "Criminal Justice and Social Control: A Japanese-American Comparative Study." Ph.D. diss., Rutgers University, 1985.

Hori, Ichiro. *Folk Religion in Japan: Continuity and Change,* edited by J. M. Kitagawa and A. L. Miller. Chicago: University of Chicago Press, 1968.

Hoshino, Kanehiro. "Organized Crime and Its Origins in Japan." Paper presented to the American Society of Criminology, Chicago, Illinois, November, 1988.

Hsu, Francis L. S., ed. *Psychological Anthropology: Approaches to Culture and Personality.* Belmont, CA: Wadsworth, 1961.

Huang, W. S. Wilson, and Wellford, Charles F. "Assessing Indicators of Crime Among International Crime Data Series." *Criminal Justice Policy Review* 3 (1989): 28–47.

Huff, C. Ronald. "Youth Gangs and Public Policy." *Crime and Delinquency* 35 (1989): 524–537.

Huggins, Martha. "Approaches to Crime and Development." In *Comparative Social Research,* Vol. 8, edited by Richard F. Tomasson, pp. 17–35. London: JAI Press, 1985.

Hughes, Everett C. "Dilemmas and Contradictions of Status." *American Journal of Sociology* 50 (1975): 353–359.

Inami, Shinnosuke. "Police Boxes and Their Officers." *Japan Quarterly* 34 (1987): 295–299.

Inciardi, James A.   *Criminal Justice.* 3rd ed. New York: Harcourt Brace Jovanovich, 1990.

Inkeles, Alex.   "National Character and Modern Political Systems." In *Psychological Anthropology,* edited by Francis L. K. Hsu, pp. 172–208. Belmont, CA: Wadsworth, 1961.

Inverarity, James M., Lauderdale, Pat, and Feld, Barry C.   *Law and Society: Sociological Perspectives on Criminal Law.* Boston: Little, Brown, 1983.

Ishida, Eiichiro.   *Japanese Culture.* Translated by Teruko Itachi. Tokyo: University of Tokyo Press, 1974.

Ishida, Takeshi.   *Japanese Society.* New York: Random House, 1971.

———.   "Conflict and Its Accommodation: Omote-Ura and Uchi-Soto Relations." In *Conflict in Japan,* edited by Ellis Krause, Thomas Rohlen, and Patricia Steinhoff, pp. 16–38. Honolulu: University of Hawaii Press, 1984.

Ito, Masami.   "The Rule of Law: Constitutional Development." In *Law in Japan: The Legal Order in a Changing Society,* edited by Arthur T. vonMehren, pp. 205–238. Cambridge, MA: Harvard University Press, 1963.

Itoh, Hiroshi.   "How Judges Think in Japan." *The American Journal of Comparative Law* 18 (1970): 775–804.

Itoh, Hiroshi, and Beer, Lawrence Ward, eds.   *The Constitutional Case Law of Japan: Selected Supreme Court Decisions, 1961–70.* Seattle: University of Washington Press, 1978.

Iwai, Hiroaki.   "Delinquent Groups and Organized Crime." In *Japanese Sociological Studies,* edited by Paul Halmos, pp. 199–212. *The Sociological Review,* Monograph 10, 1966.

———.   "Organized Crime in Japan." In *Organized Crime: A Global Perspective,* edited by Robert J. Kelly, pp. 208–233. Totowa, NJ: Rowman and Littlefield, 1986.

Jacob, Herbert.   *Justice in America: Courts, Lawyers, and the Judicial Process.* Boston: Little, Brown, 1984.

Jacobs, James B.   "The Prisoners' Rights Movement and Its Impacts, 1960–1980." In *Crime and Justice,* Vol. 2, edited by Norval Morris and Michael Tonry, pp. 229–270. Chicago: University of Chicago Press, 1980.

———.   *New Perspectives on Prisons and Imprisonment.* Ithaca, NY: Cornell University Press, 1983.

Jacoby, Joan E.   "The Changing Policies of Prosecutors." In *The Prosecutor,* edited by William F. McDonald, pp. 75–97. Newbury Park, CA: Sage, 1979.

———.   *The American Prosecutor: A Search for Identity.* Lexington, MA: Lexington Books, 1980.

Jamieson, Katherine M., and Flanagan, Timothy J., eds.   *Sourcebook of Criminal Justice Statistics—1986.* U.S. Department of Justice, Bureau of Justice Statistics. Washington, DC: USGPO, 1987.

———.   *Sourcebook of Criminal Justice Statistics—1988.* U.S. Department of Justice, Bureau of Justice Statistics. Washington, DC: USGPO, 1989.

Janowitz, Morris.   "Sociological Theory and Social Control." *American Journal of Sociology* 81 (1975): 82–108.

———.   *The Last Half-Century.* Chicago: University of Chicago Press, 1978.

Jansen, Marius B. "Tosa in the Sixteenth Century: The 100 Article Code of Chosokabe Motochika." In *Studies in the Institutional History of Early Modern Japan,* edited by John W. Hall and Marius B. Jansen, pp. 89–129. Princeton, NJ: Princeton University Press, 1967a.

———. "Tosa in the Seventeenth Century: The Establishment of Yamauchi Rule." In *Studies in the Institutional History of Early Modern Japan,* edited by John W. Hall and Marius B. Jansen, pp. 115–130. Princeton, NJ: Princeton University Press, 1967b.

Japan Institute of International Affairs. "Crime." In *White Papers of Japan, 1983–84: Annual Abstract of Official Reports and Statistics of the Japanese Government* (Ministry of Justice). Tokyo: Japan Institute of International Affairs, 1983–1984.

———. "Statistics of Japan." In *White Papers of Japan, 1984–85: Annual Abstract of Official Reports and Statistics of the Japanese Government* (Statistical Bureau). Tokyo: Japan Institute of International Affairs, 1984–1985.

Japan Society, The. "The Role of Public Prosecutors in Criminal Justice: Prosecutorial Discretion in Japan and the United States." *Public Affairs Series 14.* New York: The Japan Society, 1980.

Jaquish, G. A., and Rump, E. E. "The Generality of Attitudes Towards Authority: Cross Cultural Comparisons." *Journal of Social Psychology* 125 (1985): 307–312.

Jenkins, Philip. *Crime and Justice: Issues and Ideas.* Pacific Grove, CA: Brooks/Cole, 1984.

Johnson, David. *American Law Enforcement: A History.* Arlington Heights, IL: The Forum Press, 1981.

Johnson, Elmer H., ed. *International Handbook of Contemporary Developments in Criminology: General Issues and the Americas,* Vol. I. Westport, CT: Greenwood Press, 1983a.

———. "Criminology: Its Variety and Patterns Throughout the World." In *International Handbook of Contemporary Developments in Criminology: General Issues and the Americas,* Vol. I, edited by Elmer H. Johnson, pp. 5–30. Westport, CT: Greenwood Press, 1983b.

Johnson, Elmer H., and Hasegawa, Hisashi. "Prison Administration in Contemporary Japan: Six Issues." *Journal of Criminal Justice* 15 (1987): 65–74.

Johnstone, Ronald L. *Religion in Society.* Englewood Cliffs, NJ: Prentice-Hall, 1988.

Jon, S. T., and Quah, Stella. *Neighborhood Policing in Singapore.* Singapore: Oxford University Press, 1987.

Kadish, Sanford H. "The Crisis of Overcriminalization." *The Annals of the American Academy* 374 (1967): 157–170.

Kahn, Herman. *The Emerging Japanese Superstate: Challenge and Response.* Englewood Cliffs, NJ: Prentice-Hall, 1976.

Kahn, Mark L. "The Future of Alternative Dispute Resolution." *Pepperdine Law Review* 14 (1987): 791–793.

Kaiser, Gunther. *Prison Systems and Correctional Laws: Europe, the United States, and Japan.* Dobbs Ferry, NY: Transnational Publishers, 1984.

Kalish, Carol B. "International Crime Rates." *Bureau of Justice Statistics Special Report,* U.S. Department of Justice. Washington, DC: USGPO, 1988.

Kasai, Akio. "Some Causes of the Decrease in Crime in Japan." *Resource Materials Series* 6 (1976): 134–135.

Kato, Ryoko. "National Character Studies of Japanese." *Mid-American Review of Sociology* 13 (1988): 69–78.

Kato, Takao. "Ten Pillars for the Improvement of Police Investigation." *Japanese Resource Materials Series* 18 (1980): 115–119.

Kawashima, Takeyoshi. "The Status of the Individual and the Notion of Law, Right, and Social Order in Japan." In *The Japanese Mind: Essentials of Japanese Philosophy and Culture,* edited by Charles A. Moore, pp. 262–287. Honolulu: University of Hawaii Press, 1967.

———. "Dispute Resolution in Contemporary Japan." In *The Japanese Legal System,* edited by Hideo Tanaka, pp. 269–285. Tokyo: University of Tokyo Press, 1976.

Kelling, George L. *The Newark Foot Patrol Experiment.* Washington, DC: The Police Foundation, 1981.

———. "Police and Communities: The Quiet Revolution." *Perspectives on Policing,* no. 1, June 1988. U.S. Department of Justice. Washington, DC: USGPO, 1988.

Kelling, George L., and Moore, Mark H. "The Evolving Strategy of Policing." *Perspectives on Policing,* no. 4, November 1988. U.S. Department of Justice. Washington, DC: USGPO, 1988.

Kelling, George L., Pate, Tony, Dieckman, Duane, and Brown, Charles E. *The Kansas City Preventive Patrol Experiment: A Summary Report.* Washington, DC: The Police Foundation, 1974.

Kelling, George L., and Stewart, James K. "Neighborhoods and Police: The Maintenance of Civil Authority." *Perspectives on Policing,* no. 10, May 1989. U.S. Department of Justice. Washington, DC: USGPO, 1989.

Kelling, George L., Wasserman, Robert, and Williams, Hubert. "Police Accountability and Community Policing." *Perspectives on Policing,* no. 7, November 1988. U.S. Department of Justice. Washington, DC: USGPO, 1988.

Kelly, Robert J., ed. *Organized Crime: A Global Perspective.* Totowa, NJ: Rowman and Littlefield, 1986a.

———. "Criminal Underworlds: Looking Down on Society from Below." In *Organized Crime: A Global Perspective,* edited by Robert J. Kelly, pp. 10–31. Totowa, NJ: Rowman and Littlefield, 1986b.

Kick, Edward L., and LaFree, Gary D. "Development and the Social Context of Murder and Theft." *Comparative Social Research* 8 (1985): 37–58.

Kidder, Robert L. *Connecting Law and Society.* Englewood Cliffs, NJ: Prentice-Hall, 1983.

Kirk, Donald. "Crime, Politics, and Finger Chopping." *New York Times Magazine,* December 12, 1976, p. 61.

Kitagawa, Joseph M. *On Understanding Japanese Religion.* Princeton, NJ: Princeton University Press, 1987.

Klein, M., and Teilman, K., eds. *Handbook of Criminal Justice Evaluation.* Newbury Park, CA: Sage, 1980.

Kline, Susan. *Jail Inmates 1987.* U.S. Department of Justice, Bureau of Justice Statistics. Washington, DC: USGPO, 1988.

Koschmann, J. Victor, ed. *Authority and the Individual in Japan.* Tokyo: University of Tokyo Press, 1975.

Koshi, George M. *The Japanese Legal Advisor: Crimes and Punishment.* Rutland, VT: Tuttle, 1970.

Krahn, Harvey, Hartnagel, Timothy F., and Gartell, John W. "Income Inequality and Homicide Rates: Cross-National Data and Criminological Theory." *Criminology* 24 (1986): 269–295.

Kramer, Judith R. *The American Minority Community.* New York: Thomas Y. Crowell, 1970.

Kramer, Ronald C. "From 'Habitual Offenders' to 'Career Criminals'." *Law and Human Behavior* 6 (1982): 273–293.

Krantz, Sheldon. *The Law of Corrections and Prisoners' Rights.* 2nd ed. St. Paul, MN: West, 1981.

Krauss, Ellis S., Rohlen, Thomas P., and Steinhoff, Patricia G., eds. *Conflict in Japan.* Honolulu: University of Hawaii Press, 1984.

Krohn, Marvin D. "A Durkheimian Analysis of International Crime Rates." *Social Forces* 57 (1978): 654–670.

Krohn, Marvin, and Wellford, Charles. "A Static and Dynamic Analysis of Crime and the Primary Dimensions of Nations." *International Journal of Criminology and Penology* 5 (1977): 1–16.

Kumasaka, Y., Smith, R. J., and Aiba, H. "Crimes in New York and Tokyo: Sociocultural Perspectives." *Community Mental Health Journal* 11 (1975): 19–26.

LaFree, Gary, and Kick, Edward. "Cross-National Effects of Developmental, Distributional, and Demographic Variables on Crime: A Review and Analysis." *International Annals of Criminology* 24 (1986): 213–235.

Lambros, Thomas D. "The Future of Alternative Dispute Resolution." *Pepperdine Law Review* 14 (1987): 801–804.

Landau, S. F. "Trends in Violence and Aggression: A Cross-Cultural Analysis." *International Journal of Cross-Cultural Analysis* 24 (1984): 133–158.

Langan, Patrick A. *Felony Sentences in State Courts, 1986.* U.S. Department of Justice, Bureau of Justice Statistics. Washington, DC: USGPO, 1989.

Laufer, William S., and Adler, Freda, eds. *Advances in Criminological Theory,* Vol. I. New Brunswick, NJ: Transaction Publishers, 1989.

Leavell, James Berry. *The Development of the Modern Japanese Police System: Transition from Tokugawa to Meiji.* Ph.D. diss., Duke University, 1977.

Leavitt, Gregory C. "Relativism and Cross-Cultural Criminology: A Critical Analysis." *Journal of Research in Crime and Delinquency* 27 (1990): 5–29.

Lefkowitz, Joel. "Psychological Attributes of Policemen: A Review of Research and Opinion." *Journal of Social Issues* 1 (1975): 15–18.

Lewett, Allan E. *Centralization of City Police in Nineteenth Century United States.* Ph.D. diss., University of Michigan, 1975.

Lindsay-Hartz, J. "Contrasting Experiences of Shame and Guilt." *American Behavioral Science* 27 (1984): 689–704.

Lipset, Seymour M. "A Changing American Character?" In *Culture and Social Character,* edited by Seymour M. Lipset and Leo Lowenthal, pp. 136–171. Glencoe, IL: The Free Press, 1961.

————. "The Value Pattern of Democracy." *American Sociological Review* 28 (1963): 515–535.

Lipton, Douglas, Martinson, Robert, and Wilks, Judith. *The Effectiveness of Correctional Treatment: A Survey of Treatment Evaluation Studies.* New York: Praeger, 1975.

Lorenzo, Richard M. "The Judicial System of Japan." *Case Western Reserve Journal of International Law* 6 (1974): 294–303.

Los Angeles Daily News. "Slow Justice Is No Justice" (editorial). September 16, 1988, p. 1.

Lowry, L. Randolph. "Introduction—Symposium Issue on Alternative Dispute Resolution." *Pepperdine Law Review* 14 (1987): 771–772.

Lukes, Steven. *Emile Durkheim: His Life and Works.* New York: Penguin Books, 1977.

Lundman, Richard J. *Police Behavior: A Sociological Perspective.* New York: Oxford University Press, 1980.

Lupsha, Peter A. "Organized Crime in the United States." In *Organized Crime: A Global Perspective,* edited by Robert J. Kelly, pp. 32–58. Totowa, NJ: Rowman and Littlefield, 1986.

Maguire, M. A., and Kroliczak, A. "Attitudes of Japanese and American Workers: Convergence or Diversity?" *Sociological Quarterly* 24 (1983): 107–122.

Mahoney, Barry, Sipes, Larry L., and Ito, Jeanne A. *Implementing Delay Reduction and Delay Prevention Programs in Urban Trial Courts.* Williamsburg, VA: National Center for State Courts, 1985.

Maine, Henry. *Ancient Law.* Boston: Beacon Press, 1963.

Mannheim, H. *Comparative Criminology.* Boston: Houghton-Mifflin, 1965.

Manning, Peter K. "The Police: Mandate, Strategies, and Appearances." In *Criminal Justice in America: A Critical Understanding,* edited by Richard Quinney, pp. 175–207. Boston: Little, Brown, 1974.

————. "Deviance and Dogma." *British Journal of Criminology* 15 (1975): 14.

Manning, Peter K., and Redlinger, Lawrence J. "Invitational Edges of Corruption: Some Consequences of Narcotics Law Enforcement." In *Drugs and Politics,* edited by Paul Rock, pp. 279–310. New Brunswick, NJ: Transaction Books, 1977.

Marinin, O. "Police Performance and State Rule: Control and Autonomy in the Exercise of Coercion." *Comparative Politics* 18 (1985): 101–122.

Marshall, Robert C. *Collective Decision Making in Rural Japan.* Ann Arbor: Center for Japanese Studies, University of Michigan Press, 1984.

Martin, Robert G., and Conger, Rand D. "A Comparison of Delinquency Trends (United States and Japan)." *Criminology* 18 (1980): 53–61.

Martinson, Robert. "What Works?—Questions and Answers about Prison Reform." *Public Interest* 35 (1974): 22–54.

Marty, Martin E. *Righteous Empire*. New York: Dial Press, 1970.

———. *A Nation of Behavers*. Chicago: University of Chicago Press, 1976.

———. *Pilgrims in Their Own Land*. Boston: Little, Brown, 1984.

———. *Religion and Republic: The American Circumstance*. Boston: Beacon Press, 1987.

Maruyama, Masao. *Studies in the Intellectual History of Tokugawa Japan*. Translated by Mikiso Hane. Princeton, NJ: Princeton University Press, 1974.

Marvell, Thomas B. "Is There an Appeal from the Caseload Deluge?" *Judges Journal* 24 (3) (1985): 35–37, 52–54.

———. "Caseload Growth—Past and Future Trends." *Judicature* 71 (1987): 151–159.

Masatsugu, Mitsuyuki. *The Modern Samural Society: Duty and Dependence in Contemporary Japan*. New York: American Management Associations, 1982.

Mather, Lynn, and Yngvesson, Barbra. "Language, Audience, and the Transformation of Disputes." *Law and Society Review* 15 (1981): 775–821.

Matsuda, Jiro. "The Japanese Legal Training and Research Institute." *American Journal of Comparative Law* 1 (1958): 366–390.

Matsumoto, Yoshie, Kamahara, Keiko, Shirai, Toshiko, and Katkura, Eiko. "Resistance in Prisoners to Group Psychotherapy." In *International Summaries*, Vol. 2, translated by Keiko Nishimoto, 56–74. National Criminal Justice Reference Service. Washington, DC: USGPO, 1978.

Matsushita, Teruo. "Crime in Japan—A Search for the Causes of Low and Decreasing Criminality." *Material Resource Series* 12 (1976): 36.

Mayer, Cynthia. "Japan: Behind the Myth of Japanese Justice." *American Lawyer* 6 (1984): 113–124.

Mayhew, Leon, and Reiss, Albert. "The Social Organization of Legal Contacts." *American Sociological Review* 34 (1969): 309–318.

McCampbell, Michael S. "Field Training for Police Officers: State of the Art." *Research in Brief*, November, National Institute of Justice. Washington, DC: USGPO, 1986.

McCarthy, Belinda Rogers, and McCarthy, Bernard J. *Community-Based Corrections*. Pacific Grove, CA: Brooks/Cole, 1984.

McDonald, Lynn. *The Sociology of Law and Order*. Boulder, CO: Westview Press, 1976.

McGillis, Daniel. *Community Dispute Resolution Programs and Policy*. Issues and Practices Series, National Institute of Justice. Washington, DC: USGPO, 1986.

McKelvey, Blake. *American Prisons: The History of Good Intentions*. Montclair, NJ: Patterson Smith, 1977.

McLemore, Dale S. *Racial and Ethnic Relations in America*. Boston: Allyn & Bacon, 1980.

McMahon, Margaret Mary. "Legal Education in Japan." *American Bar Association Journal* 60 (1974): 1376–1380.

Meier, Robert F. "Perspectives on the Concept of Social Control." *Annual Review of Sociology* 8 (1982): 35–65.

———. *Crime and Society*. Boston: Allyn & Bacon, 1989.

Melton, J. Gordon. *The Encyclopedia of American Religion,* Vols. 1 and 2. Wilmington, NC: McGrath, 1978.

Merton, Robert K. *Social Theory and Social Structure.* New York: The Free Press, 1957.

Messner, Steven F. "Societal Development, Social Equity, and Homicide: A Cross-National Test of a Durkheimian Model." *Social Forces* 61 (1982): 225–240.

———. "Economic Discrimination and Societal Homicide Rates: Further Evidence on the Cost of Inequality." *American Sociological Review* 54 (1989): 597–611.

Meyers, John C. "Methodological Issues in Comparative Criminal Justice Research." *Criminology* 10 (1972): 295–313.

Michalowski, Raymond J. *Order, Law, and Crime: An Introduction to Criminology.* New York: Random House, 1985.

Mikazuki, Akira. "Problems in the Japanese Judicial System." In *The Japanese Legal System,* edited by Hideo Tanaka, pp. 444–474. Tokyo: University of Tokyo Press, 1976.

Minami, Ken R. "Japanese Thought and Western Law: A Tangential View of the Japanese *bengoshi* and the Japanese American Attorney." *Loyola of Los Angeles International and Comparative Law Journal* 8 (1986): 301–326.

Minear, Richard H. *Japanese Tradition and Western Law.* Cambridge, MA: Harvard University Press, 1970.

Ministry of Justice–Japan. *Criminal Justice in Japan.* Tokyo: Ministry of Justice, 1981.

———. *Annual Report on Crime 1986 (Summary).* Tokyo: Foreign Press Center, 1986.

———. *Summary of the White Paper on Crime, 1988.* Tokyo: Research and Training Institute, 1988.

———. *Summary of the White Paper on Crime, 1989.* Tokyo: Research and Training Institute, 1989.

Minor-Harper, Stephanie. *State and Federal Prisoners, 1925–85.* U.S. Department of Justice, Bureau of Justice Statistics. Washington, DC: USGPO, 1986.

Mitchell, Richard H. *Thought Control in Prewar Japan.* Ithaca, NY: Cornell University Press, 1976.

Miyazawa, Setsuo. "Taking Kawashima Seriously: A Review of Japanese Research on Japanese Legal Consciousness and Disputing Behavior." *Law and Society Review* 21 (1987): 219–241.

———. "Scandal and Hard Reform: Implications of a Wiretapping Case to the Control of Organizational Police Crimes in Japan." Paper presented to the American Society of Criminology, Chicago, Illinois, 1988.

Monkkonen, Eric H. *Police in Urban America 1860–1920.* Cambridge, England: Cambridge University Press, 1981.

Moore, Mark H., and Kelling, George L. "To Serve and Protect: Learning from Police History." *The Public Interest* 70 (1983): 49–65.

Moore, Mark H., and Trojanowicz, Robert C. "Policing and the Fear of

Crime." *Perspectives on Policing*, no. 3 (June). U.S. Department of Justice. Washington, DC: USGPO, 1988a.

———. "Corporate Strategies for Policing." *Perspectives on Policing*, no. 6 (November). U.S. Department of Justice. Washington, DC: USGPO, 1988b.

Moore, Mark H., Trojanowicz, Robert C., and Kelling, George L. "Crime and Policing." *Perspectives on Policing*, no. 2 (June). U.S. Department of Justice. Washington, DC: USGPO, 1988.

Moore, Merlyn D. "The Police: In Search of Direction." In *Managing the Police Organization*, edited by Larry K. Gaines and Truett A. Ricks, pp. 50–72. St. Paul, MN: West, 1977.

More, Harry W., Jr., ed. *Critical Issues in Law Enforcement*. Cincinnati, OH: Anderson, 1980.

Morris, Norval. "Reordering Priorities Would Free Police and Criminal Courts to Deal with Predatory Crime." *The Center Magazine*, July/August 1977, pp. 39–42.

———. "Alternatives to Imprisonment: Failures and Prospects." *Criminal Justice Research Bulletin* 3, no. 7 (1987).

Morris, Norval, and Hawkins, Gordon. *The Honest Politician's Guide to Crime Control*. Chicago: University of Chicago Press, 1970.

Morris, Norval, and Tonry, Michael. *Between Prison and Probation—Intermediate Punishments in a Rational Sentencing System*. New York: Oxford University Press, 1990a.

———. "Between Prison and Probation—Intermediate Punishments in a Rational Sentencing System." *NIJ Reports*, no. 218 (February 1990), pp. 8–10, 1990b.

Mouer, Ross, and Sugimoto, Yoshio. *Images of Japanese Society: A Study in the Structure of Social Reality*. London: KPI, 1986.

Muir, William K., Jr. *Police: Streetcorner Politicians*. Chicago: University of Chicago Press, 1977.

Murray, John S. "Lawyers and Alternative Dispute Resolution Success." *Pepperdine Law Review* 14 (1987): 771–772.

Myren, Richard A. *Law and Justice: An Introduction*. Pacific Grove, CA: Brooks/Cole, 1988.

Nader, Laura, ed. *Law in Culture and Society*. Chicago: Aldine, 1969.

Nagashima, Atsushi. "The Accused and Society: The Administration of Justice in Japan." In *Law in Japan: The Legal Order in a Changing Society*, edited by Arthur T. vonMehren, pp. 297–323. Cambridge, MA: Harvard University Press, 1963.

Nakahara, Hidenori. "The Japanese Police." *The Journal of Criminal Law, Criminology and Police Science* 46 (1955): 583–594.

Nakane, Chie. *Japanese Society*. Berkeley: University of California Press, 1970.

Nakayama, Kinichi. "Japan." In *Major Criminal Justice Systems*, edited by George F. Cole, S. J. Frankowski, and M. G. Gertz, pp. 132–146. Newbury Park, CA: Sage, 1981.

National Council on Crime and Delinquency. "Probation in the United States, 1979." National Probation Reports. San Francisco: National Council on Crime and Delinquency, 1981.

National Manpower Survey of the Criminal Justice System. Washington, DC: USGPO, 1978.

National Police Agency, The.   *The Police of Japan.* Tokyo: The National Police Agency, 1989.

Nelson, Dorothy W.   "The Immediate Future of Alternative Dispute Resolution." *Pepperdine Law Review* 14 (1987): 777–780.

Nettler, Gwen.   *Explaining Crime.* New York: McGraw-Hill, 1974.

Neubauer, David W.   "Are We Approaching Judicial Gridlock?" *Justice System Journal* 2 (1986): 363–381.

New York Law Journal.   "City's New Anti-drug Drive to Jam Courts." November 14, 1988, p. 1.

Newman, Donald J.   "Public Attitudes toward a Form of White Collar Crime." *Social Problems* 4 (1957): 228–232.

Newman, Graeme.   *Comparative Deviance: Perception and Law in Six Cultures.* New York: Elsevier North–Holland, 1976.

Niederhoffer, Arthur.   *Behind the Shield: The Police in Urban Society.* Garden City, NY: Doubleday, 1967.

———.   "Police Cynicism." In *The Ambivalent Force,* edited by Abraham S. Blumberg and Elaine Niederhoffer, pp. 208–210. New York: Holt, Rinehart & Winston, 1985.

Nishi, Toshio.   *Unconditional Democracy: Education and Politics in Occupied Japan 1945–1952.* Palo Alto, CA: Hoover Institution Press, 1982.

Noda, Yosiyuki.   *Introduction to Japanese Law.* Translated and edited by Anthony H. Angelo. Tokyo: University of Tokyo Press, 1976a.

———.   "The Character of the Japanese People and Their Conception of Law." In *The Japanese Legal System,* edited by Hideo Tanaka, pp. 295–310. Tokyo: University of Tokyo Press, 1976b.

Nomura, Jiro.   *Japan's Judicial System.* "About Japan Series" (#15). Tokyo: Foreign Press Center, 1981.

Norbeck, Edward, and DeVos, George.   "Japan." In *Psychological Anthropology,* edited by Francis L. S. Hsu, pp. 19–47. Belmont, CA: Wadsworth, 1961.

Ochiai, Kiyotaka.   "Offenders Rehabilitation in Japan." *New Zealand Law Journal* (1984): 407–409.

Ogawa, Tara.   "Japan." In *Criminology: A Cross-Cultural Perspective,* Vol. II, edited by Dae H. Chang, pp. 586–652. Durham, NC: Carolina Academic Press, 1976.

Packer, Herbert L.   *The Limits of the Criminal Sanction.* Palo Alto, CA: Stanford University Press, 1968.

Park, Robert E., Burgess, Ernest W., and McKenzie, Roderick D.   *The City.* Chicago: University of Chicago Press, 1967.

Parker, L. Craig.   *The Japanese Police System Today: An American Perspective.* New York: Kodansha, 1984.

———.   *Parole and Community Based Treatment of Offenders in Japan and the United States.* New Haven, CT: University of New Haven Press, 1986.

Parsons, Talcott.   *The Social System.* Glencoe, IL: The Free Press, 1951.

———.   *Economy and Society.* Glencoe, IL: The Free Press, 1957.

Patrick, Hugh, ed. *Japanese Industrialization and Its Social Consequences.* Berkeley: University of California Press, 1976.

Pederson, William D. "Inmate Movements and Prison Uprisings: A Comparative Study." *Social Science Quarterly* 59 (1978): 509–524.

Pfohl, Stephen J. *Images of Deviance and Social Control: A Sociological History.* New York: McGraw-Hill, 1985.

Phillipson, M. *Understanding Crime and Delinquency: A Sociological Introduction.* Chicago: Aldine, 1974.

Pontell, Henry N. *A Capacity to Punish: The Ecology of Crime and Punishment.* Bloomington: Indiana University Press, 1984.

Posner, Richard A. "The Summary Jury Trial and Other Methods of Dispute Resolution: Some Cautionary Observations." *University of Chicago Law Review* 53 (1986): 366–393.

President's Commission on Law Enforcement and the Administration of Justice. *Task Force Report: The Courts.* Washington, DC: USGPO, 1967a.

———. *Task Force Report: Corrections.* Washington, DC: USGPO, 1967b.

Pruyser, Paul W. *A Dynamic Psychology of Religion.* New York: Harper & Row, 1968.

Pulley, F. "Cross-Cultural Reflections of Organized Crime." *Police Chief* 50 (1983): 62–65.

Rabinowitz, Richard W. "The Historical Development of the Japanese Bar." *Harvard Law Review* 70 (1956): 61–78.

Ramseyer, Mark J. "Japan's Myth of Non-Litigiousness." *National Law Journal* 5 (1983): 13, 36.

———. "Reluctant Litigant Revisited: Rationality and Disputes in Japan." *Journal of Japanese Studies* 14 (1988): 111–123.

Ramseyer, Mark, J., and Nakazato, Minoru. "The Rational Litigant: Settlement Amounts and Verdict Rates in Japan." *Journal of Legal Studies* 18 (1989): 263–289.

Reaves, Brian. *Profile of State and Local Law Enforcement Agencies, 1987.* U.S. Department of Justice, Bureau of Justice Statistics. Washington, DC: USGPO, 1989.

Rehabilitation Bureau. *Non-Institutional Treatment of Offenders in Japan.* Tokyo: Ministry of Justice, 1970.

———. *Community-Based Treatment of Offenders in Japan.* Tokyo: Ministry of Justice, 1981.

Reid, Sue Titus. *Criminal Justice: Procedures and Issues.* St. Paul, MN: West, 1987.

———. *Criminal Law.* New York: Macmillan, 1989.

Reischauer, Edwin O. "Japanese Feudalism." In *Feudalism in History,* edited by Rushton Coulborn, pp. 26–44. Princeton, NJ: Princeton University Press, 1956.

———. *The Japanese.* Cambridge, MA: Harvard University Press, 1977.

———. *The Japanese Today.* Cambridge, MA: Harvard University Press, 1988.

Reiser, Martin. "Some Organizational Stresses on Policemen." In *Managing the*

Police Organization, edited by Larry K. Gaines and Truett A. Ricks, pp. 240–245. St. Paul, MN: West, 1977.

Reiss, Albert J. *The Police and the Public.* New Haven, CT: Yale University Press, 1971.

———. "Why Are Communities Important in Understanding Crime?" In *Communities and Crime,* Vol. 8 of *Crime and Justice,* edited by A. J. Reiss, Jr., and Michael Tonry, pp. 1–33. Chicago: University of Chicago Press, 1986.

Reppetto, Thomas A. "The Influence of Police Organizational Style on Crime Control Effectiveness." *Journal of Police Science and Administration* 3 (1975): 274–279.

Reuss-Ianni, Elizabeth. *Two Cultures of Policing: Street Cops and Management Cops.* New York: Transaction Books, 1983.

Riesman, David, Denney, Reuel, and Glazer, Nathan. *The Lonely Crowd.* New Haven, CT: Yale University Press, 1950.

Rinalducci, Ralph J. *The Japanese Police Establishment.* Tokyo: Obun Intereurope, 1972.

Riskin, Leonard. "The Special Place of Mediation in Alternative Dispute Processing." *University of Florida Law Review* 37 (1985): 19–27.

Robertson, Roland, and Taylor, Laurie. *Deviance, Crime and Socio-Legal Control: Comparative Perspectives.* South Hackensack, NJ: Fred B. Rothman, 1973.

Rokumato, K. "Legal Problems and the Use of Law in Tokyo and London—A Preliminary Study in International Comparison." *Zeitzchrift fur Soziologie* 7 (1978): 228–250.

Rome, Florence. *The Tattooed Men.* New York: Delacorte Press, 1975.

Roof, Wade Clark, and McKinney, William. *American Mainline Religion: The Changing Shape and Future.* New Brunswick, NJ: Rutgers University Press, 1987.

Rosch, Joel. "Institutionalizing Mediation: The Evolution of the Civil Liberties Bureau in Japan." *Law and Society Review* 21 (1987): 243–266.

Roscoe, B. "Battles in the Brotherhood." *Far Eastern Economic Review* 127 (1985): 47.

Rose, Arnold M., and Prell, Arthur E. "Does the Punishment Fit the Crime? A Study in Social Valuation." *American Journal of Sociology* 61 (1955): 247–259.

Rosenbaum, Dennis P. *Community Crime Prevention: Does It Work?* Newbury Park, CA: Sage, 1986.

———. "Community Crime Prevention: A Review and Synthesis of the Literature." *Justice Quarterly,* 5 (1988): 323–395.

Rosenbaum, Dennis P., Lewis, D. A., and Grant, J. A. *The Impact of Community Crime Prevention Programs in Chicago: Can Neighborhood Organizations Make a Difference?* Evanston, IL: Northwestern University, Center for Urban Affairs and Policy Research, 1985.

Ross, Edward A. *Social Control.* New York: Macmillan, 1901.

Ross, Ruth A., and Benson, George C. S. "Criminal Justice from East to West." *Crime and Delinquency* 25 (1979): 76–86.

Rossi, Peter H., Waite, Emily, Bose, Christine E., and Berk, Richard E.

"The Seriousness of Crimes: Normative Structure and Individual Differences." *American Sociological Review* 39 (1974): 224–237.

Rothman, David J. *The Discovery of the Asylum: Social Order and the Republic.* Boston: Little, Brown, 1971.

———. *Conscience and Convenience: The Asylum and Its Alternatives in Progressive America.* Boston: Little, Brown, 1980.

Rumbaut, Rubin G., and Bittner, Egon. "Changing Conditions of the Police Role: A Sociological Review." *Crime and Justice* 1 (1979): 239–288.

Rutherford, Andrew. *Prisons and the Process of Justice: The Reductionist Challenge.* Portsmouth, NH: Heinemann Educational Books, 1984.

Sales, James B. "Alternative Dispute Resolution—the Wave of the Future." *Corporate Counsel* 7 (1988): 47–59.

Sander, Frank E. A. "Alternative Methods of Dispute Resolution: An Overview." *University of Florida Law Review* 37 (1985): 1–18.

Sarat, Austin. "The Litigation Explosion." *Rutgers Law Review* 37 (1985): 319–337.

Sato, Kinko. "Why Is There Less Crime in Japan? *Crime and Criminology* 15 (1984): 1–11.

Satsumae, Takeshi. "Suspension of Prosecution: A Japanese Practice Designed to Screen Out Offenders." *UNAFEI Resource Materials Series* 15 (1978): 100–111.

Scheiner, Irwin. *Modern Japan: An Interpretive Anthology.* New York: Macmillan, 1974.

Schembri, Anthony J. "An Overview of the Japanese Police System." *The Police Chief* 52, no. 5 (1985): 40–43.

Schlesinger, Steven R. "Prison Crowding in the United States: The Data." *Criminal Justice Research Bulletin* 3 (no. 1). Sam Houston State University, Criminal Justice Center, 1987.

Schumacher, Michael Allen. *Mightier than the Sword: The Social Control of Crime in Japan and the United States.* Ph.D. diss., United States International University, 1978.

Schur, Edwin M. *Crimes Without Victims.* Englewood Cliffs, NJ: Prentice-Hall, 1965.

———. *Law and Society: A Sociological View.* New York: Random House, 1968.

Schwartz, Richard, and Miller, James. "Legal Evolution and Societal Complexity." *American Journal of Sociology* 70 (1964): 159–169.

Schwartz, Richard, and Skolnick, Jerome. *Society and the Legal Order.* New York: Basic Books, 1970.

Scott, Carolyn, and Zatz, Marjorie S. "Comparative Deviance and Criminology." *International Journal of Comparative Sociology* 22 (1982): 237–256.

Scott, Eric J. *Calls for Service: Citizen Demand and Initial Police Response.* U.S. Department of Justice. Washington, DC: USGPO, 1981.

See, Harold. "The Judiciary and Dispute Resolution in Japan: A Survey." *Florida State University Law Review* 10 (1982): 339–368.

Sellin, Thorsten.   "Culture Conflict and Crime." *Social Science Research Bulletin* 41, Social Science Research Council, 1938.

Senna, Joseph J., and Siegel, Larry J.   *Introduction to Criminal Justice.* 5th ed. St. Paul, MN: West, 1990.

Shane, Paul G.   *Police and People: A Comparison of Five Countries.* St. Louis, MO: Mosby, 1980.

Shannon, Douglas.   "Correctional Executives: Who's Leading the Way?" *Corrections Today* 49 (1987): 48, 94.

Shaw, Clifford, and McKay, Henry D.   *Juvenile Delinquency and Urban Areas: A Study of Rates of Delinquency in Relation to Differential Characteristics of Local Communities in American Cities.* Chicago: University of Chicago Press, 1929.

Shelley, Louise I., ed.   *Readings in Comparative Criminology.* Carbondale: Southern Illinois University Press, 1981.

Sherman, Lawrence W.   "The Sociology and Social Reform of the American Police: 1950–1973." *Journal of Police Science and Administration* 2 (1974): 255–262.

———.   *The Quality of Police Education.* San Francisco: Jossey-Bass, 1978.

———.   "Police in the Laboratory of Criminal Justice." In *Critical Issues in Policing,* edited by Roger G. Dunham and Geoffrey P. Alpert, pp. 48–70. Prospect Heights, IL: Waveland Press, 1989.

Shikita, M., and Tsuchiya, S.   "The Juvenile Justice System in Japan." *Juvenile Justice: An International Survey* 12 (1976): 55–81.

Shikita, Minoru.   "Law Under the Rising Sun: How Lawyers, Prosecutors and Judges Are Educated and Trained in Japan." *Judges Journal* 20 (1981): 42–47.

Shinnosuke, Ianmi.   "Police Boxes and Their Officers." *Japan Quarterly* 34 (1986): 295–300.

Siegal, M., and Shwalb, D.   "Economic Justice in Adolescence: An Australian Japanese Comparison." *Journal of Economic Psychology* 6 (1985): 313–326.

Seigel, Larry J.   *Criminology.* 3rd ed. St. Paul, MN: West, 1989.

Sith, Robert J.   "Lawyers, Litigiousness, and the Law in Japan." *Cornell Law Forum* 11 (1984): 53–55.

Skogan, W. G.   "The Validity of Official Crime Statistics: An Empirical Investigation." *Social Science Quarterly* 55 (1974): 25–38.

———.   "Community Organizations and Crime." In *Crime and Justice: A Review of Research,* Vol. 10, edited by M. Tonry and Norval W. Morris, pp. 39–78. Chicago: University of Chicago Press, 1987.

Skogan, W. G., and Antunes, G.   "Information, Apprehension, and Deterrence: Exploring the Limits of Police Productivity." *Journal of Criminal Justice* Fall (1979): 217–242.

Skolnick, Jerome H.   *Justice Without Trial: Law Enforcement in a Democratic Society,* 2nd ed. New York: Wiley, 1975.

Skolnick, J. H., and Bayley, D. H.   *The New Blue Line: Police Innovation in Six American Cities.* New York: The Free Press, 1986.

————. *Community Policing: Issues and Practices Around the World*. Washington, DC: National Institute of Justice, 1988a.

————. "Theme and Variation in Community Policing." In *Crime and Justice: A Review of Research*, Vol. 10, edited by Michael Tonry and Norval Morris, pp. 1–37. Chicago: University of Chicago Press, 1988b.

Slovak, Jeffery S. *Styles of Urban Policing: Organization, Environment, and Police Styles in Selected American Cities*. New York: University Press, 1986.

Smith, Robert J. *Japanese Society: Tradition, Self, and the Social Order*. New York: Cambridge University Press, 1983.

————. "Lawyers, Litigiousness, and the Law in Japan." *Cornell Law Forum*, 11 (1984): 53–55.

Smith, Thomas C. *The Agrarian Origins of Modern Japan*. Palo Alto, CA: Stanford University Press, 1959.

Smith, W. Eugene, and Smith, Aileen. *Minimata*. New York: Holt, Rinehart & Winston, 1975.

Snarr, Richard W., and Wolford, Bruce I. *Introduction to Corrections*. Dubuque, IA: William C. Brown, 1985.

Sorrentino, C. "Japan's Low Unemployment: An In-Depth Analysis." *Monthly Labor Review* 107 (1984): 18–27.

Souryal, Sam S. *Police Organization and Administration*. New York: Harcourt Brace Jovanovich, 1981.

Sparrow, Malcolm K. "Implementing Community Policing." *Perspectives on Policing* (November 1988). U.S. Department of Justice. Washington, DC: USGPO.

Spelman, W., Oshima, M., and Kelling, G. L. *Crime Suppression and Traditional Police Tactics*. (Final report to the Florence W. Burden Foundation.) Cambridge, MA: Harvard University Program in Criminal Justice Policy and Management, 1985.

Standish, Miles, and Villalon, Luis J. A., eds. *Tokyo: One City Where Crime Does Not Pay*. Philadelphia: The Citizens Crime Commission of Philadelphia, 1975.

Statistics Bureau. *Statistical Handbook of Japan*. Tokyo: Prime Minister's Office, 1980.

————. *Statistical Handbook of Japan*. Tokyo: Prime Minister's Office, 1986.

Sugai, Suichi. "The Japanese Police System." In *Five Studies in Japanese Politics*, edited by Robert E. Ward, University of Michigan, Center for Japanese Studies, 7 (1957): 1–14.

Summers, Robert S., Clermont, Kevin M., Hillman, Robert A., Johnson, Sheri Lynn, Barcelo, John J., III, and Provine, Doris Marie. *Law: Its Nature, Functions and Limits*. St. Paul, MN: West, 1986.

Supreme Court of Japan. *Outline of Japanese Judicial System*. Tokyo: Supreme Court of Japan, 1961.

————. *The Constitution of Japan*. Tokyo: Supreme Court of Japan, 1972.

————. *Court Organization in Japan*. Tokyo: Supreme Court of Japan, 1975.

————. *Justice in Japan*. Tokyo: Supreme Court of Japan, 1982.

————. *Outline of Japanese Judicial System*. Tokyo: Supreme Court of Japan, 1983.

Suzuki, Chuichi. "Problems of Disqualification of Judges in Japan." *The American Journal of Comparative Law* 18 (1970): 727–743.

Suzuki, Sadatoshi. "Opening General Session Address, ICAP Convention." *The Police Chief* 50 (1983): 38–41.

Suzuki, Yoshio. "Politics of Criminal Law Reform—Japan." *Journal of Comparative Law* 212 (1973): 287–303.

———. "Criminal Law Reform in Japan." *UNAFEI Resource Materials Series* 13 (1977): 84–96.

———. "Some Thoughts on Decriminalization and Depenalization." *UNAFEI Resource Materials Series* 14 (1978a): 24–31.

———. "Speedy Administration of Criminal Justice: The Right of the Accused and the Interest of Society." *UNAFEI Resource Materials Series* 15 (1978b): 91–99.

———. "Dispositional Decision-Making in the Criminal Justice Process: Objectives, Discretion and Guidelines." *UNAFEI Resource Materials Series* 16 (1979a): 184–196.

———. "Corrections in Japan." In *International Corrections*, edited by Robert J. Wicks and H. H. A. Cooper, pp. 141–161. Lexington, MA: Lexington Books, 1979b.

———. "Crime." In *Encyclopedia of Japan*, Vol. II, pp. 44–46. Tokyo: Kodansha, 1985.

Sykes, Richard E., and Brent, Edward E. *Policing: A Social Behavior Perspective*. New Brunswick, NJ: Rutgers University Press, 1983.

Taft, Philip B., Jr. "Fighting Fear: The Baltimore County COPE Project." Washington, DC: Police Executive Research Forum, 1986.

Takagi, Masayuki. "Pride and Prosperity Among Yakuza." *Japan Quarterly* 32 (1985): 320–323.

Takayanagi, Kenso. "A Century of Innovation: The Development of Japanese Law." In *Law in Japan: The Legal Order in a Changing Society*, edited by Arthur T. vonMehren, pp. 5–40. Cambridge, MA: Harvard University Press, 1963.

Tanabe, Kohji. "The Processes of Litigation: An Experiment with the Adversary System." In *Law in Japan: The Legal Order in a Changing Society*, edited by Arthur T. vonMehren, pp. 73–110. Cambridge, MA: Harvard University Press, 1963.

Tanaka, Hideo, ed. *The Japanese Legal System*. Tokyo: University of Tokyo Press, 1976a.

———. "Introduction: Divided Profession." In *The Japanese Legal System*, edited by Hideo Tanaka, pp. 459–553. Tokyo: University of Tokyo Press, 1976b.

———. "Emphasis Upon Repentence." In *The Japanese Legal System*, edited by Hideo Tanaka, p. 316. Tokyo: University of Tokyo Press, 1976c.

Tanaka, Hideo. "The Role of Law and Lawyers in Japanese Society." In *The Japanese Legal System*, edited by Hideo Tanaka, pp. 254–268. Tokyo: University of Tokyo Press, 1976d.

———. "The Role of Law in Japanese Society: Comparisons with the West."

Speech to the Vancouver Institute, September 15, 1981. *University of British Columbia Law Review* 19 (1985): 375–388.

Tanigawa, Akira.   "Public Participation and the Integrated Approach in Japanese Rehabilitative Services." In *Criminal Justice in Asia: The Quest for an Integrated Approach*, pp. 328–350. Tokyo: United Nations Asia and Far East Institute for the Prevention of Crime and Treatment of Offenders, 1982.

Tanizawa, Tadhiro.   "Sentencing Standards in Japan." *UNAFEI Resource Materials Series* 16 (1979): 197–221.

Terrill, Richard J.   *World Criminal Justice Systems: A Survey.* Cincinnati, OH: Anderson, 1984.

Thomas, Jim, Keeler, Devin, and Harris, Kathy.   "Issues and Misconceptions in Prisoner Litigation." *Criminology* 24 (1986): 775–797.

Thomas, W. I., and Znaniecki, Florian.   "The Concept of Social Disorganization." In *Theories of Deviance,* 3rd ed., edited by Stuart H. Traub and Craig B. Little, pp. 44–50. Itasca, IL: Peacock, 1920 (1985).

Thompson, Michael Nishikahama.   "Dispute Resolution in Japan: The Non-litigious Way." *Law Society Journal* 24 (1986): 30–35.

Tiedeman, Arthur E., ed.   *An Introduction to Japanese Civilization.* New York: Columbia University Press, 1974.

Tifft, Larry L.   "Control Systems, Social Bases of Power and Power Exercise in Police Organizations." In *Managing the Police Organization,* edited by Larry K. Gaines and Truett K. Ricks, pp. 232–240. St. Paul, MN: West, 1977.

Tipton, Elise K.   *The Civil Police in the Suppression of the Prewar Japanese Left.* Ph.D. diss., Indiana University, 1977.

Töennies, Ferdinand.   *Community and Society.* New York: Harper & Row, 1887 (1963).

Tokyo Metropolitan Police Department.   *Keishico—1982.* Tokyo: Metropolitan Police Department, 1982.

Tonry, Michael, and Morris, Norval, eds.   *Crime and Justice: A Review of Research,* Vol. 10. Chicago: University of Chicago Press, 1988.

Totman, Conrad.   *The Collapse of the Tokugawa Bakufu 1862–1868.* Honolulu: University of Hawaii Press, 1980.

Traub, Stuart H., and Little, Craig B.   *Theories of Deviance.* 3rd ed. Itasca, IL: Peacock, 1985.

Trojanowicz, Robert.   *An Evaluation of the Neighborhood Foot Patrol Program in Flint, Michigan.* East Lansing: National Foot Patrol Center, Michigan State University Press, 1980.

Trojanowicz, Robert, and Bucqueroux, Bonnie.   *Community Policing.* Cincinnati, OH: Anderson, 1990.

Tsubouchi, Toshihiko.   "Diversion in the Criminal Justice System of Japan." *UNAFEI Resource Materials Series* 6 (1973): 151–156.

Tsunoda, Ryusaku, de Bary, William Theodore, and Keene, Donald, compilers.   *Sources of Japanese Tradition.* New York: Columbia University Press, 1958.

Ueno, Haruo.   "The Japanese Police: Education and Training." *Police Studies* 2 (1979): 11–17.

Umbreit, Mark. *Crime and Reconciliation: Creative Options for Victims and Offenders.* Nashville, TN: Abingdon, 1985a.

―――. "Victim Offender Mediation and Judicial Leadership." *Judicature* 69 (1985b): 202–204.

Upham, Frank. "Litigation and Moral Consciousness in Japan: An Interpretive Analysis of Four Japanese Pollution Suits." *Law and Society Review* 10 (1976): 579–619.

―――. *Law and Social Change in Postwar Japan.* Cambridge, MA: Harvard University Press, 1987.

―――. "Instrumental Violence and Social Change: The Buraku Liberation League and the Tactic of 'Denunciation Struggle'." In *Law and Society in Contemporary Japan: American Perspectives,* edited by John O. Haley, pp. 289–305. Dubuque, IA: Kendall/Hunt, 1988.

―――. "What's Happening in Japan, Sociolegalwise." *Law and Society Review* 23 (1989): 879–889.

Vago, Steven. *Law and Society.* Englewood Cliffs, NJ: Prentice-Hall, 1988.

VanMaanen, John. "The Asshole." In *The Ambivalent Force,* edited by Abraham S. Blumberg and Elaine Niederhoffer, pp. 146–158. New York: Holt, Rinehart & Winston, 1985a.

―――. "Observations on the Making of Policemen." In *The Ambivalent Force,* edited by Abraham S. Blumberg and Elaine Niederhoffer, pp. 91–103. New York: Holt, Rinehart & Winston, 1985b.

van Wolferen, Karel. *The Enigma of Japanese Power.* New York: Vintage Books, 1990.

Varley, H. P. *Japanese Culture.* Honolulu: University of Hawaii Press, 1984.

Verba, Sidney, Kelman, Steven, Orren, Gary, Miyake, Ichiro, Watanuki, Joji, Kabashima, Ikuo, and Feree, G. Donald, Jr. *Elites and the Idea of Equality: A Comparison of Japan, Sweden, and the United States.* Cambridge, MA: Harvard University Press, 1987.

Verkko, V. "General Theoretical Viewpoints in Criminal Statistics Regarding Real Crime." In *Transactions of the Westermarck Society,* pp. 47–75. Copenhagen, Denmark: E. Munksgard, 1953.

―――. "Survey of Current Practice in Criminal Statistics." In *Transactions of the Westermarck Society,* pp. 5–33. Copenhagen, Denmark: E. Munksgard, 1956.

Viano, Emilio C., and Reiman, J. H., eds. *National Symposium on the Humanities and the Police.* Lexington, MA: Lexington Books, 1975.

Viccia, Antoinette D. "World Crime Trends." *International Journal of Offender Therapy and Comparative Criminology* 24 (1982): 270–277.

Vigderhous, Gideon. "Methodological Problems Confronting Cross-Cultural Criminological Research Using Official Data." *Human Relations* 31 (1978): 229–247.

Vogel, E. F. *Japan as Number ONE: Lessons for America.* Boston: Harvard University Press, 1979.

Voigt, Lydia, and Thornton, William E., Jr. *The Limits of Justice: A Sociological Analysis.* Lanham, MD: University Press of America, 1984.

Vold, George B., and Bernard, Thomas J. *Theoretical Criminology.* 3rd ed. New York: Oxford University Press, 1986.

vonHirsch, Andrew. *Doing Justice: The Choice of Punishments.* New York: Hill and Wang, 1976.

vonMehren, A., ed. *Law in Japan: The Legal Order in a Changing Society.* Cambridge, MA: Harvard University Press, 1963.

Wagatsuma, Hiroshi, and Rosett, Arthur. "The Implications of Apology: Law and Culture in Japan and the United States." *Law and Society Review* 20 (1986): 461–507.

Wagner, Allen E. "Police Storefront Centers: Then and Now." Paper presented to the Midwestern Criminal Justice Association, Chicago, Illinois, October 1988.

Wahrhaftig, Paul. "An Overview of Community-Oriented Citizen Dispute Resolution Programs in the United States." In *The Politics of Informal Justice, Vol. I,* pp. 75–98. New York: Academic Press, 1982.

———. "Nonprofessional Conflict Resolution." Symposium on alternative dispute resolution. *Villanova Law Review* 29 (1984): 1463–1476.

Walker, Migel, and Hough, Mike, eds. *Public Attitudes to Sentencing: Surveys from Five Countries.* Brookfield, VT: Gower, 1988.

Walker, Samuel. *A Critical History of Police Reform: The Emergence of Professionalism.* Lexington, MA: Lexington Books, 1977.

———. *Popular Justice: A History of American Criminal Justice.* New York: Oxford University Press, 1980.

———. *The Police in America.* New York: McGraw-Hill, 1983.

———. *Sense and Nonsense About Crime: A Policy Guide.* 2nd ed. Pacific Grove, CA: Brooks/Cole, 1989.

Ward, Robert E. *Five Studies in Japanese Politics.* Freeport, NY: Books for Libraries Press, 1957.

———, **ed.** *Political Development in Modern Japan.* Princeton, NJ: Princeton University Press, 1968.

Warr, Mark, Gibbs, Jack P., and Erickson, Maynard. "Contending Theories of Criminal Law: Statutory Penalties versus Public Preferences." *Journal of Research in Crime and Delinquency* 19 (1982): 25–46.

Wasserman, Robert, and Moore, Mark H. "Values in Policing." *Perspectives on Policing,* no. 8 (November 1988). U.S. Department of Justice. Washington, DC: USGPO.

Watson, D., Clark, Lee Anna, and Tellegen, Auke. "Cross-Cultural Convergence in the Structure of Mood: A Japanese Replication and a Comparison with U.S. Findings." *Journal of Personality and Social Psychology* 47 (1984): 127–144.

Weatherhead, Leslie D. *Psychology, Religion, and Healing.* New York: Abingdon-Cokesbury Press, 1951.

Webb, J. "What We Can Learn from Japan's Prisons." *Parade Magazine,* January 15, 1984.

Webb, S. D. "Crime and the Division of Labor: Testing a Durkheimian Model." *American Journal of Sociology* 78 (1972): 643–656.

Weber, Max. *Economy and Society,* edited by Guenther Roth and Claus Wittich. Berkeley: University of California Press, 1978.

Weinstein, Jack B. "Warning: Alternative Dispute Resolution May Be Dangerous to Your Health." *Litigation* 12 (1986): 5.

Weisz, J. R. "Standing Out and Standing In: The Psychology of Control in America and Japan." *American Psychologist* 39 (1984): 955–969.

Wellford, Charles F. "Crime and the Dimensions of Nations." *International Journal of Criminology and Penology* 2 (1974): 1–10.

Westermann, Ted, and Burfeind, James. "Crime in Two Societies: Cultural Influences on Crime and Control in Japan and the United States." Paper presented at the American Society of Criminology, November 1988, Chicago, Illinois.

Westley, William A. "Violence and the Police." *American Journal of Sociology* 59 (1953): 34–41.

Weston, Paul B., and Wells, Kenneth M. *The Administration of Justice.* 5th ed. Englewood Cliffs, NJ: Prentice-Hall, 1987.

White, Leslie A. *The Evolution of Culture.* New York: McGraw-Hill, 1959.

Whitehead, John T., and Lindquist, Charles A. "Correctional Officer Burnout: A Test of Two Theories." *Journal of Research in Crime and Delinquency* 22 (1986): 23–42.

Whitehouse, Jack E. *A Police Bibliography.* New York: AMS Press, 1980.

Whitmore, Gray, ed. *Current Studies in Japanese Law.* Ann Arbor: University of Michigan Press, 1979.

Whyte, William H., Jr. *The Organization Man.* Garden City, NY: Doubleday Anchor Books, 1957.

Wiatrowski, Michael D., Griswold, David B., and Roberts, Mary K. "Social Control Theory and Delinquency." *American Sociological Review* 46 (1981): 525–541.

Wilkins, Leslie T. "World Crime: To Measure or Not to Measure." In *Crime and Deviance: A Comparative Perspective,* edited by Graeme Newman, pp. 17–41. Newbury Park, CA: Sage, 1980.

Wilkinson, John H. "Alternative Dispute Resolution—The Summary Jury Trial." *New York Law Journal,* April 13, 1987, p. 1.

Williams, Kirk R., Gibbs, Jack P., and Erickson, Maynard. "Public Knowledge of Statutory Penalties: The Extent and Basis of Accurate Perception." *Pacific Sociological Review* 23 (1980): 105–128.

Williams, Robin. *American Society: A Sociological Interpretation.* 2nd ed. New York: Knopf, 1960.

Wilson, Bryan. *Religion in Sociological Perspective.* New York: Oxford University Press, 1982.

Wilson, James Q. *Varieties of Police Behavior.* Cambridge, MA: Harvard University Press, 1968.

Wilson, James Q., and Kelling, George L. "Broken Windows: The Police and Neighborhood Safety." *Atlantic Monthly* (March, 1982): 29–38.

Wilson, John. *Religion in American Society: The Effective Presence.* Englewood Cliffs, NJ: Prentice-Hall, 1978.

Wilson, Orlando W. *Police Administration.* New York: McGraw-Hill, 1950.

Winter, J. Alan. *Continuities in the Sociology of Religion: Creed, Congregation, and Community.* New York: Harper & Row, 1977.

Wise, Daniel. "Flip Side of Anti-Drug Drive Is Understaffed Court System." *New York Law Journal,* March 23, 1989, p. 1.

Wolf, P. "Crime and Development: An International Comparison of Crime Rates." *Scandinavian Studies in Criminology* 38 (1971): 501–508.

Wolff, Robert Paul. *The Rule of Law.* New York: Simon & Schuster, 1971.

Wolfgang, M. E. "International Crime Statistics: A Proposal." *Journal of Criminal Law, Criminology and Police Science* 58 (1963): 65–69.

———, **ed.** *Crime and Culture: Essays in Honor of Thorsten Sellin.* New York: Wiley, 1968.

Wren, Harold G. "The Legal System of Pre-Western Japan." *Hastings Law Journal* 20 (1968): 217–244.

Wright, J. D., and Rossi, P. H. "The Armed Criminal in America." *Research in Brief,* National Institute of Justice. Washington, DC: USGPO, 1985.

Wright, J. D., Rossi, P. H., and Daly, K. *Under the Gun: Weapons, Crime, and Violence in America.* New York: Aldine, 1983.

Wrobleski, Henry M., and Hess, Karen M. *Introduction to Law Enforcement and Criminal Justice.* 2nd ed. St. Paul, MN: West, 1986.

Wrong, Dennis H. "The Oversocialized Concept of Man in Modern Sociology." *American Sociological Review* 26 (1961): 183–193.

Yanagimoto, Masaharu. "Some Features of the Japanese Prison System." *British Journal of Criminology* 10 (1970): 209–224.

———. "The Juvenile Delinquent in Japan." *British Journal of Criminology* 24 (1973): 170–177.

Yokoo, Toshio. "The Japanese Police Campaign Against the Boryokudan." *International Criminal Police Review* 395 (1986): 38–45.

Yokoyama, Minoru. "Delinquency Control Programs in the Community in Japan." *International Journal of Applied Criminal Justice* 5 (1981): 169–178.

Zawitz, Marianne W., ed. *Report to the Nation of Crime and Justice.* 2nd ed. U.S. Department of Justice, Bureau of Justice Statistics. Washington, DC: USGPO, 1988.

Zedlewski, Edwin W. "Making Confinement Decisions." *Research in Brief,* National Institute of Justice. Washington, DC: USGPO, 1987.

Zymanski, Albert. *Class Structure: A Critical Perspective.* New York: Praeger, 1983.

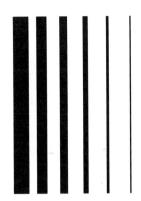

INDEX

TO THE OWNER OF THIS BOOK:

We hope that you have found *Crime and Justice in Two Societies: Japan and the United States*, by Ted D. Westermann and James W. Burfeind, useful. So that this book can be improved in a future edition, would you take the time to complete this sheet and return it? Thank you.

Instructor's name: _____

Department: _____

School and address: _____

_____

1. The name of the course in which I used this book is: _____

_____

2. My general reaction to this book is: _____

_____

_____

3. What I like most about this book is: _____

_____

_____

4. What I like least about this book is: _____

_____

_____

5. Were all of the chapters of the book assigned for you to read?   Yes   No

   If not, which ones weren't? _____

6. Do you plan to keep this book after you finish the course?   Yes   No

   Why or why not? _____

_____

7. On a separate sheet of paper, please write specific suggestions for improving this book and anything else you'd care to share about your experience in using the book.

Optional:

Your name: _____ Date: _____

May Brooks/Cole quote you, either in promotion for *Crime and Justice in Two Societies: Japan and the United States* or in future publishing ventures?

Yes: _____ No: _____

Sincerely,
Ted D. Westermann
James W. Burfeind

FOLD HERE

FOLD HERE